IMAGES
of America

OGDEN DUNES

7/20/14

Emily – Thank you for your contributions this past year and for your future efforts.

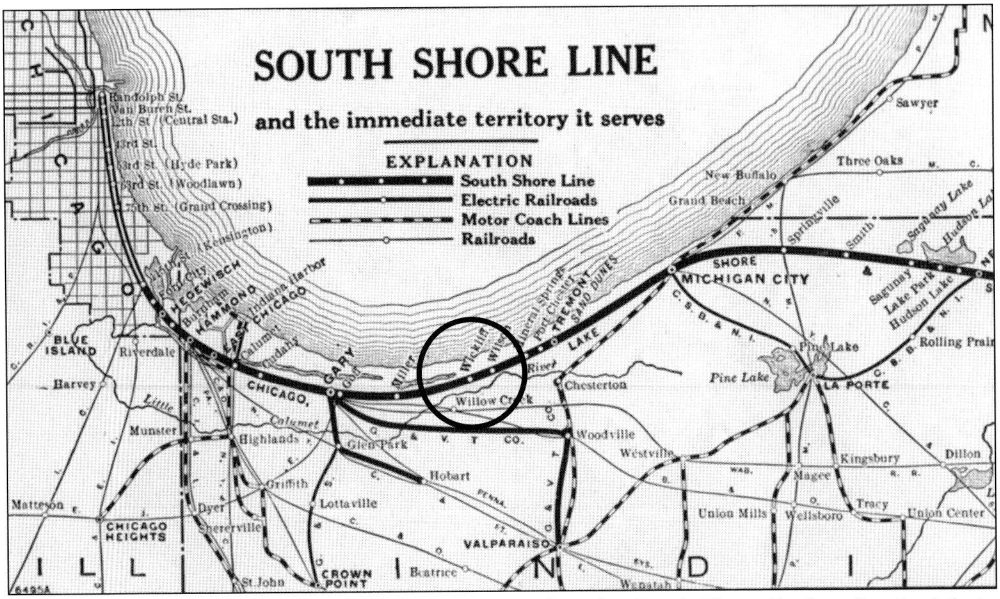

SOUTH SHORE LINE, 1925. This route map appeared in the South Shore Railroad's schedule in 1925. It shows the stops along the electric line that ran from the Chicago Loop to South Bend, Indiana. In 1923, Samuel Reck of Gary, Indiana, led a group of investors who purchased 500-plus acres of duneland from the Ogden estate, north of the Wickliffe South Shore stop (circled). This purchase led to the incorporation of the Town of Ogden Dunes in 1925. (Courtesy of the Calumet Regional Archives, Indiana University Northwest.)

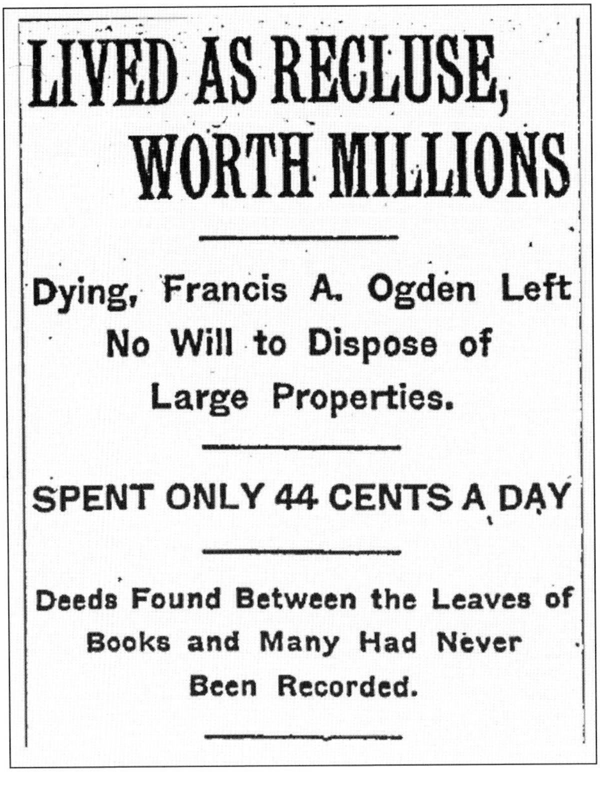

LIVED AS RECLUSE, WORTH MILLIONS

Dying, Francis A. Ogden Left No Will to Dispose of Large Properties.

SPENT ONLY 44 CENTS A DAY

Deeds Found Between the Leaves of Books and Many Had Never Been Recorded.

FRANCIS A. OGDEN'S DEATH NOTICE. In 1914, a reclusive Wisconsin real-estate speculator and millionaire, Francis A. Ogden, died in a Houston hotel room. Hundreds of property deeds worth more than $12 million were found in his room. Part of his holdings on the southern shore of Lake Michigan became Ogden Dunes; much of the rest ultimately became part of the Indiana Dunes National Lakeshore. (Courtesy of the Historical Society of Ogden Dunes.)

IMAGES
of America

OGDEN DUNES

Dick Meister, Ken Martin, and
the Historical Society of Ogden Dunes

ARCADIA
PUBLISHING

ISBN 978-1-4671-1189-8

Published by Arcadia Publishing
Charleston, South Carolina

Printed in the United States of America

Library of Congress Control Number: 2013952749

For all general information, please contact Arcadia Publishing:
Telephone 843-853-2070
Fax 843-853-0044
E-mail sales@arcadiapublishing.com
For customer service and orders:
Toll-Free 1-888-313-2665

Visit us on the Internet at www.arcadiapublishing.com

To those who have saved the past for the future.

On the Cover: In the late 1930s, a group of young men and women, high school and college students whose families lived or spent the summers in Ogden Dunes, called themselves the "rafters." They were known for spending their leisure time during this era of innocence prior to World War II on sailboats or a man-made raft. (Courtesy of the Historical Society of Ogden Dunes, Thompson.)

Contents

ACKNOWLEDGMENTS

Bringing together the fragments of history—photographs, oral remembrances, and written stories—is a daunting challenge. In our case, it would not have been possible if a small group of dedicated individuals had not the will to establish the Historical Society of Ogden Dunes and the Hour Glass Museum in the early 1990s. We wish to thank Linda Simon and Jane Ammeson, the authors of *Miller Beach*, for sharing their excitement for local history at a program sponsored by our historical society. They also introduced us to Arcadia Publishing and the Images of America series. In turn, Amy Perryman and Kelsey Jones of Arcadia Publishing encouraged us to submit a proposal for a book on Ogden Dunes. And the rest is history.

We wish to thank fellow historians and archivists who shared their knowledge, time, and resources to ensure that this book was completed. These include Steve McShane of the Calumet Regional Archives, Indiana University Northwest; Eva Hopkins and Serena Sutliff of the Westchester Township Historical Museum; Kathy Heckman and Lois Mollick of the Portage Community Historical Society; and Kevin Pazour and his staff at Porter County Museum of History. We also thank the many current and former residents and friends of Ogden Dunes who contributed stories and photographs: Barbara Ahrens, Jack Ahrens, Arthur Cash, Carol Chepko, Rick Collins, Mary Gasser, Dena Green, Richard Hallman, Lisa Hartlund, Tom Hendrix, Lee Hibbs, Julia Hoham, Hank Kazmier, Don and Dorothy Kurtz, David Larson, Ted Lelek, Alec Mackenzie, Joella Jean Mahoney, Laura Bucko Mallonee, Jean Manna, Steve Mark, Joan Meister, Laura Cash Mitchell, Noel Nicholas, John Peterson, Starr Rohrman, Ian Roseen, the late Jack Simmerling, Stephanie Smith, George Svihla, Tom Tittle, Mildred Tracht, Randi Vogt, Bill Warrick, Carol Wise, Tom Woodward, and Tony Wrann.

We also thank the following fellow researchers who directly assisted us on this project: Ken Schoon, author of the recently published *Dreams of Duneland*; Peter B. Campbell, Roger J. Barski, and Thomas J. Loebel for their recent study on the 19th-century schooner that remains buried along the Ogden Dunes beach; Steve Shook for his amazing collection of historical photographs of Porter County; and Emilie Cardoso-Seerup for her technical and photographic skills. For assisting us on this project, we thank Allen Johnson, president of the town board; members of the board; and Jean Manna. We are grateful to the following for permission to use photographs: Robert Graham of the Historical Collections of the Great Lakes; Bowling Green State University; the *Chicago Tribune*; the Town of Ogden Dunes; the Ogden Dunes Community Church; the Prairie Club Archives; and the Indiana Historical Society. We, the authors, are responsible for any errors. Please let us know of these so that we may correct our records.

This book would not have been possible without the support that we received from our fellow board members of the historical society. They contributed their time to collecting and sorting photographs and to proofreading the many versions of this book. They kept us from committing errors of fact and grammar, and they patiently allowed us to take over the museum while we worked on this project. Most importantly, we express our gratitude and love to our families and our spouses, Joan and Curt, as we worked to meet our deadlines. They were patient, understanding, and supportive throughout this project.

We use abbreviations in acknowledging the following sources of photographs: Historical Society of Ogden Dunes (HSOD, plus the name of the donor of the collection, if known); Calumet Regional Archives, Indiana University Northwest (CRAIUN); Westchester Township Historical Museum (WTHM); and Prairie Club Collection, Westchester Township Historical Museum (PCCWTHM). In all other cases, we provide the full name of the source.

We also thank the unknown photographers who captured the moments within this book.

Introduction

In August 1925, the Porter County commissioners approved the petition to incorporate the Town of Ogden Dunes. Signed by 20 landowners, the petition for incorporation covered approximately 500 acres of sand dunes, oak savannas, and sloughs with a mile of Lake Michigan shoreline. The new town was approximately one mile east of the Lake/Porter county line. This was also the eastern boundary of the "City of the Century," Gary, Indiana, founded in 1906.

This book traces the history of this lakefront community from the early 20th century to the 1990s through photographs, documents, and personal stories. This history is the story of how a small community reacted and contributed to the larger history of the United States. The story begins at a time when many saw northern Porter County as offering little but useless sand and disease-breeding swamps. By the early 20th century, this view of the dunes slowly began to change. Given the success of the industrialization of northern Lake County, industrial interests saw northern Porter County as ripe for exploitation. "Big steel" and land speculators purchased large tracts of land. Sand mining, which began as early as the mid-1850s, also expanded. Scientists and environmentalists began to see the sand dunes as one of earth's great natural wonders. Thus began a nearly century-long battle between those favoring industrialization and those wishing to protect nature. The history of Ogden Dunes reflects these economic and political battles, as well as the struggle of how to deal with the intended and unintended consequences of decisions made over the course of this conflict.

Chapter one documents the early efforts of those who wished to preserve the dunes, and those who sought to conquer nature. The Prairie Club supported the preservation of the dunes. This led to the establishment in 1916 of the National Dunes Park Association, which lobbied for a national park. One of the most interesting of the early naturalists was Alice Mabel Gray, also known as "Diana of the Dunes." At the same time, transportation improvements increased access to the dunes for recreational and economic purposes. In the mid-1920s, Samuel Insull purchased and upgraded the Chicago, South Shore & South Bend electric railroad. State and federal funds were used to build Dunes Highway, US 12. The counties of Porter and Lake also funded the construction of Burns Ditch, a waterway that linked the Little Calumet River to Lake Michigan just east of Ogden Dunes. The drained lowlands created thousands of acres of land for development.

Chapter two develops the story of the founding of Ogden Dunes. Samuel Reck, Colin Mackenzie, and others purchased 500-plus acres in 1923 from the Francis Ogden estate to establish a highly restricted lakefront community. Because of its proximity to Gary and to Chicago and its access to transportation, Ogden Dunes was to be both a residential suburb and a summer/weekend retreat.

Chapter three focuses on the early compromises that Ogden Dunes Realty made, as well as the community's first encounter with the forces of industrialization. To stimulate sales, land was sold to a group of ski enthusiasts who erected the largest man-made ski jump in North America. The ski jump, despite its brief existence, has become an iconic image of Ogden Dunes. "Big steel" became interested in the uninhabited sand dunes. National Steel announced plans to create a mill, lake port, and a town just east of Ogden Dunes. The Depression, however, destroyed both visions.

The images in Chapter four carry the story to the last years of the 1930s. Just as the country slowly recovered from the Great Depression, so did Ogden Dunes. The influx of permanent and part-time residents created a dynamic and supportive community. This effort was led by the Woman's Club, organized in 1938, and it was supported by a community newsletter, the *Ogden Dunes Sandpiper*. O.D. and Tillie Frank also left their mark on the community. O.D., a member of the Prairie Club and a biology instructor at the University of Chicago Laboratory School, built their cottage, The Hour Glass, in 1933.

Chapter five traces the impact of World War II and its aftermath on Ogden Dunes. Over 30 young men who had connections with Ogden Dunes served in the military. Their families supported the war on the home front. Then, postwar recovery changed the very character of the community. Ogden Dunes became a residential community, with affordable housing for returning veterans and their families. The community, like many others, was also forced to give up its legal restrictions on selling property to Jews and nonwhites because of a 1948 Supreme Court decision. As an increasing number of their children attended Portage Township schools, parents became more involved with the larger township community. New organizations appeared, including the volunteer fire department, an American Legion post, and Scout troops. Beginning on Memorial Day in 1947, American Legion Post 132 sponsored a parade, memorial ceremony, and picnic that remain the major communal events of the year.

Chapter six resurrects the battle over the dunes. Big steel and the State of Indiana planned a deepwater port and the leveling of the dunes between Ogden Dunes and Dune Acres, five miles to the east. Dorothy Richardson Buell and a group of women organized the Save the Dunes Council at a meeting in her home on Cedar Court in June 1952. Other communal activities became institutionalized: the establishment of the Ogden Dunes Community Church in 1953, the Town Planning Commission in 1956, the Home Owners Association in 1957, and the Lions Club in 1959. Another woman also left her mark. Dale Messick, creator of the comic strip *Brenda Starr*, moved into the community in 1952 and remained a resident until the late 1960s. Midwest Steel's plans in 1960 for a mill on Ogden Dunes' eastern border resulted in the closing of the Gary Boat Club and the demolition of small cottages east of Ogden Dunes.

The community was badly divided as it entered the 1960s. Chapter seven begins with the bitterly fought town board election in November 1959. The town divided into the "resisters," who supported the lawsuits against the steel companies and the new town of Portage, and the "accommodators," who favored negotiation. The latter slate carried the election. This ultimately resulted in the lessening of conflict. Tensions were further reduced with congressional action in 1966 that created a Burns Harbor Port and an Indiana Dunes National Lake Shore and that ensured Bethlehem Steel's future.

The war in Vietnam impacted the families of Ogden Dunes, even more so than did World War II, as three young men from the area died in action. The decade ended with a number of extravagant New Year's Eve parties at the firehouse. And it marked the end of an era, as Nelson and Helen Reck donated their remaining holdings to the University of Chicago and planned their move to California.

Chapter eight focuses on activities that brought the community together, including the soccer mania that resulted from local boys' teams playing in Russia and Great Britain, as well as the successful scouting programs. The community accepted the reality of living next door to steel mills and a national park. Its major challenges dealt with the consequences of the creation of the Burns Harbor Port and the Indiana Dunes National Lake Shore. The first resulted in the erosion of the beach, which threatened homes along Shore Drive. The second resulted in the purchase of undeveloped and developed land within Ogden Dunes. The community also came to terms with the National Park Service's decision to build a public beach a half-mile west of Ogden Dunes.

The book ends with an epilogue, which recognizes the traditions, memories, and lasting friendships that bring former residents back to Ogden Dunes. The community has stabilized. It is aging; it is more diverse. The spirit of the community remains. Memorial Day celebrations, the Community Church, the Women's Club, the Home Owners Association, the Lions Club, and the Volunteer Fire Department continue to bind people together.

One

Before the Town

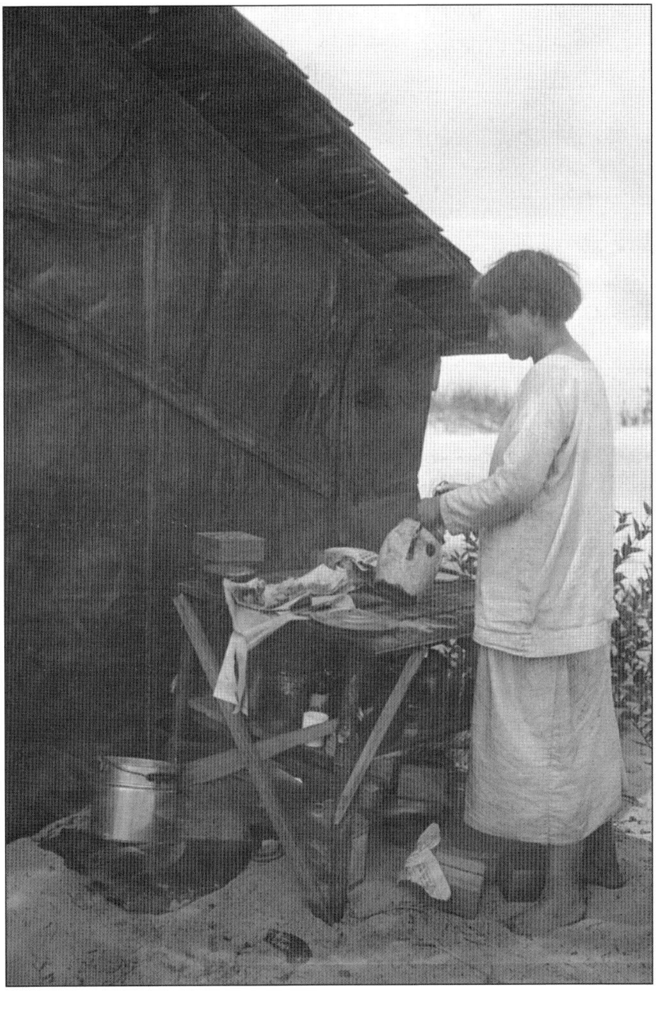

Alice Mabel Gray. Better known as Diana of the Dunes, Gray (1881–1925) was the iconic figure of the Indiana dunes in the early 20th century. This photograph was taken in May 1917. Raised in a struggling, working-class family near the Back of the Yards community in Chicago, Gray, with the support of a wealthy uncle, attended the University of Chicago. She graduated Phi Beta Kappa with a degree in mathematics. (PCCWTHM.)

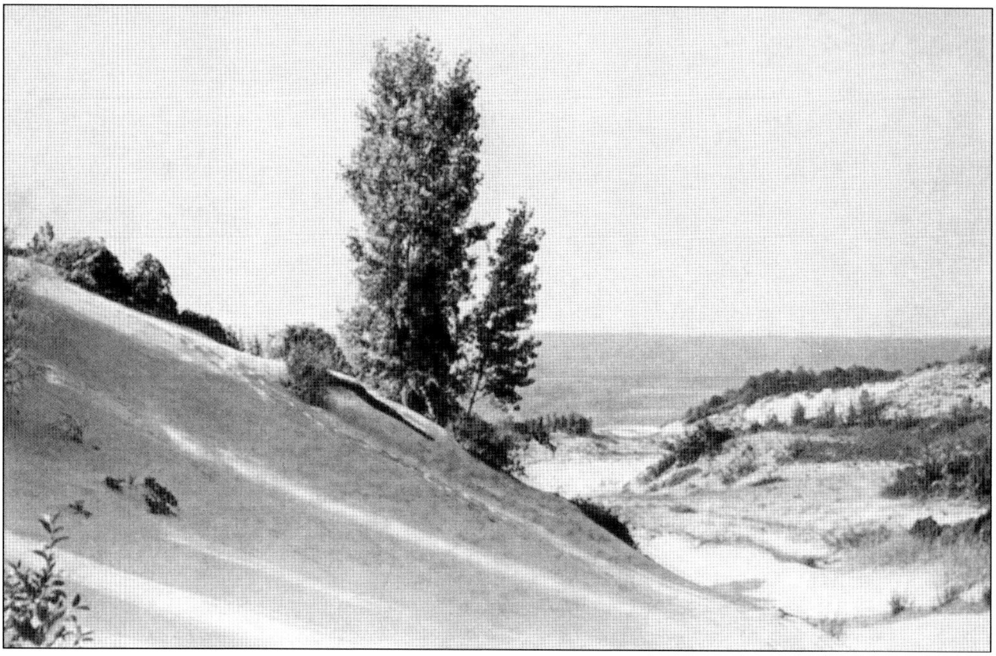

The Dunes. In the early 19th century, the lakeshore, sand dunes, and marshes of northern Porter County were sparsely populated. Native Americans hunted, trapped, fished, and established small, temporary settlements in the area. (WTHM.)

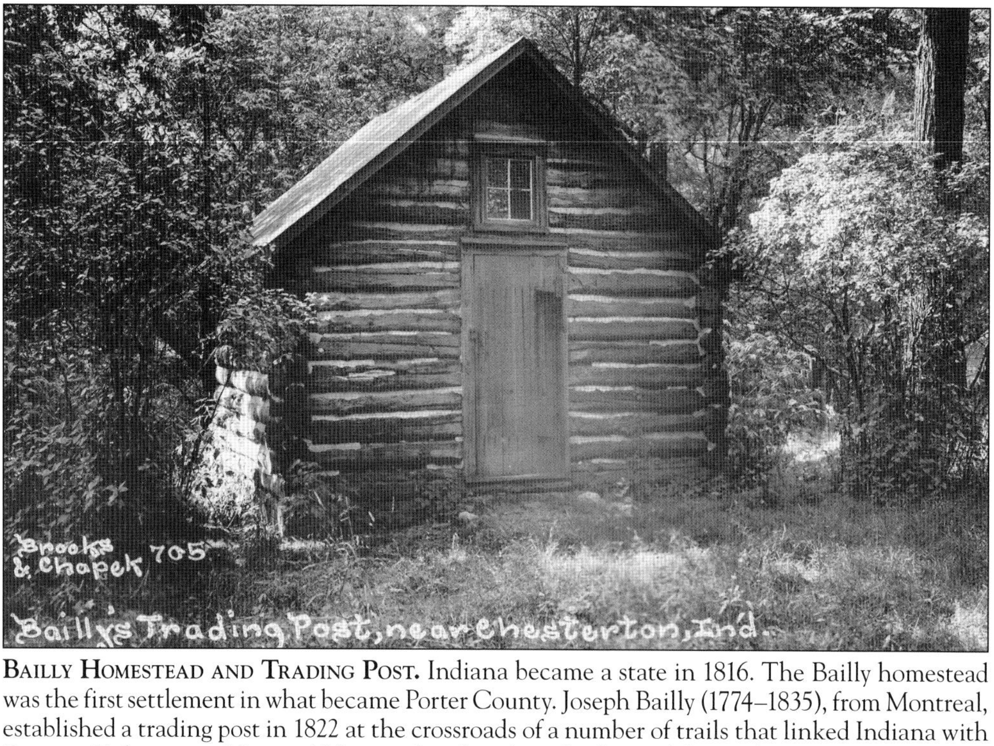

Bailly Homestead and Trading Post. Indiana became a state in 1816. The Bailly homestead was the first settlement in what became Porter County. Joseph Bailly (1774–1835), from Montreal, established a trading post in 1822 at the crossroads of a number of trails that linked Indiana with Detroit. Today, it is a National Historic Landmark and is located five miles southeast of Ogden Dunes. (WTHM.)

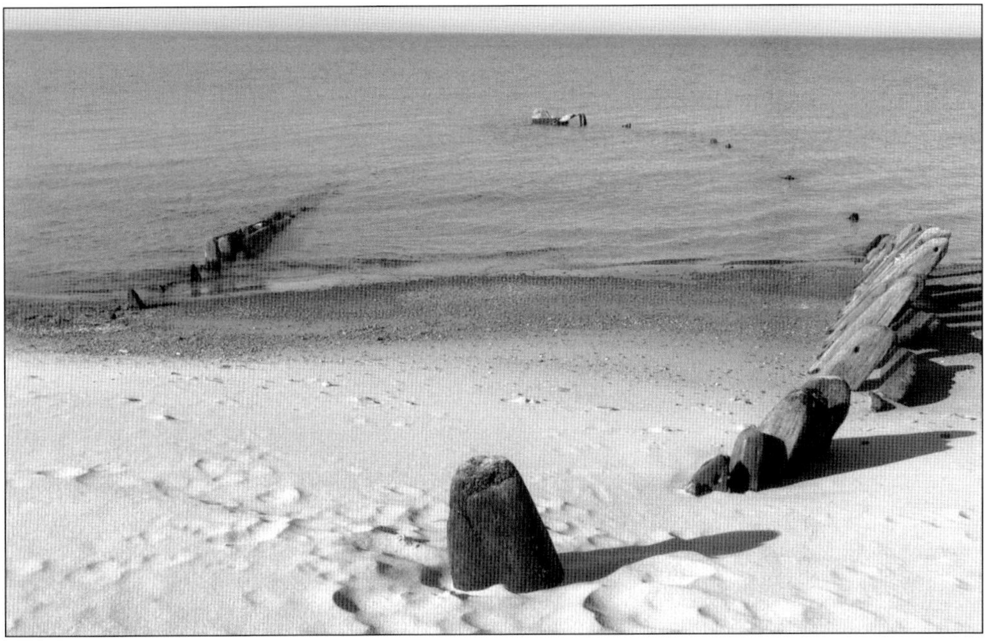

SHIPWRECK. Within the boundaries of Ogden Dunes, only one artifact remains that reflects human activity in the 19th century: the buried half-hull of a timber ship. In 1936, a historian wrote, "It is not always visible; I have seen it; I know it's there." Changes in the shifting sands and in lake levels have resulted in its reappearance in the 1980s and again after 2006. (Courtesy of Richard Hallman.)

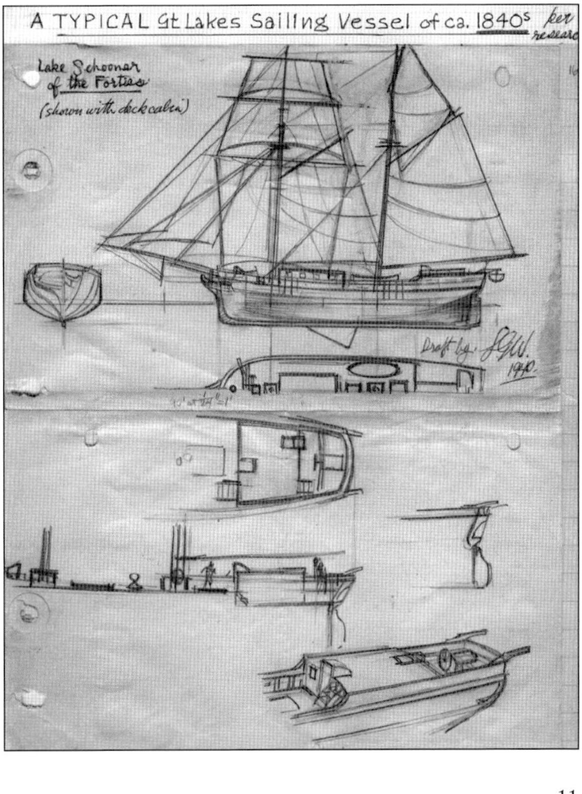

GREAT LAKES SAILING VESSEL. Since 2006, a number of scientific studies have been done of the remains of the ship. It is believed to have been a two-masted vessel, approximately 90 feet in length and 24 feet across. The latest study, by Peter B. Campbell and others in 2012–2013, included this 1910 composite drawing by Loudon G. Wilson. It is a recreation of how a Great Lakes ship might have looked in the mid-19th century. (Courtesy of the Loudon G. Wilson Collection, Historical Collections of the Great Lakes, Bowling Green State University.)

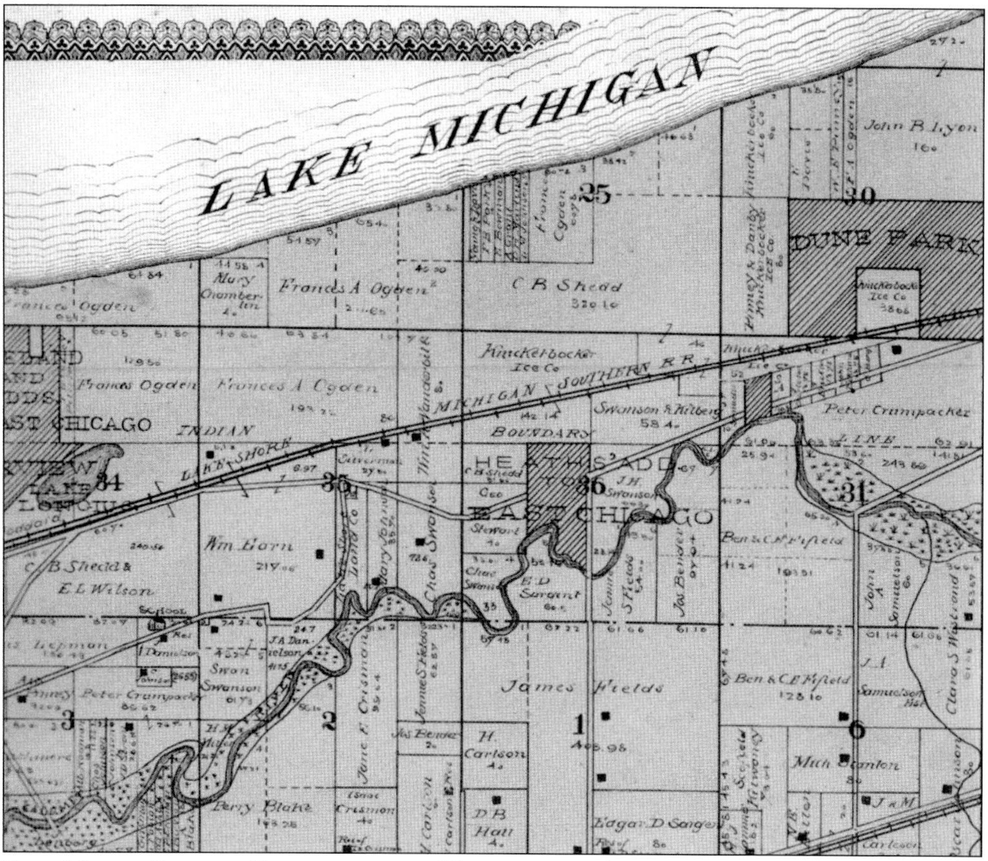

Plat Map of Portage Township, 1906. This map provides a view of land ownership in what became Ogden Dunes and its immediate environs. Francis Ogden, a real-estate speculator from Wisconsin, purchased a large tract of land that would become Ogden Dunes and the West Beach of the Indiana Dunes National Lakeshore. The maps shows railroads crossing through the area and the neighboring settlements, for example, Dune Park. (HSOD.)

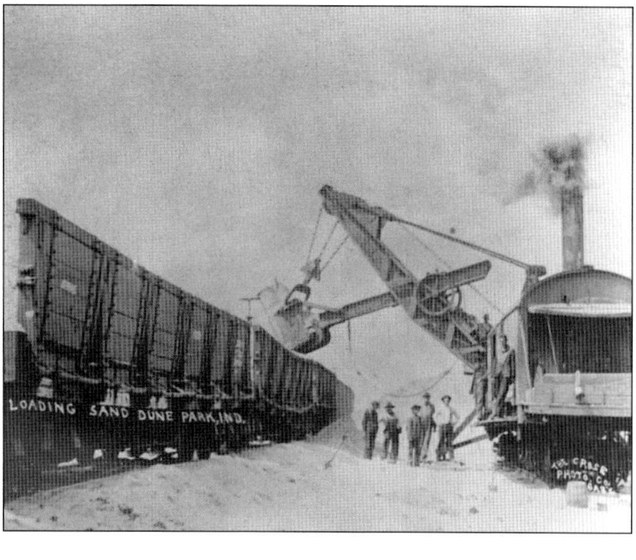

Sand Mining. A major area of sand mining in Porter County was in Section 34, a mile west of Ogden Dunes. The New York Central Railroad established Dune Park as a station and a railroad siding. This siding allowed the railroad to lay tracks into the dunes in order for steam shovels to load sand for landfill and for industrial purposes. (CRAIUN.)

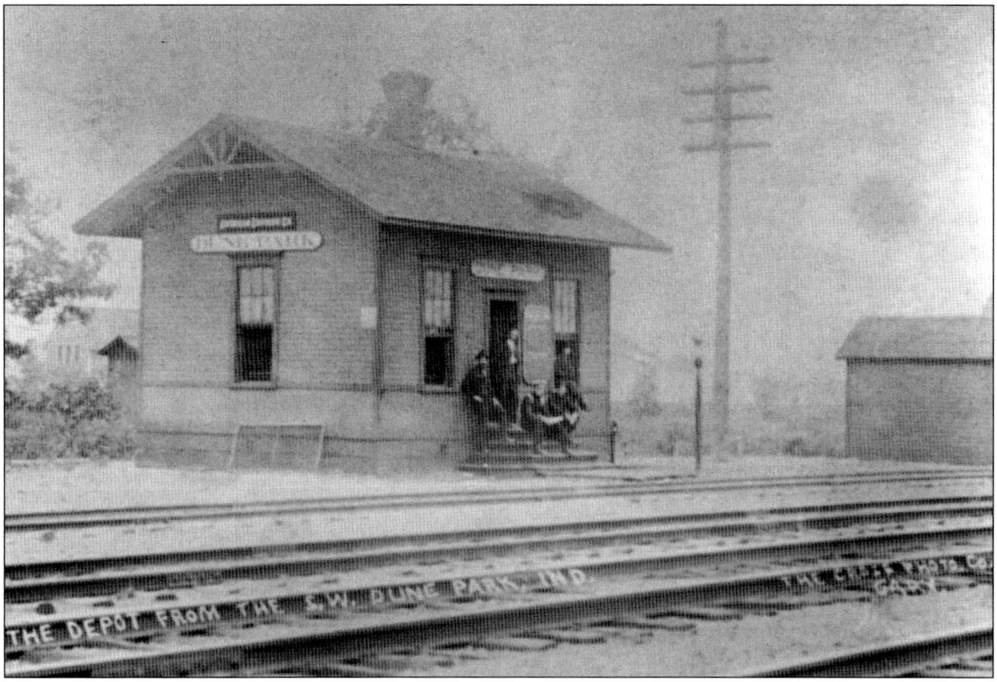

Dune Park Station. This New York Central station became a regular stop for nature enthusiasts. Chicagoans would come to hike, swim, and picnic in the dunes. The beach was a mile north of the station. (HSOD.)

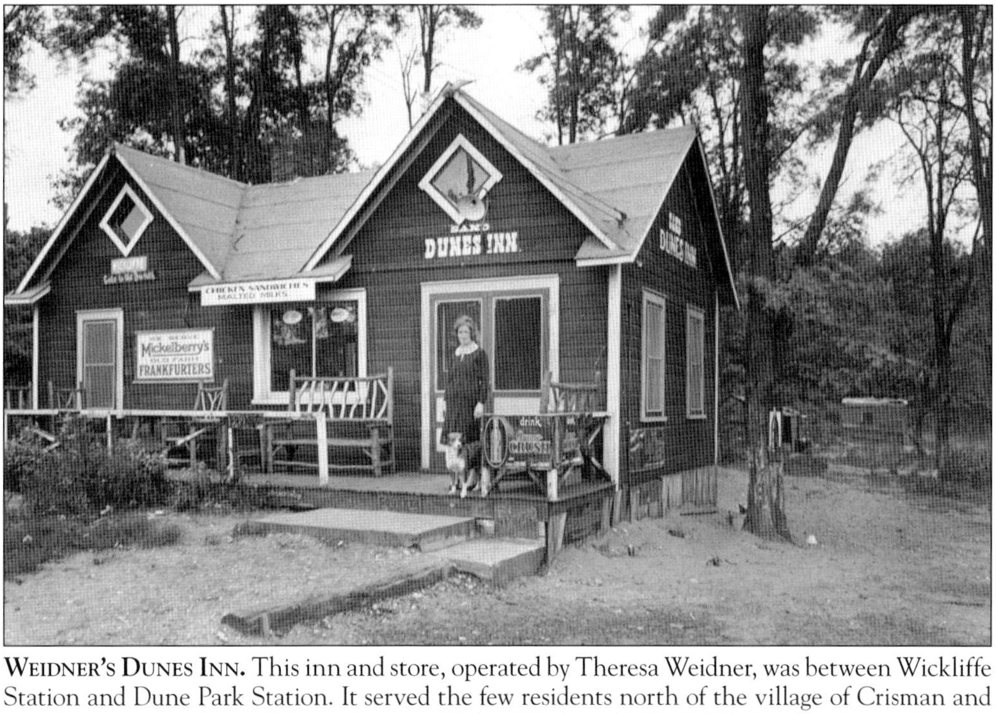

Weidner's Dunes Inn. This inn and store, operated by Theresa Weidner, was between Wickliffe Station and Dune Park Station. It served the few residents north of the village of Crisman and the visitors to the dunes. Weidner's niece, Helen Wachter (1909–1996), lived on Diana Road in Ogden Dunes from 1961 until her death. (HSOD, Wachter family.)

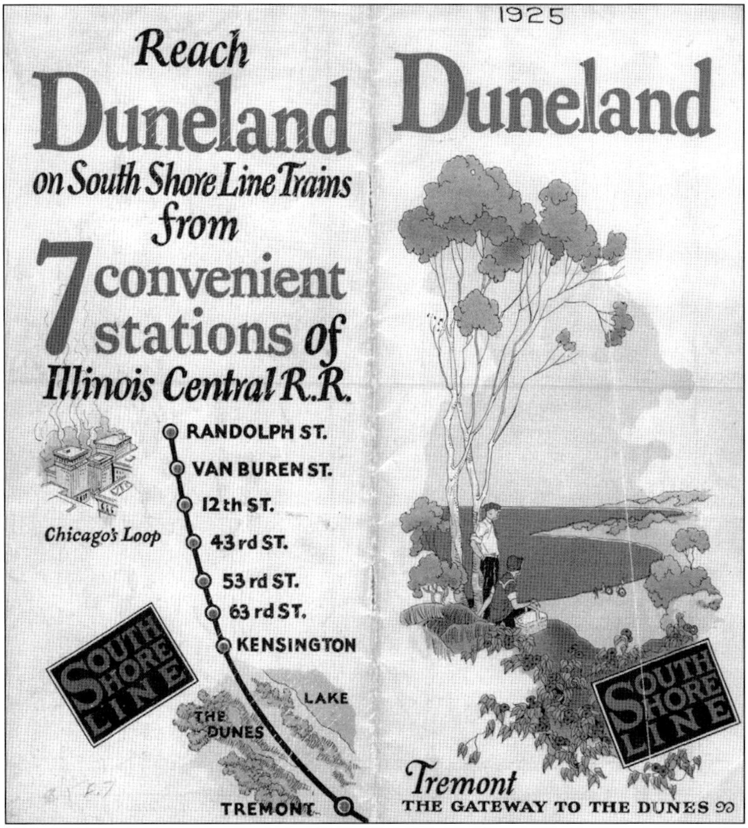

SOUTH SHORE RAILROAD SCHEDULE, 1925. This schedule of the Chicago, South Shore & South Bend Railroad features Tremont, a station one mile south of the Prairie Club's camp. In 1925, Samuel Insull (1859–1939), a successful Chicago utilities magnate, took over the bankrupt electric railway that ran between Chicago and South Bend. Insull then invested millions in changing the power system to 1,500 volts DC, building electric substations along the rail line, and adding a number of stops. (CRAIUN.)

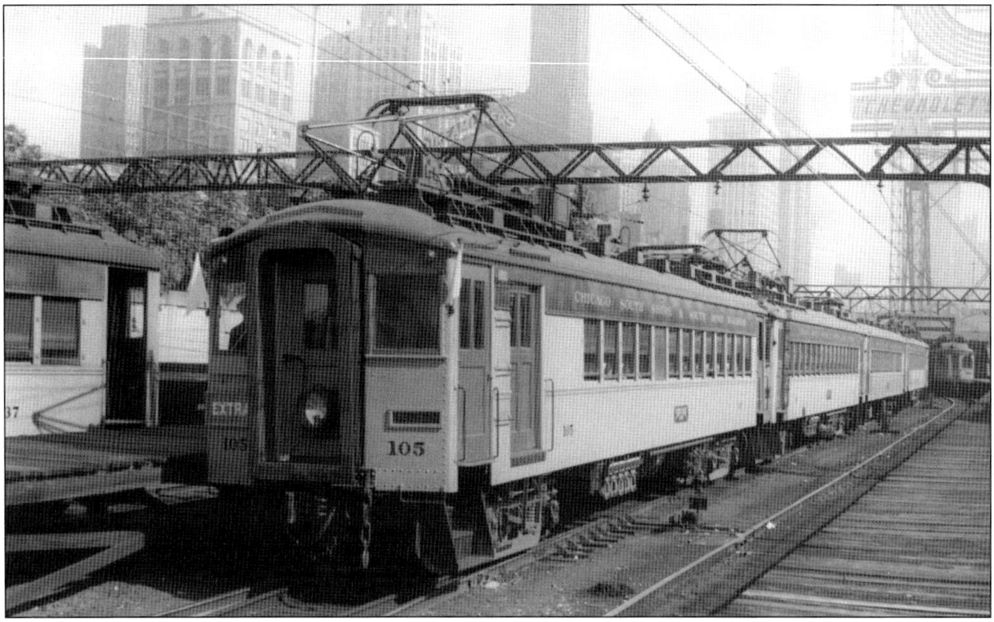

SOUTH SHORE RAILROAD PASSENGER CARS. The South Shore's terminus in Chicago is located in the Loop. The electric railcars, built originally by the Pullman Company in 1926, remained in use, largely unchanged, until 1983, when new cars were added. (CRAIUN.)

RAILROAD POSTER. Samuel Insull invested significant money in advertising this railroad, which linked Chicago and South Bend. To generate passengers, Insull created the image of Northwest Indiana (from Chicago to South Bend) as a region for recreation and bedroom communities. Artists designed nearly 50 posters between 1925 and 1932. Oscar Rabe Hanson created this lithograph in 1925. (CRAIUN.)

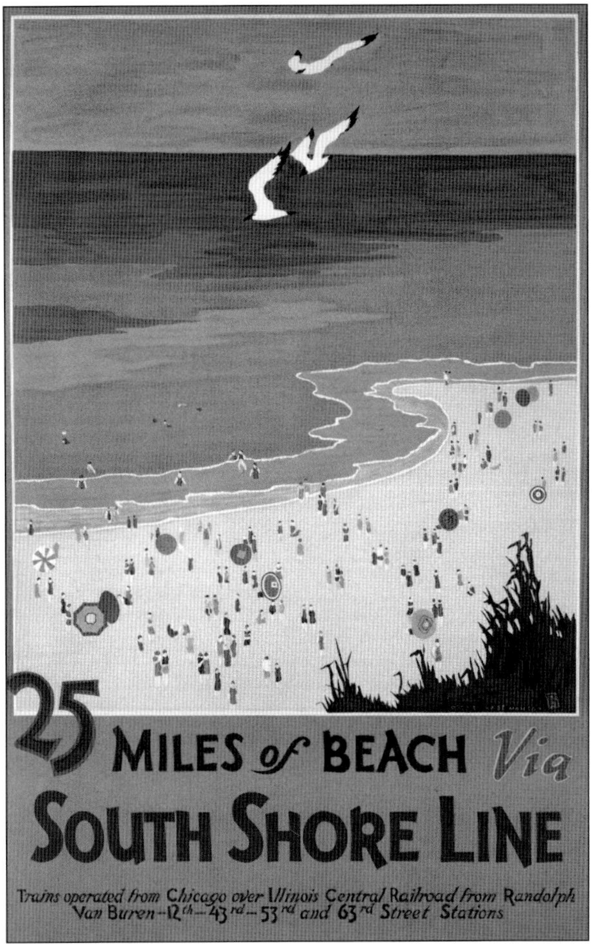

WICKLIFFE STATION. Wickliffe was one of the electric substations upgraded in 1925–1926 to power Samuel Insull's railroad. Wickliffe, the original name for the stop that was to become Ogden Dunes, was supposedly named after the electrical engineer in charge of building the substation. Today, the electric substation looks almost the same as it did when it was built. (HSOD.)

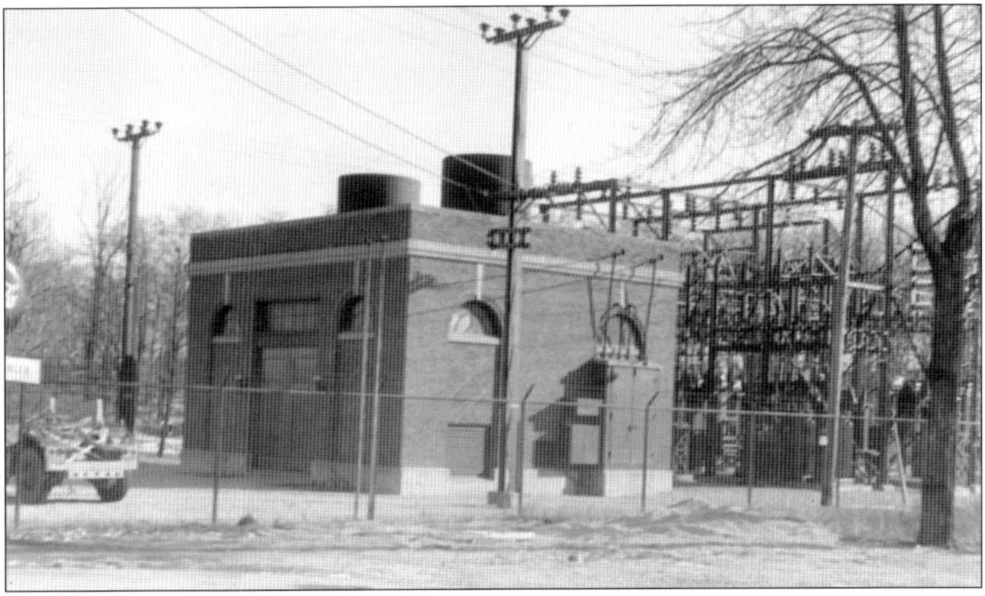

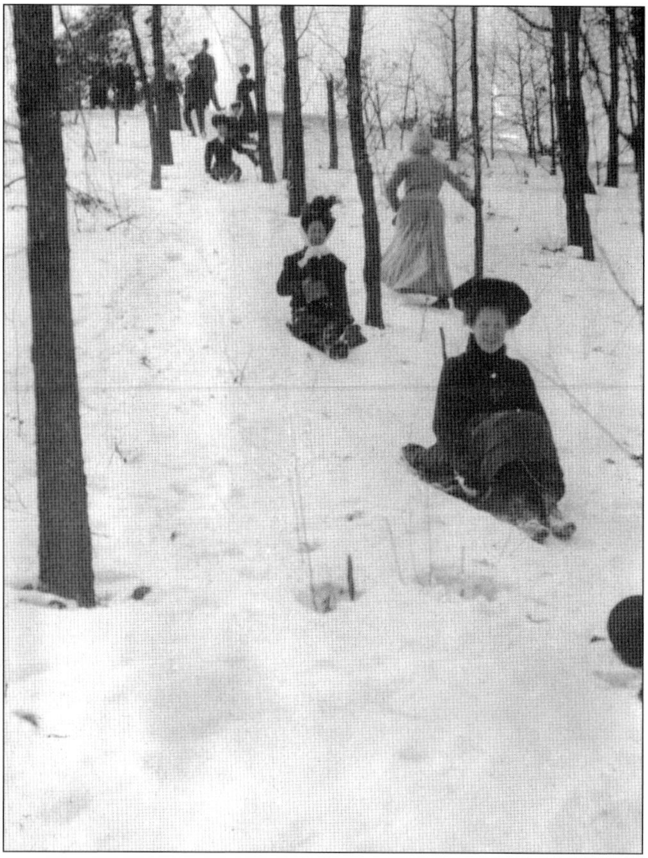

Fun with the Prairie Club. The Prairie Club, formed in 1908 in Chicago, provided its members and guests with opportunities to explore nature in and near Chicago. The first walk attracted 120 hikers. By 1929, the club had more than 1,400 members. Also in 1908, the South Shore Railway began to offer service to the Indiana dunes, making it a popular area for hiking. Here, hikers in their Sunday best enjoy sledding. (Prairie Club, WTHM.)

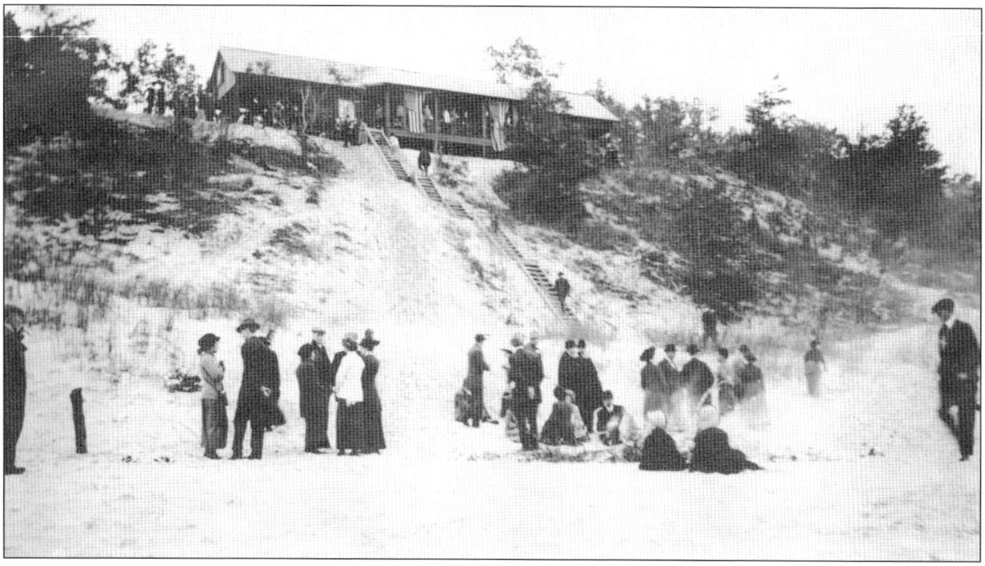

Prairie Club Clubhouse. The dunes became so popular that, by 1914, the club had built a clubhouse about one mile north of the Tremont South Shore stop. Members also had the opportunity to build temporary cabins nearby in order to enjoy the benefits of the clubhouse. (PCCWTHM.)

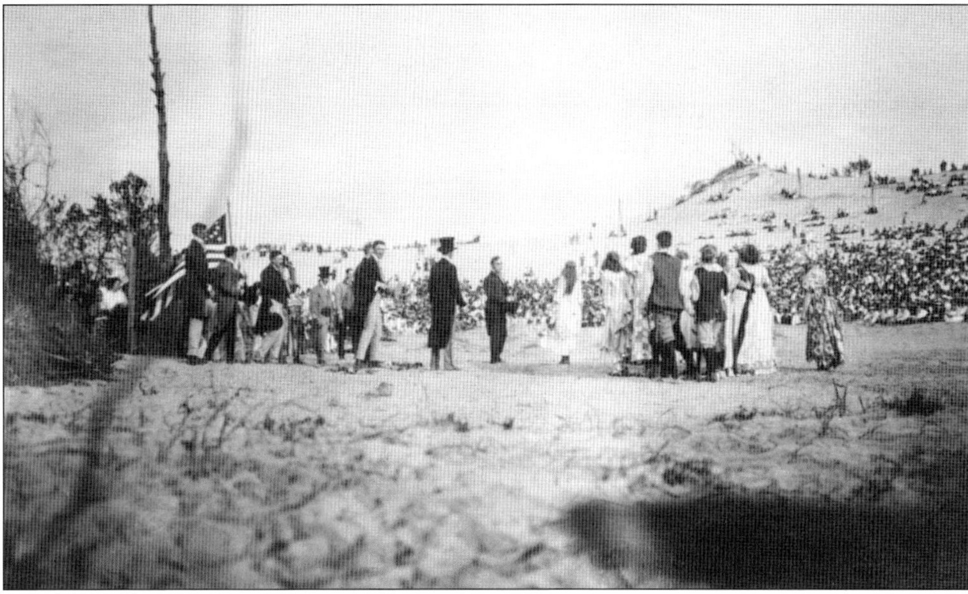

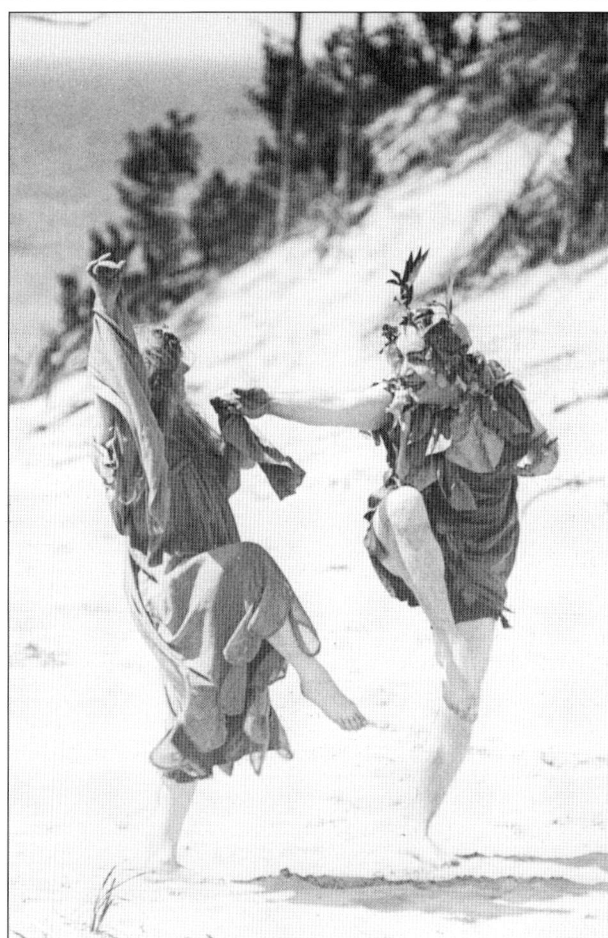

"The Dunes Under Four Flags." The 1917 Memorial Day pageant, sponsored by the Prairie Club and others, involved almost a year of planning and attracted over 700 participants. It was an effort to lobby for the creation of a national park. At least two early residents of Ogden Dunes participated in this extravaganza: Ethel Durfee, who served as secretary of Dunes Pageant Association, an outgrowth of the Prairie Club; and Anita Bailey Cassidy (1890–1976), who played one of the daughters of Joseph Bailly of Bailly Town. (PCCWTHM.)

Nymphs. One of the most well known of the hundreds of photographs of the pageant is this one, depicting the nymphs. The pageant was planned for Memorial Day as well as for June 3, 1917. Rain on the holiday caused this performance to be cancelled. Some observers estimated that nearly 40,000 attended the second performance. (PCCWTHM.)

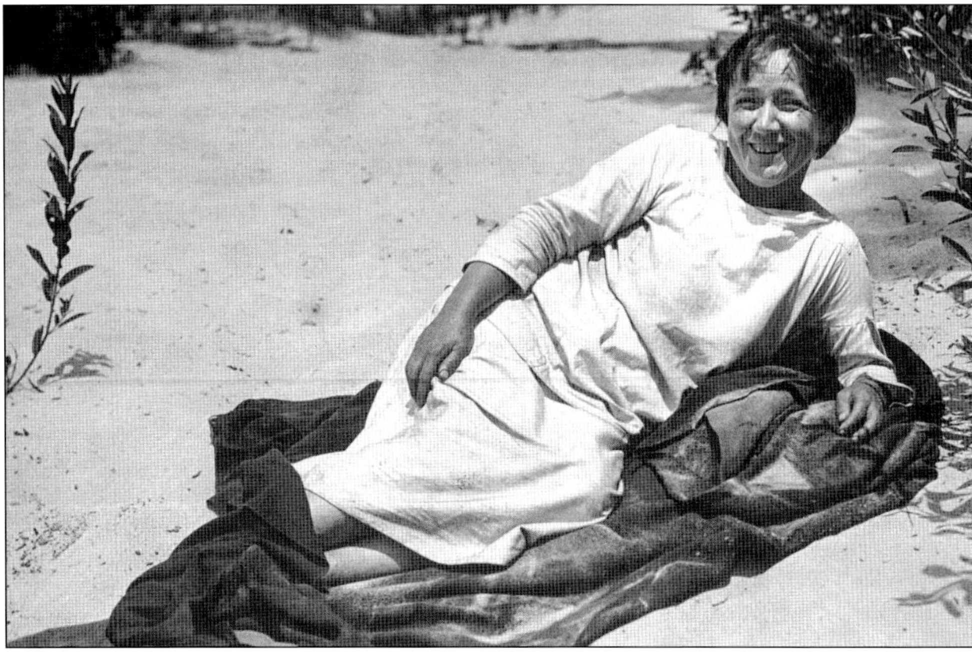

Leaving Society Behind. After graduating from the University of Chicago, Alice Gray worked in Washington, DC, and then studied in Germany. She dropped out of society in 1915. She was later quoted as saying, "I wanted to live my own life—a free life. The life of a salary earner in the city is slavery, a constant fight for the means of living. Here it is so different." (Courtesy of the *Chicago Tribune*.)

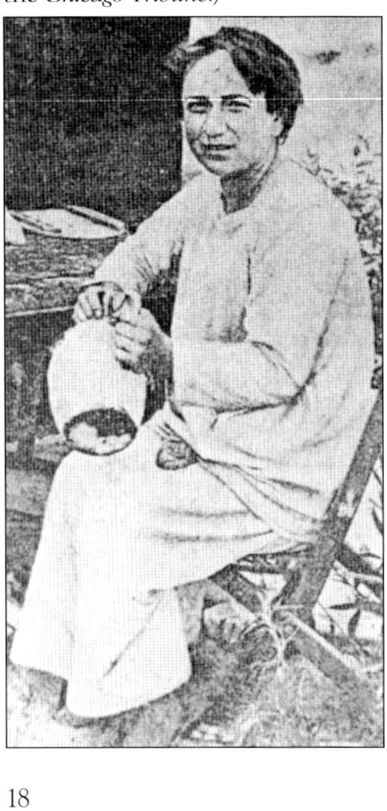

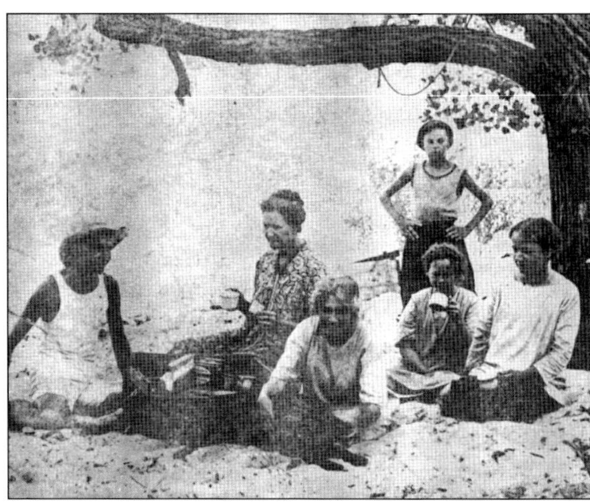

Diana of the Dunes. Above, Alice Gray and a group of friends enjoy the Indiana dunes. Although Gray lived alone in the dunes in the early years, she kept in contact with friends. She even spoke in favor of protecting the dunes at a meeting in the Art Institute's Fullerton Hall in April 1917. At left, the cottage behind Gray may be the Wren's Nest, or an earlier one located near Dune Acres. (Above, PCCWTHM; left, WTHM.)

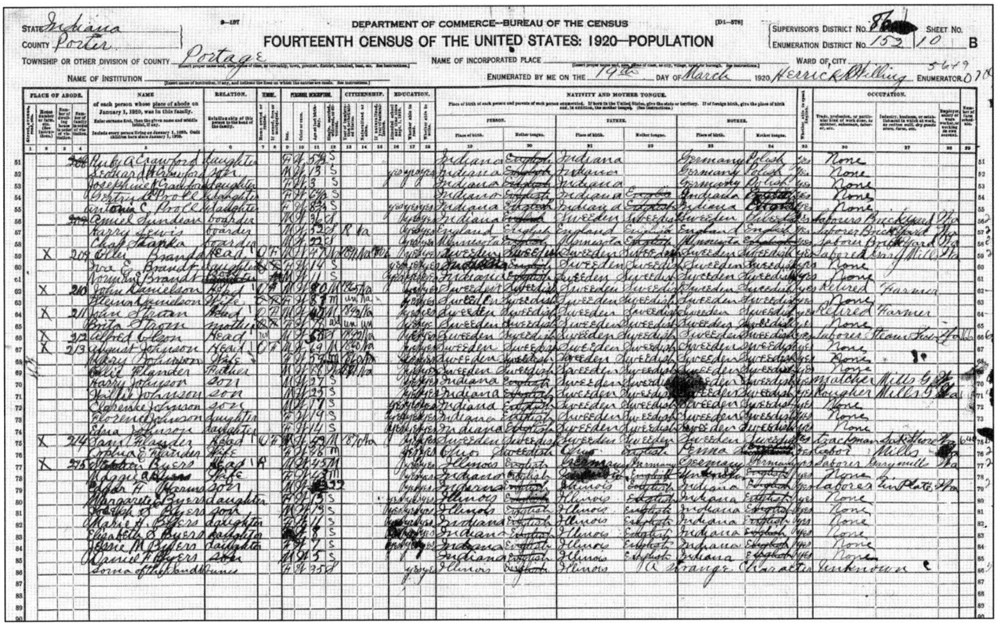

DEPARTMENT OF COMMERCE—BUREAU OF THE CENSUS

FOURTEENTH CENSUS OF THE UNITED STATES: 1920—POPULATION

STATE Indiana
COUNTY Porter
TOWNSHIP OR OTHER DIVISION OF COUNTY Portage
SUPERVISOR'S DISTRICT NO.
ENUMERATION DISTRICT NO. 152
SHEET NO. 10 B
NAME OF INCORPORATED PLACE
WARD OF CITY
NAME OF INSTITUTION
ENUMERATED BY ME ON THE 19th DAY OF March 1920.

1920 Census. In the 1920 manuscript census for Portage Township of Porter County, the census taker identified the last person listed as "Lorna of the Sand Dunes," age 35, single, born in Illinois, and "a strange character." Most likely, this was Alice Gray.

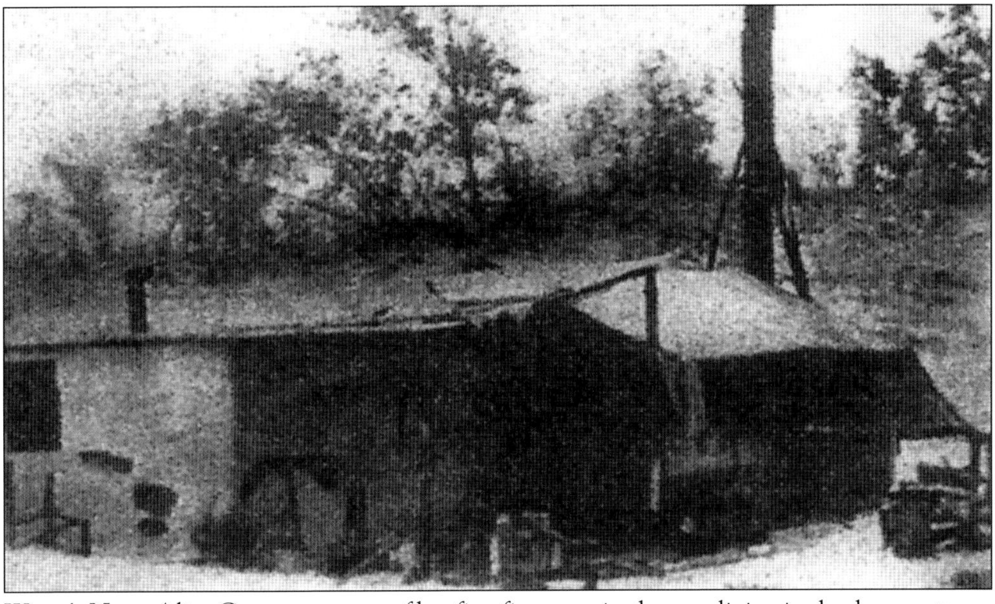

Wren's Nest. Alice Gray spent most of her first five years in the area living in shacks or cottages in the area east of Ogden Dunes. During that time, she was interviewed by Chicago reporters, who described her as a free spirit; they came to refer to her as "Diana of the Dunes." Around 1920, she and her common-law husband, Paul Wilson, settled near Polliwog Pond at the western edge of what became Ogden Dunes. She called her cottage Wren's Nest. Gray died there on February 9, 1925, at the age of 43. She was buried without a tombstone in Oak Hill Cemetery, south of Glen Park, near the graves of several prominent Gary families. A tombstone was erected in 1996 as a result of a local fundraising effort. (PCCWTHM.)

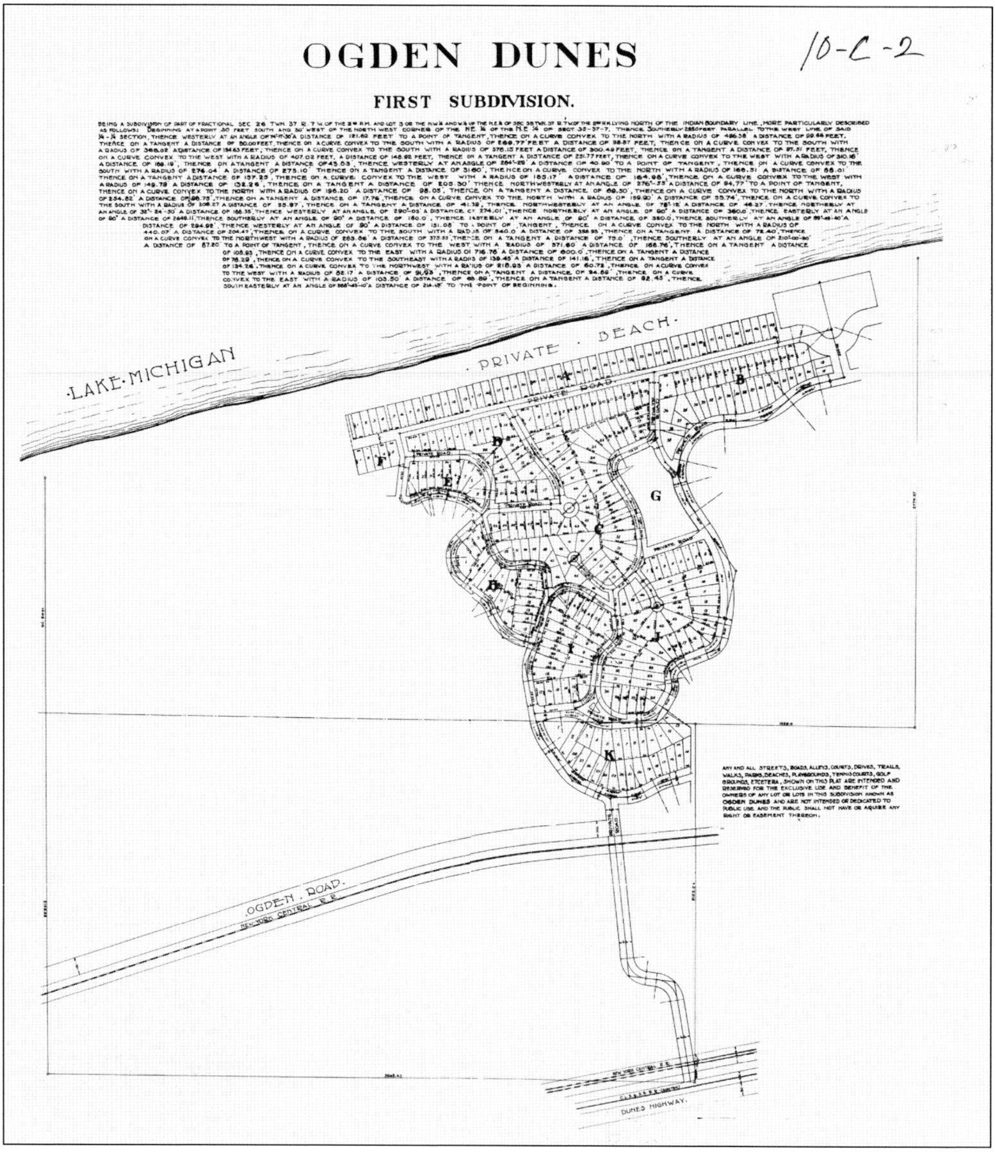

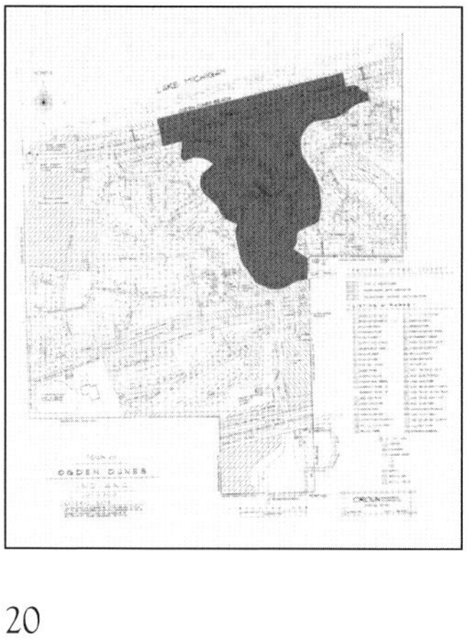

Map of First Subdivision, 1924. After the purchase of the 500-plus acres from the Francis Ogden Estate in 1923 by Ogden Dunes Incorporated, Colin Mackenzie (1892–1931), a civil engineer and a partner in the enterprise, undertook to survey the land and to lay out streets and lots. The map above, filed with the Porter County commissioners, became the basis for incorporation in 1925. The map at left shows the First Subdivision within the 1994 boundaries of Ogden Dunes, which remain the same today. (Above, courtesy of Alec Mackenzie; left, HSOD.)

Two

THE RIGHT MOMENT 1923–1927

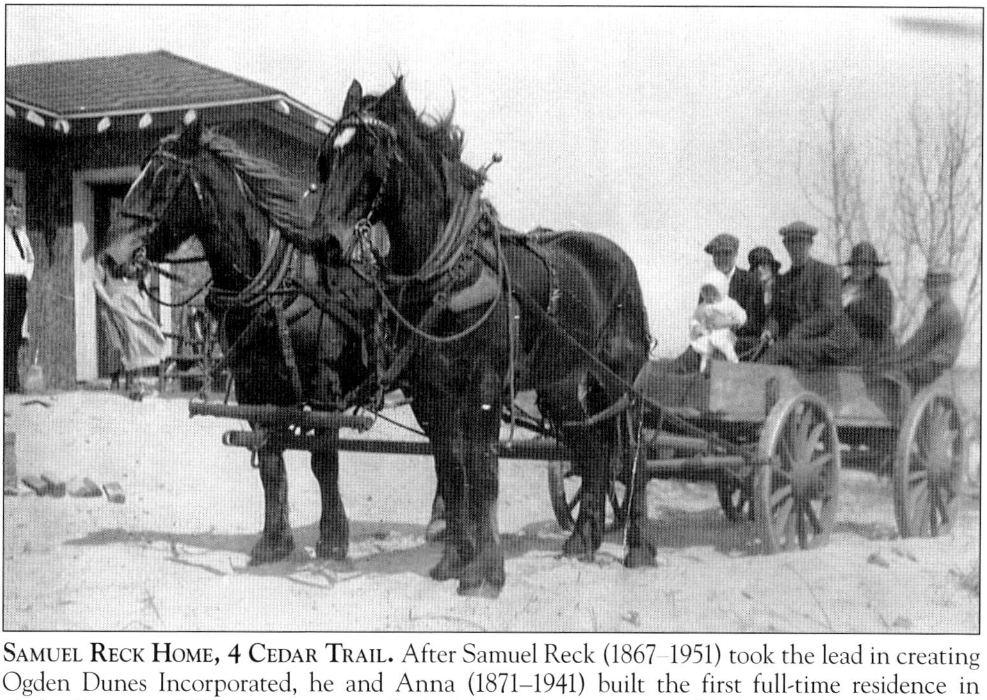

SAMUEL RECK HOME, 4 CEDAR TRAIL. After Samuel Reck (1867–1951) took the lead in creating Ogden Dunes Incorporated, he and Anna (1871–1941) built the first full-time residence in Ogden Dunes in 1923. The home overlooked Shore Drive and Lake Michigan. This photograph was taken in January 1924. Because of the lack of roads, most guests had to come by horse and wagon. (HSOD.)

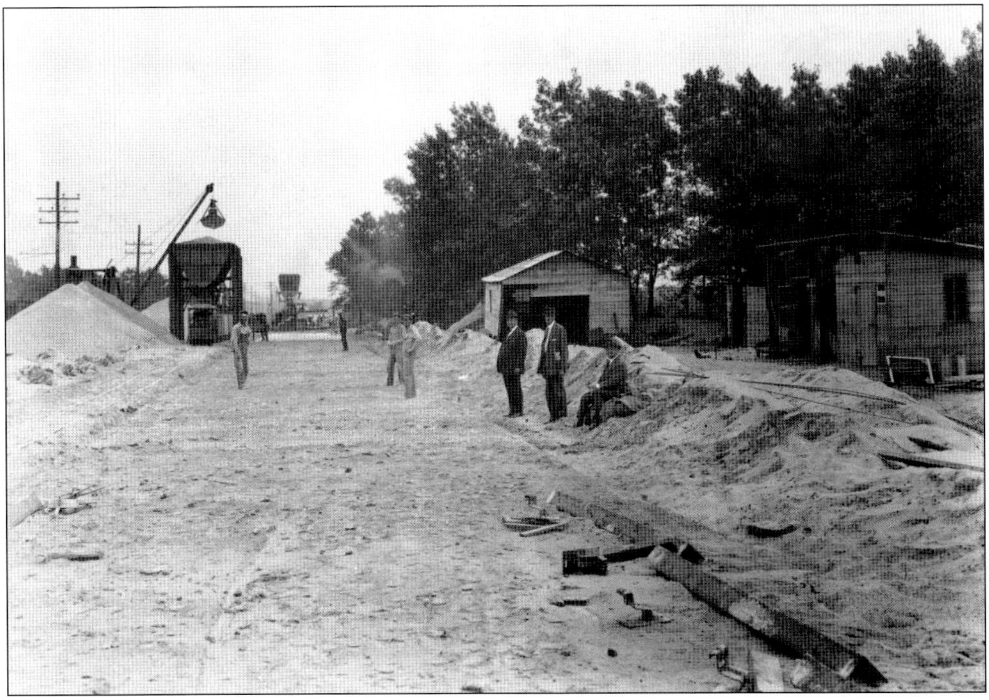

Dunes Highway. The key to the successful development of northern Porter County was transportation. By 1925, the South Shore Railroad was being upgraded and a new federal highway between Chicago and Detroit was being completed. This photograph was taken near Wickliffe Station. (CRAIUN.)

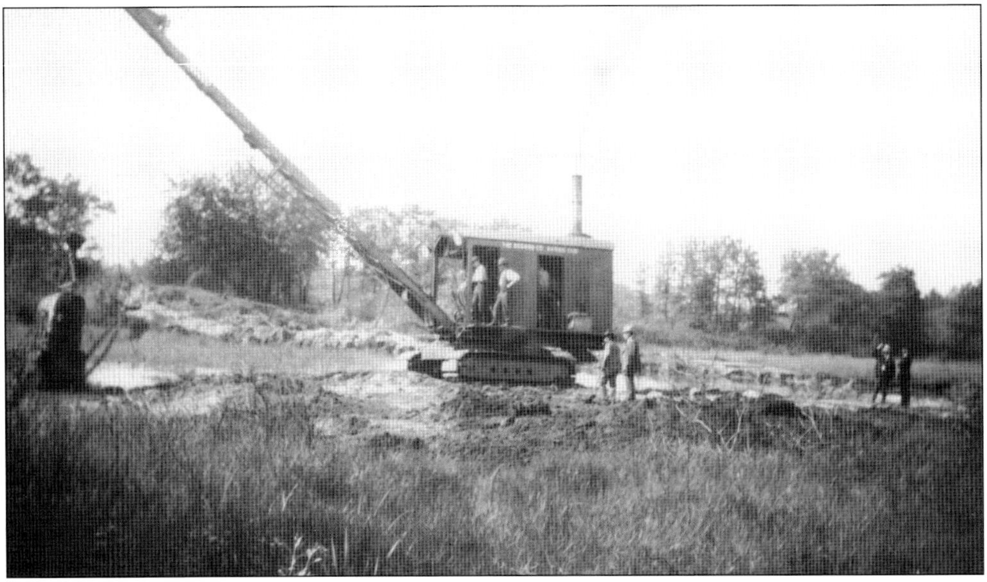

Draining Marshlands. The development of the area around Ogden Dunes required the draining of thousands of acres of marshland. The commissioners of Lake and Porter Counties approved a plan to create a channel along the Little Calumet River and to link this to Burns Ditch. Later referred to by some as Burns Waterway or Burns Canal, Burns Ditch was completed in the mid-1920s. It flows into Lake Michigan, one-fourth of a mile east of Ogden Dunes. (CRAIUN.)

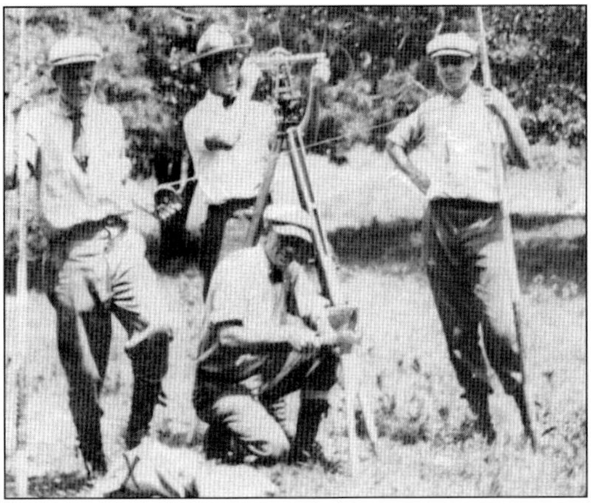

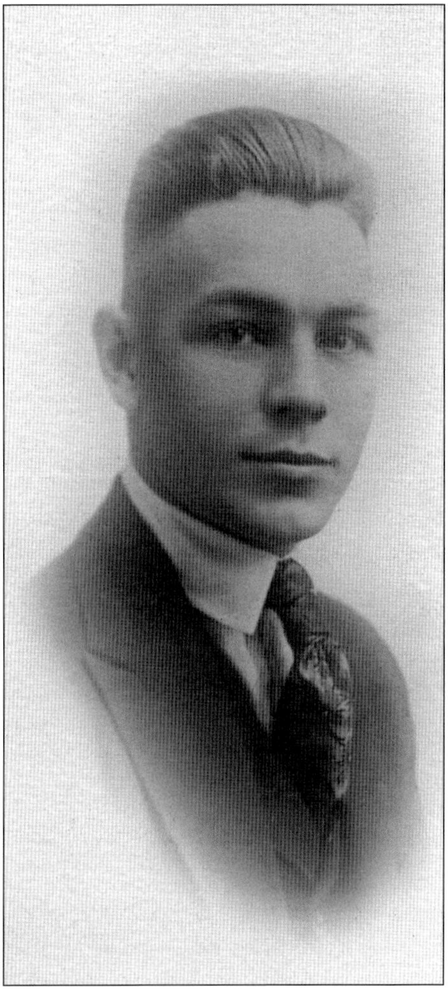

Colin Mackenzie. Mackenzie (1892–1931) and his family emigrated from Scotland, coming first to Illinois and then to Gary in 1910. His father, Alexander, was a successful sea captain before he became a civil engineer. He established the Gary Engineering Company with his two sons, Colin and Godfrey. Colin (right) had graduated from Gary Emerson High School and then earned an engineering degree from the University of Cincinnati in 1915. Around 1922, he interested the Reck family (Samuel and his son Nelson) in a plan to purchase land from the Ogden estate, which became Ogden Dunes. Samuel Reck raised the funds for the purchase in 1923 and then organized Ogden Dunes Realty to sell the lots. Colin Mackenzie laid out the First Subdivision. Mackenzie's surveying crew is shown above. Colin Mackenzie oversaw the platting of the roads and lots. (Courtesy of Alec Mackenzie.)

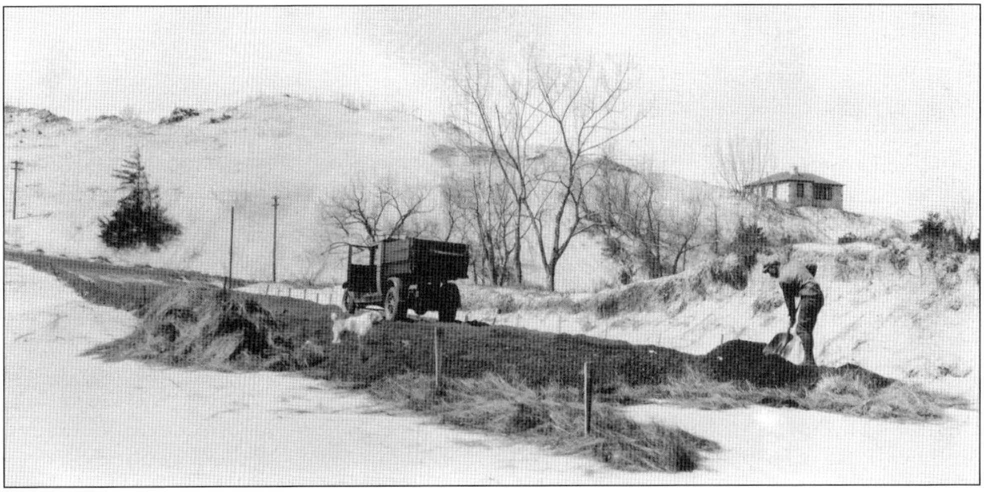

Road Building. The road crew of Ogden Dunes Realty is at work. An early home is visible in the background. (HSOD.)

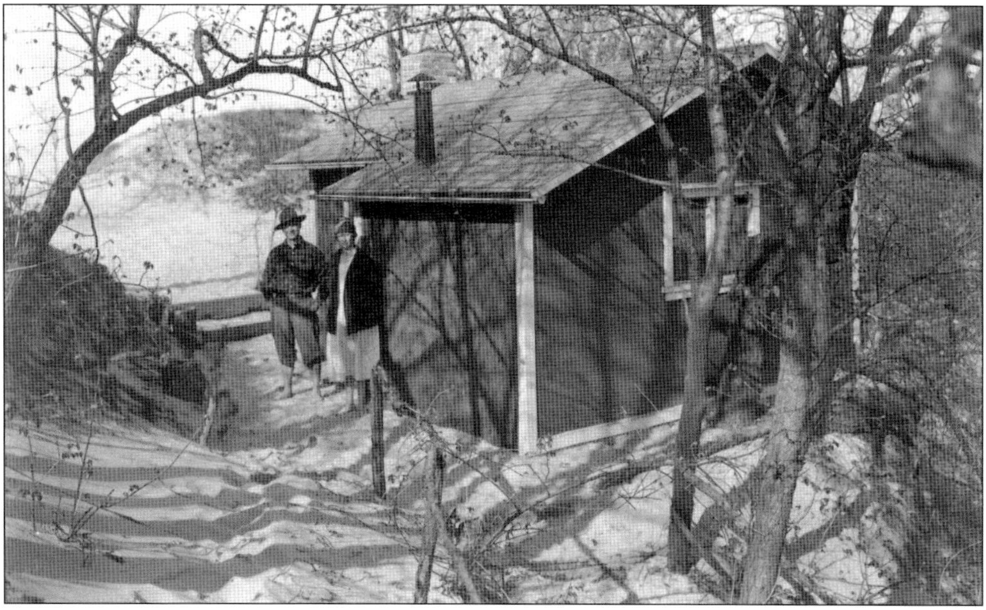

LINNBERG COTTAGE. Nils and Emma Linnberg, Swedish immigrants who lived in Chicago, were drawn to the Indiana dunes. By the early 1920s, they built a squatter's cottage on a high dune on land owned by the Ogden estate. It was one of a number of such cottages or shacks on the property purchased by Ogden Dunes Incorporated. (Courtesy of Dave Larson.)

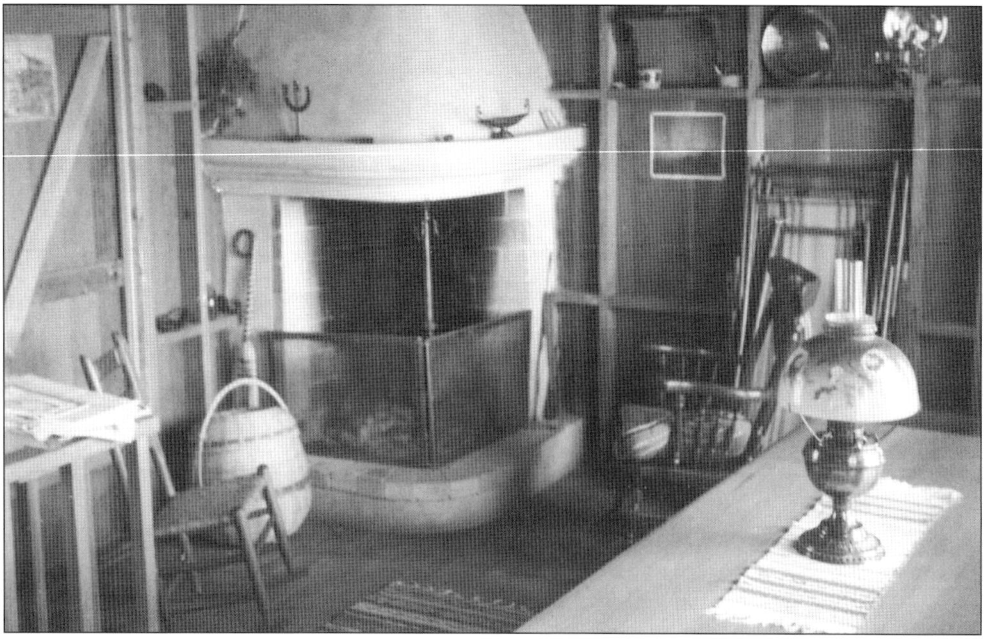

STAMPEN COTTAGE INTERIOR, 9 COTTONWOOD LANE. This cottage, built in 1923, is on land just east of the First Subdivision. Jacob and Kari Stampen emigrated from Norway in 1902 with their daughter Ingrid. Their daughter Marie was born in 1903. She was listed as the owner in 1938, when the town extended East Hill Road to this and another cottage. Marie, who was listed as a librarian in 1940, traveled extensively with Ingrid. She sold the cottage in 1946. The interior of the cottage is very simple, but it has a magnificent fireplace. (HSOD, Vogt.)

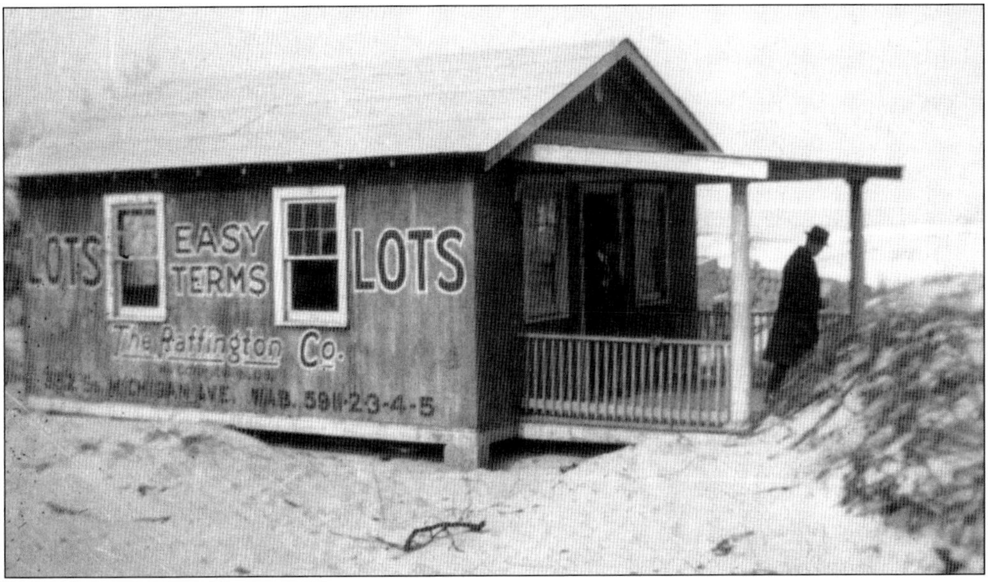

Temporary Sales Office. This old sales office building was transported by barge from Chicago to a dune near the Reck home. Ogden Dunes Realty's main office was in downtown Gary. Later, an on-site office was established near the entrance, in a building that served as office and home of the Whelpley family. Harold Whelpley managed on-site sales; his wife, Lucille, handled the telephone exchange, which served six residences in 1931. (HSOD.)

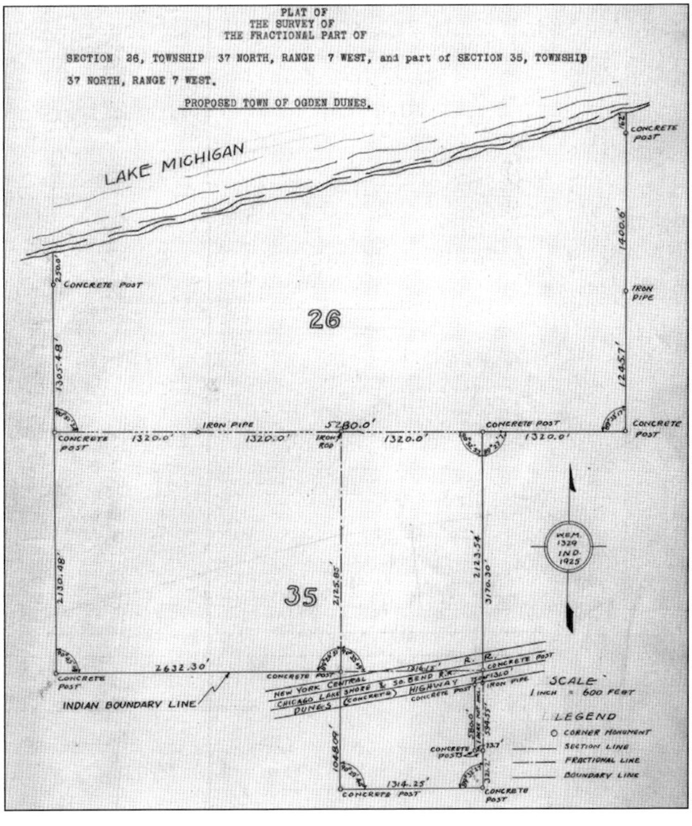

Incorporation Map, 1925. The realty company was unable to obtain a right-of-way across the New York Central tracks. As a result, 20 landowners petitioned the county commissioners to approve the incorporation of the town. The petition was approved in August 1925. The new entrance was not built until 1927, when a court decided in favor of the town. (Courtesy of the Town of Ogden Dunes.)

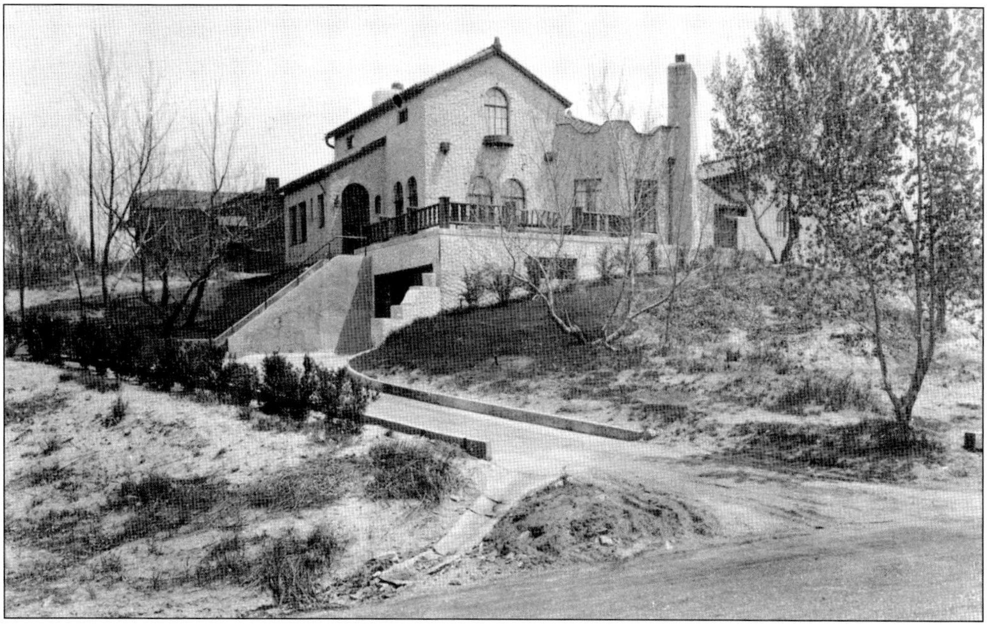

Glover Home, 3 Cedar Trail. The Lynn Glover family of Gary built a large Spanish-style home around 1925 across from the Samuel Reck home. Glover, who had an insurance business in Gary, was elected to serve on the first town board in 1925, along with Samuel Reck and R.B. "Pete" Nicholson, a local builder. The DeLong cottage, built in 1924 by a Gary physician, was directly behind the Glover home. The Glovers sold their home to Guy and Mary Burroughs in the mid-1930s. (HSOD.)

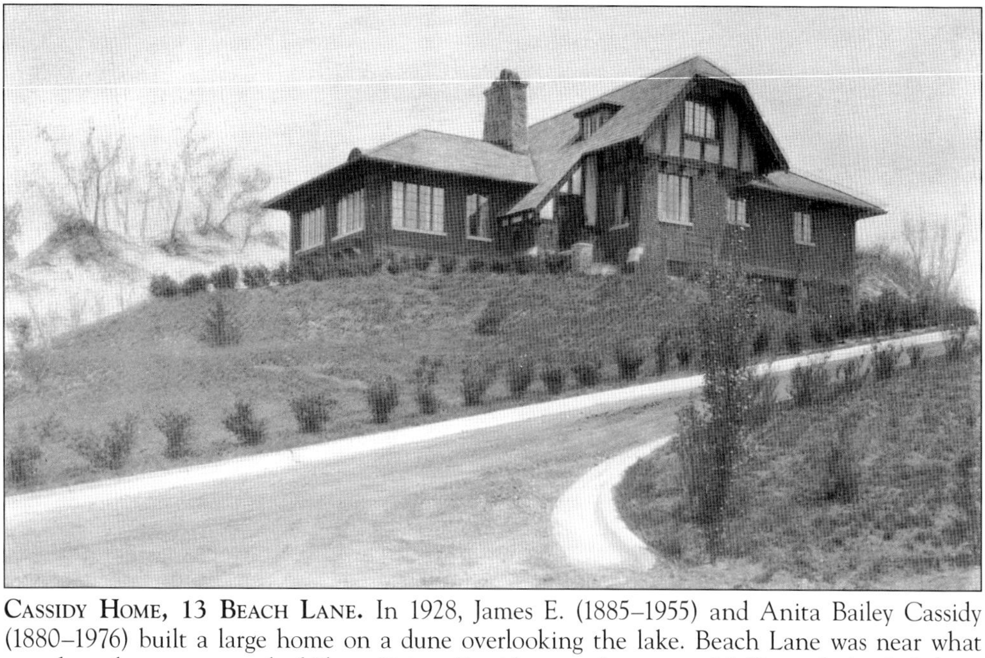

Cassidy Home, 13 Beach Lane. In 1928, James E. (1885–1955) and Anita Bailey Cassidy (1880–1976) built a large home on a dune overlooking the lake. Beach Lane was near what was then the western end of Shore Drive. Cassidy owned a successful Gary wholesale baking company. His wife, Anita, played the role of one of Joseph Bailly's daughters in the 1917 Prairie Club pageant. (HSOD.)

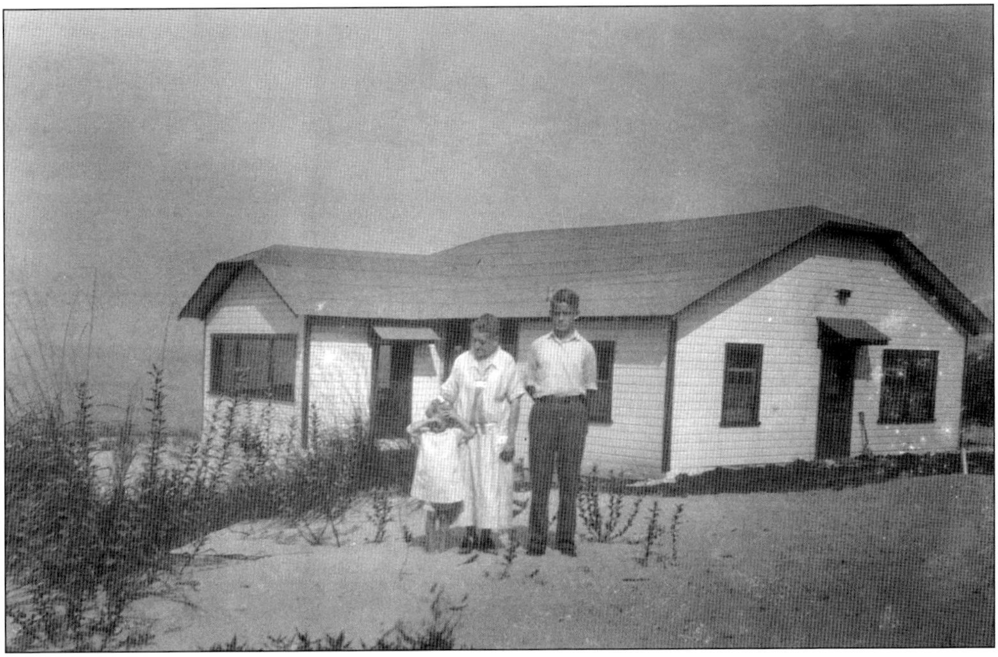

Dalby Cottage, 67 Shore Drive. Harry Dalby and his wife, Mabel, built a cottage in 1925 on Shore Drive, overlooking the lake. Their cottage was adjacent to Samuel Reck's. They had two sons and a daughter, Neysa, who was one of the "rafters." Their son, George M. (1913–1999), and his wife, Margaret, later took ownership of the cottage. They had seven children. For many years, the Dalby family spent its summers in the dunes. The cottage was demolished around 2007. (HSOD, Dalby.)

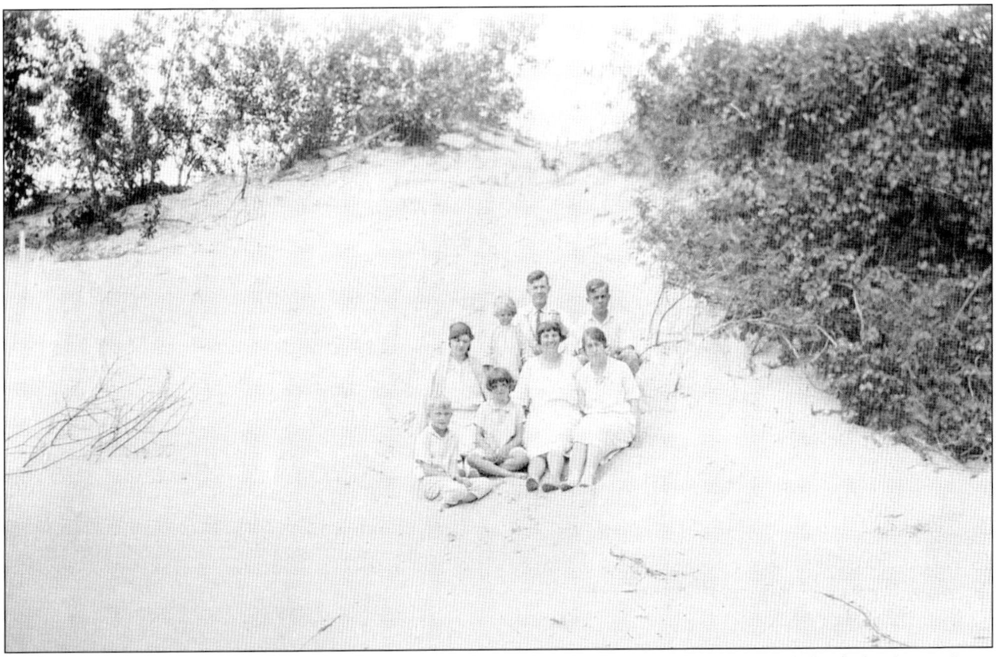

Dalby Family. Harry and Mabel and their extended family enjoy the view of the lake from their property. (HSOD, Dalby.)

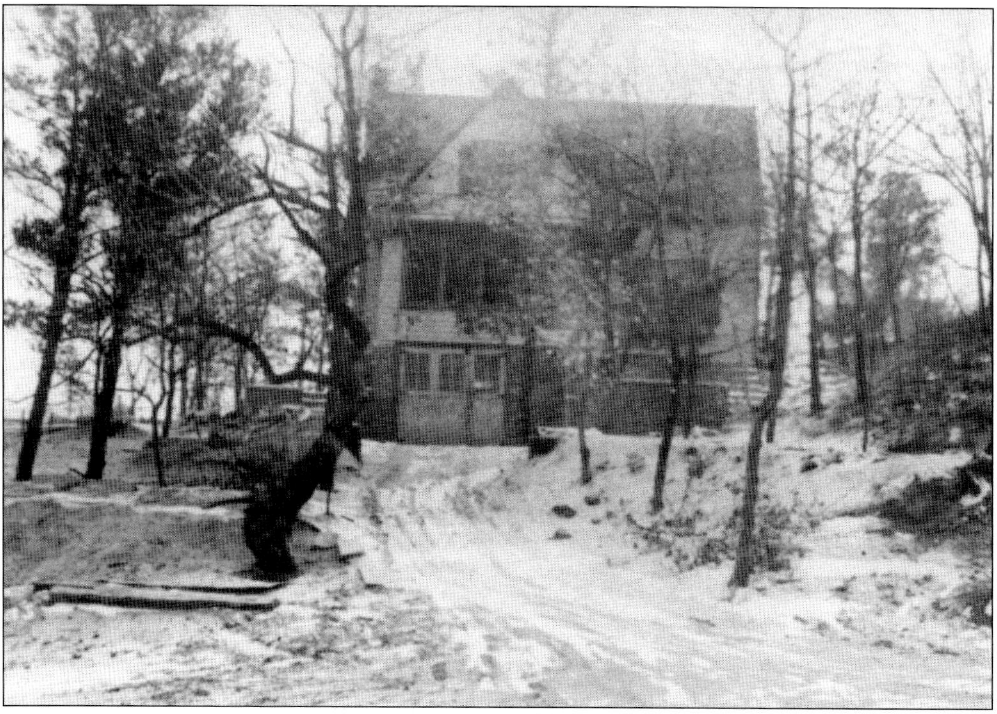

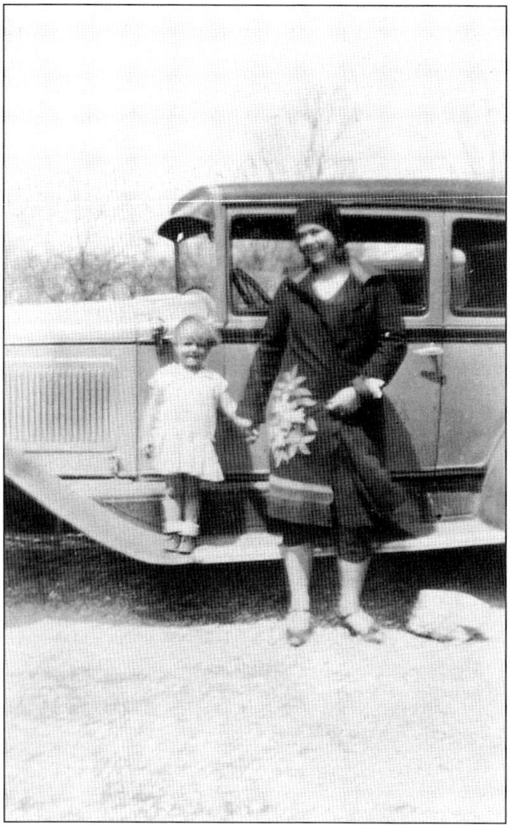

NICKERSON HOME, 89 OGDEN ROAD. Ogden Nickerson (1904–1987), an electrician for the South Shore Railroad, and his wife, Louisa (1909–1993), were married in 1927. The following year, they ordered a Sears house kit and had it delivered and erected on their lot, near what was then the end of Ogden Road. Ogden served on the town board for many years. (HSOD, Nickerson.)

LOUISA AND MARY LOUISE NICKERSON. The Nickersons had two children, Mary Louise, born in 1928, and Ogden Jr., born in 1934. (HSOD, Nickerson.)

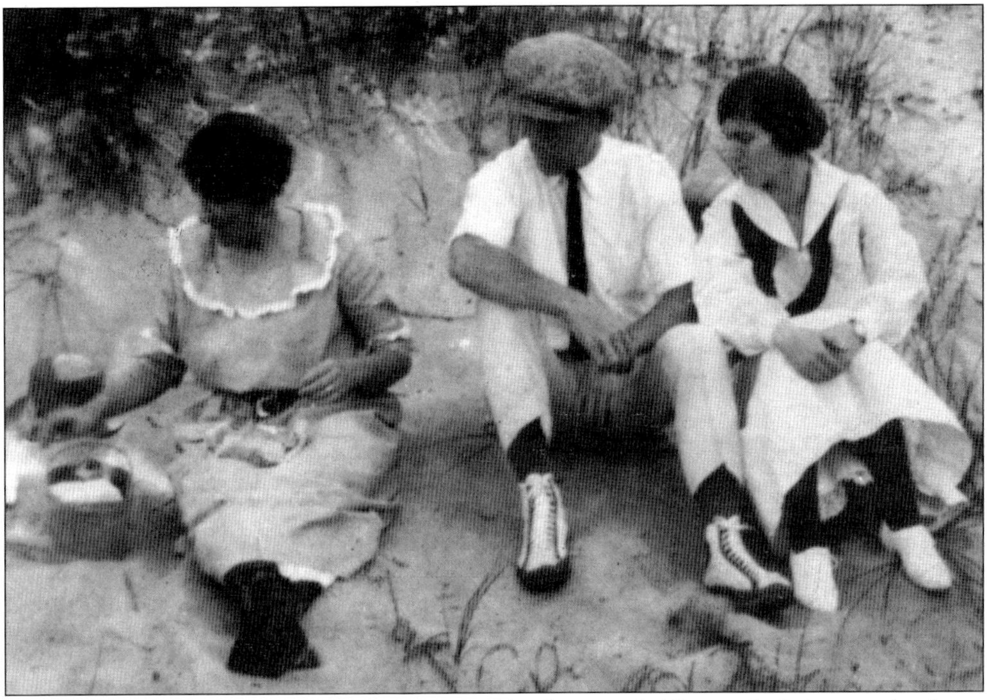

COLIN MACKENZIE FAMILY. Colin Mackenzie and his future wife, Harriet (right), enjoy the dunes with Colin's mother, Elizabeth (left). Colin and Harriet had four children, three of whom lived beyond infancy. They settled in Miller Beach. After Colin's death in 1931 as a result of an assault and then a hospital staph infection, Harriet and her children lived with her in-laws in Miller. Their son Colin moved to 59 Hillcrest in Ogden Dunes in 1964 and became president of the town board in the 1970s. (Courtesy of Alec Mackenzie.)

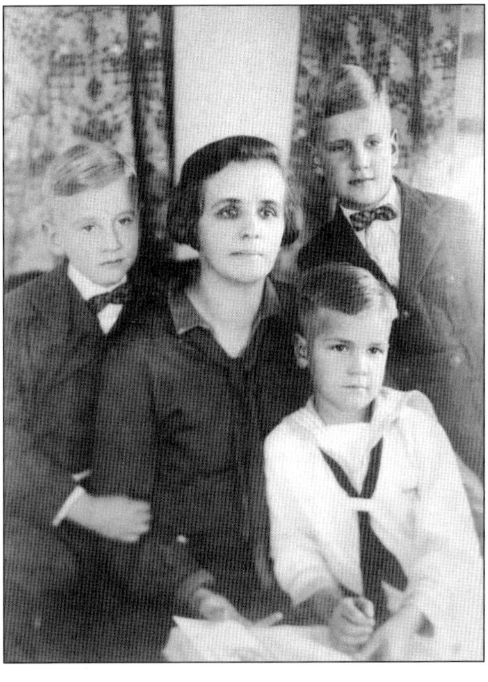

A.L. AND DESS CASH FAMILY. This portrait shows Dess and her three sons, from left to right, Webster (1920–1999), Arthur, and Mitchell (1918–2011). A.L. Cash (1886–1966), a Gary contractor, bought a small cottage in Ogden Dunes about 1928. Over the years, he built scores of homes in Ogden Dunes, and in 1937, he moved permanently there. Dess Cash (1887–1983) organized book and dramatic reading groups and served as the first president of the Woman's Club in 1938. (Courtesy of Laura Cash Mitchell.)

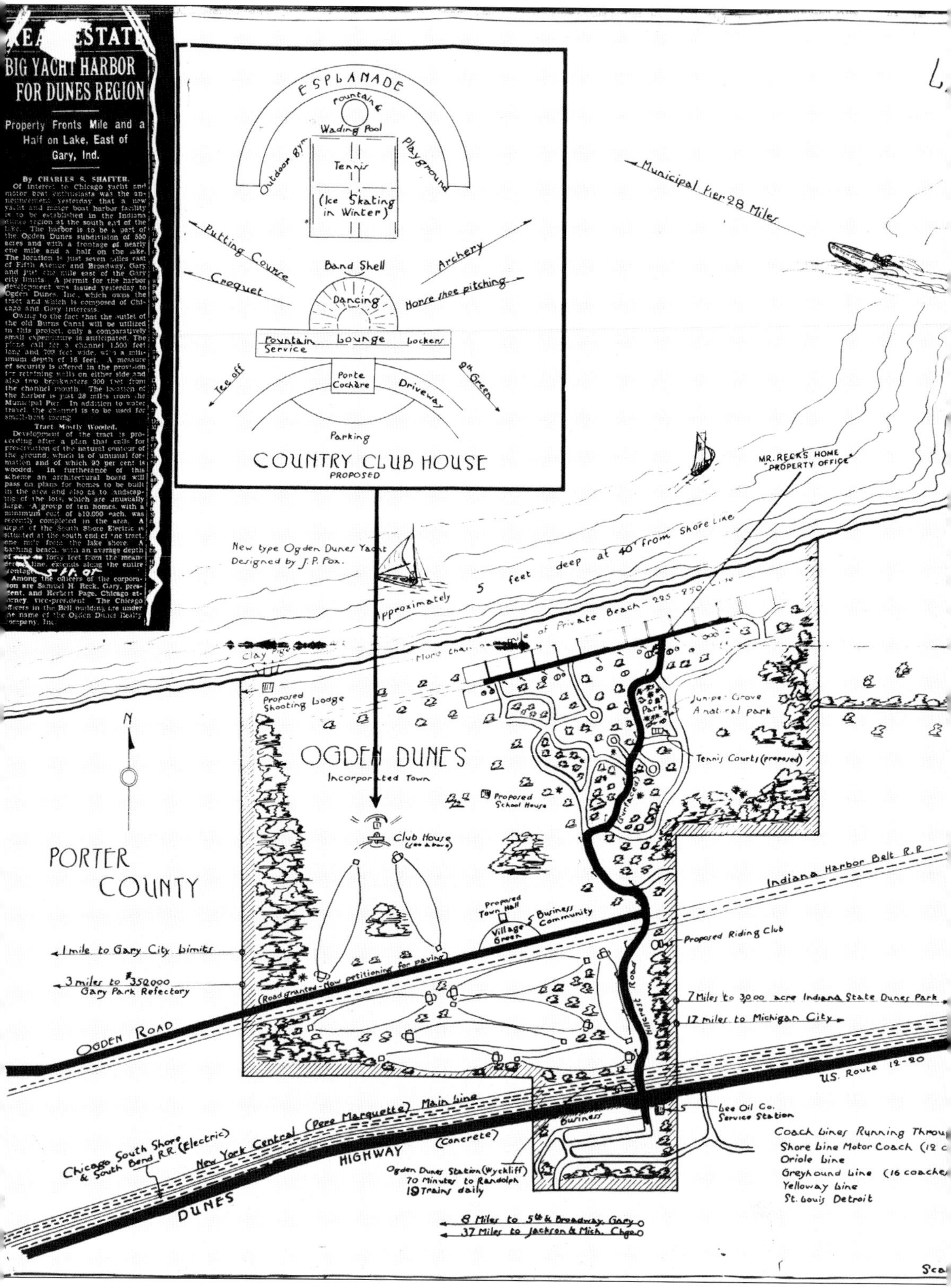

REA ESTATE

BIG YACHT HARBOR FOR DUNES REGION

Property Fronts Mile and a Half on Lake, East of Gary, Ind.

By CHARLES S. SHAFFER.

Of interest to Chicago yacht and motor boat enthusiasts was the announcement yesterday that a new yacht and motor boat harbor facility is to be established in the Indiana dunes region at the south end of the lake. The harbor is to be a part of the Ogden Dunes subdivision of 550 acres and with a frontage of nearly one mile and a half on the lake. The location is just seven miles east of Fifth Avenue and Broadway, Gary and just one mile east of the Gary city limits. A permit for the harbor development was issued yesterday to Ogden Dunes, Inc., which owns the tract and which is composed of Chicago and Gary interests.

Owing to the fact that the outlet of the old Burns Canal will be utilized in this project, only a comparatively small expenditure is anticipated. The plans call for a channel 1,500 feet long and 700 feet wide, with a minimum depth of 16 feet. A measure of security is offered in the provision for retaining walls on either side and also two breakwaters 300 feet from the channel mouth. The location of the harbor is just 28 miles from the Municipal Pier. In addition to water travel, the channel is to be used for small-boat racing.

Tract Mostly Wooded.

Development of the tract is proceeding after a plan that calls for preservation of the natural contour of the ground, which is of unusual formation and of which 90 per cent is wooded. In furtherance of this scheme an architectural board will pass on plans for homes to be built in the area and also as to landscaping of the lots, which are unusually large. A group of ten homes, with a minimum cost of $10,000 each, was recently completed in the area. A depot of the South Shore Electric is situated at the south end of the tract, one mile from the lake shore. A bathing beach, with an average depth of [illegible] forty feet from the meander line, extends along the entire frontage. 5 ft. or

Among the officers of the corporation are Samuel H. Reck, Gary, president, and Herbert Page, Chicago attorney, vice-president. The Chicago offices in the Bell building are under the name of the Ogden Dunes Realty Company, Inc.

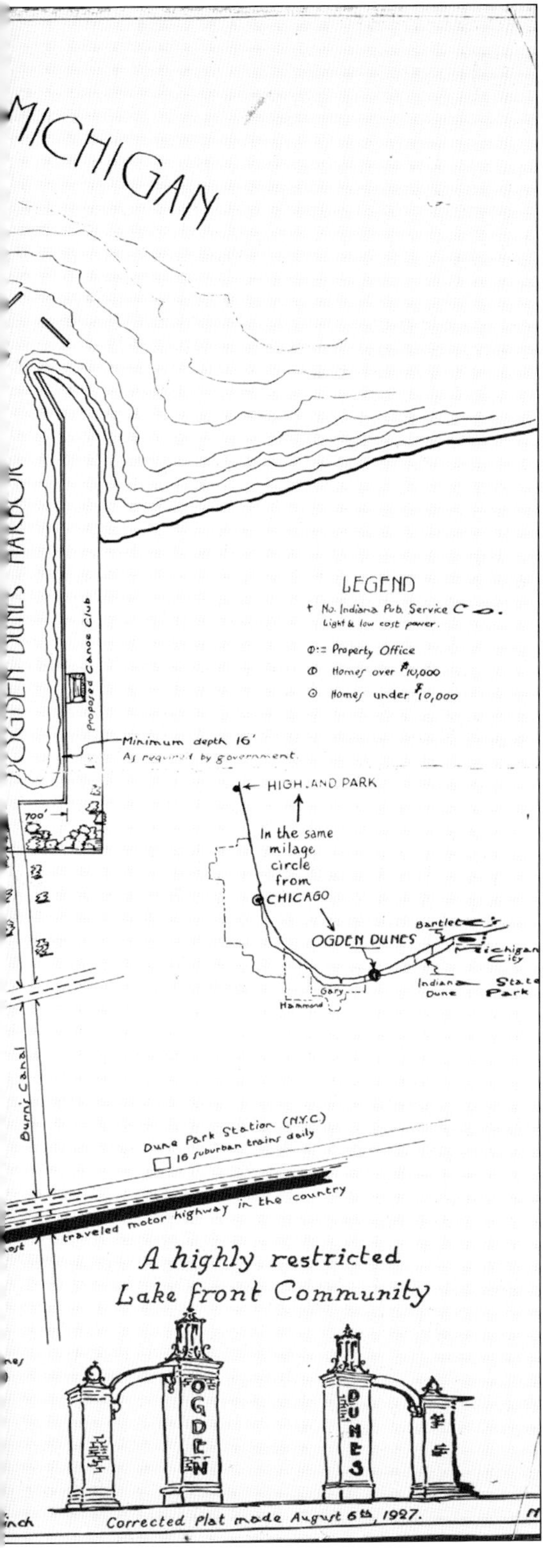

Sales Brochure. In 1927, Ogden Dunes Realty, following the final approval for an easement to cross the railroads at the new entrance, began to advertise the community as a highly restricted residential suburb. A brochure, a page of which is shown here, promised a country club with a nine-hole golf course on the southwest side, as well as a town hall, village green, and school. The map shows the First Subdivision, with circles indicating the 10 homes valued at $10,000 or more, and a number of cottages under $10,000. At the mouth of the Burns Canal (Ditch) is the proposed yacht harbor, 1,500 feet long and 700 feet wide. The land along the canal never became part of Ogden Dunes. An article describing the brochure appeared in the *Chicago Journal of Commerce* on August 16, 1927. (HSOD.)

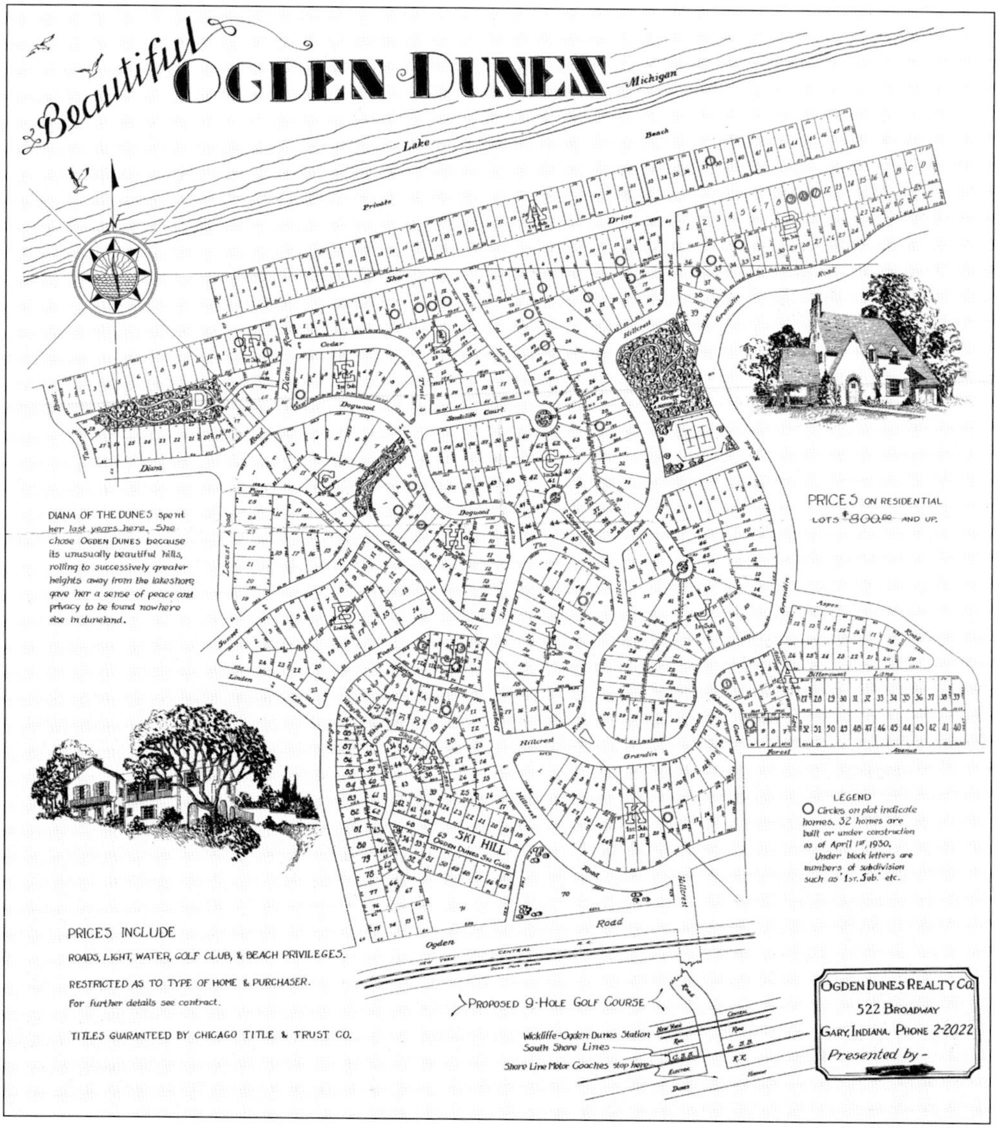

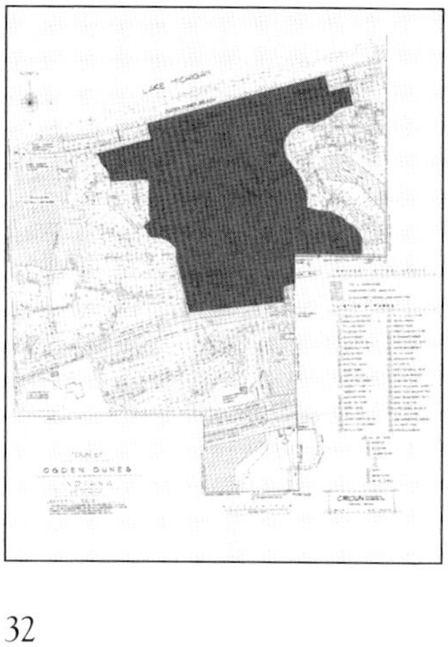

1930 MAP. Along with the First Subdivision, the map above shows the Second Subdivision, the area near the ski jump and west of Hillcrest that was developed after 1929. The map shows 32 homes and cottages, approximately half of which were summer cottages. The 1930 census lists 14 families and 50 individuals as full-time residents. The 1930 map at left shows the First and Second Subdivisions within Ogden Dunes' 1994 boundaries, which remain the same today. (Both, HSOD.)

Three

Ups and Downs 1928–1934

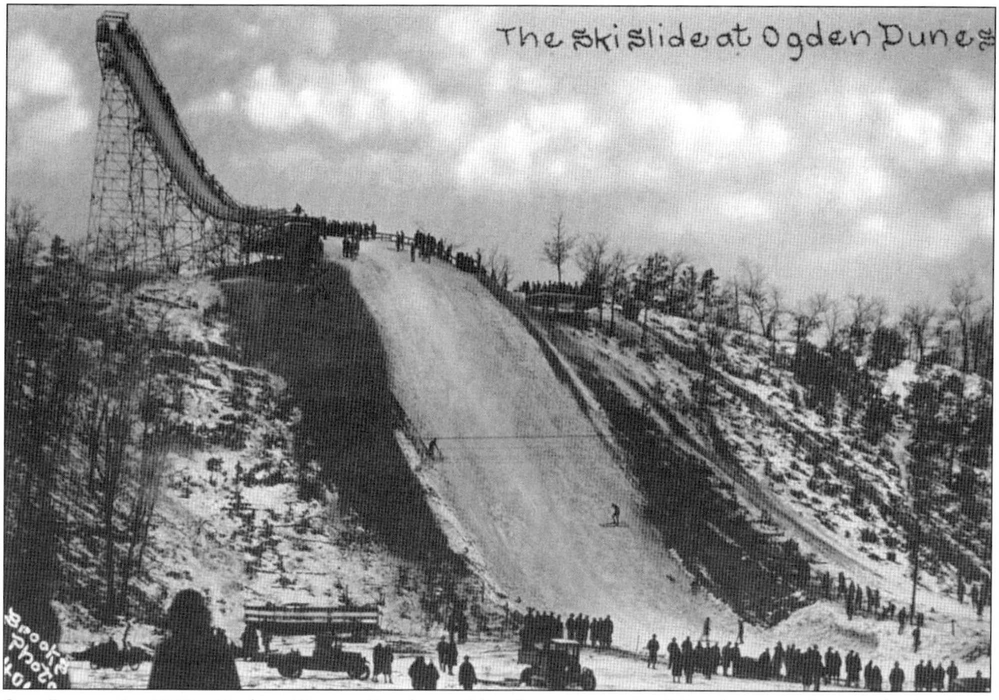

Ski Jump. In 1927, Ogden Dunes Realty sold a large parcel of land situated on a high dune near the town's entrance to the Ogden Dunes Ski Club. The club was organized by Norwegian-American ski enthusiasts from Chicago. That fall, the club built the largest man-made ski jump in North America. The first international competition was held on January 22, 1928, with an audience of nearly 10,000. (Courtesy of Steve Shook.)

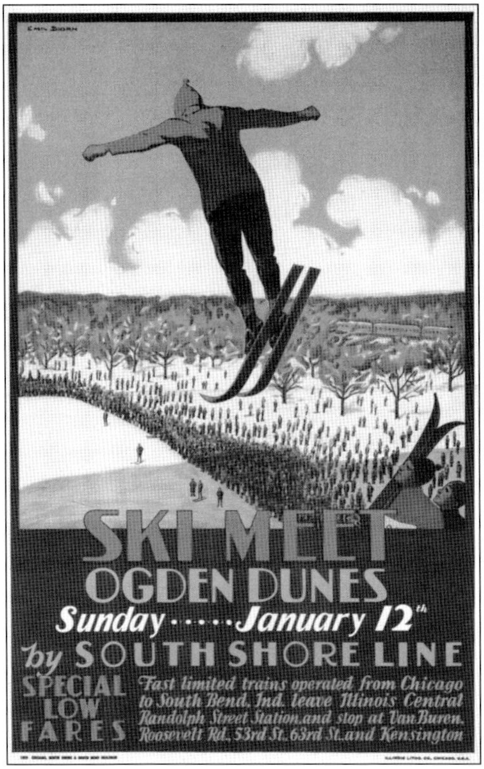

SOUTH SHORE RAILROAD POSTER. Samuel Insull's advertising campaign for his South Shore Railroad found willing partners in Samuel Reck and the Ogden Dunes Ski Club. This lithograph, created by Emil Biorn in 1929, helped to attract thousands of attendees to watch the international competitions that were held between 1928 and 1932. (CRAIUN.)

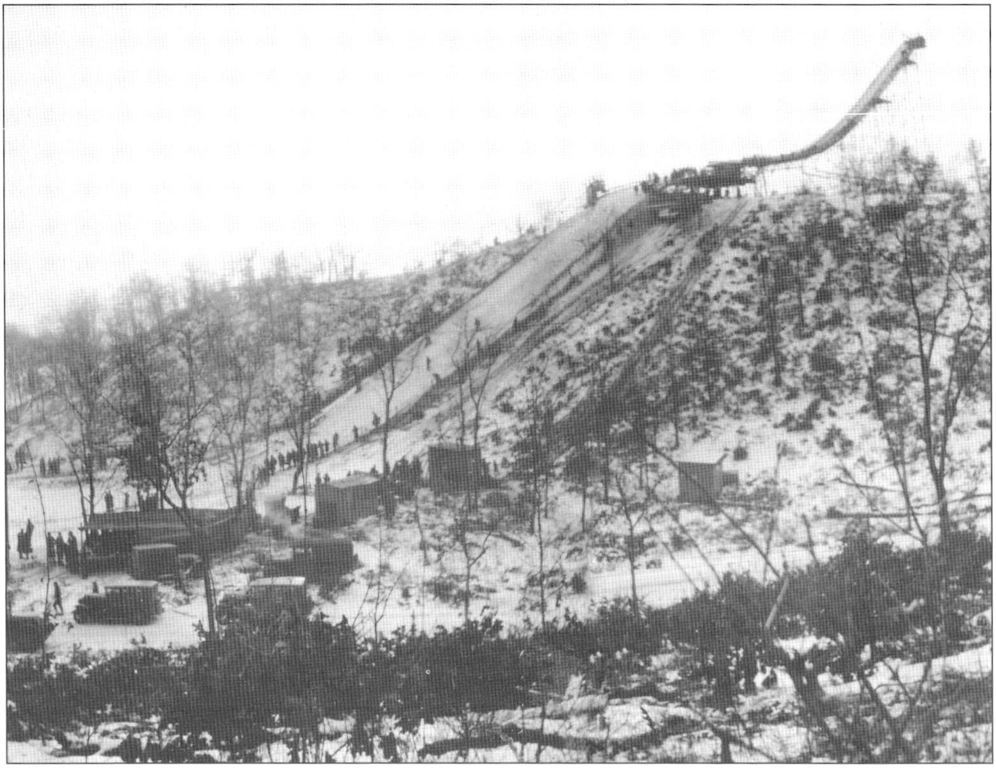

SKI COMPETITION. The Linnberg family, which purchased a lot and built on Hillcrest, took this photograph. For each international competition, the ski club published a program that also advertised Ogden Dunes as an attractive lakeshore community. "Then will come those who will buy and build with us and near us, to enjoy the huge, weird, fascinating hills of golden sand—a luxurious forest of trees, ferns and flowers—the Dunes Switzerland." (Courtesy of David Larson.)

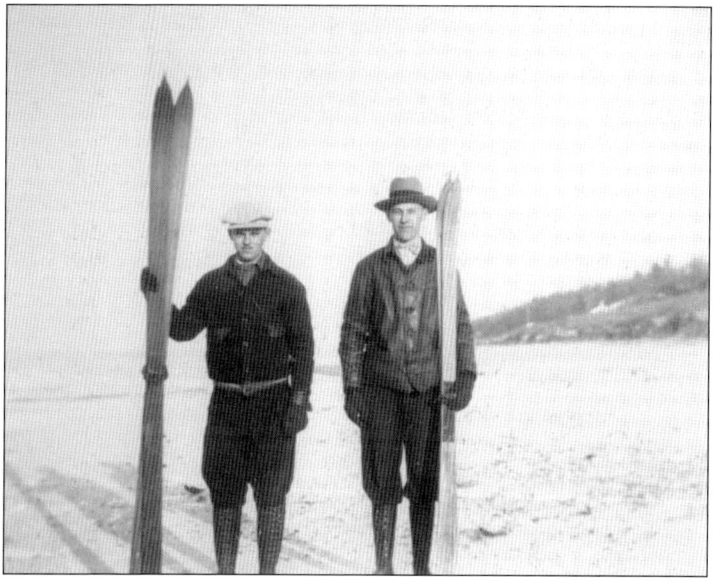

Two Skiers. This photograph, taken in December 1929, shows Laverne Borg (left) and an unidentified skier on the beach. They competed in the January 1930 contest. (Courtesy of Carol Chepko.)

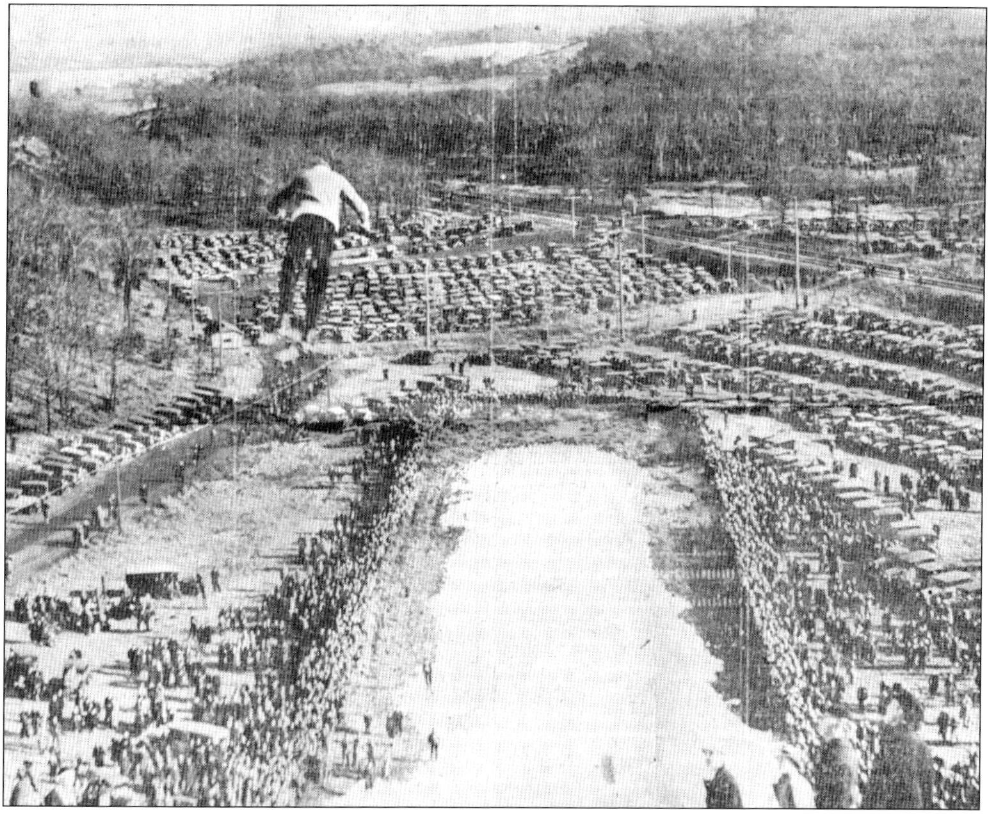

Ski Jumper. This amazing photograph offers the viewer a skier's perspective, showing the thousands of attendees. Many drove cars to the site. The jump's tower was 195 feet above the dune, which was 115 feet high. The 345-foot slide allowed skiers to reach speeds of 60 miles per hour at the time they began their jumps of up to 200 feet. The competition attracted large crowds, estimated between 10,000 and 20,000 during each of its five years of operation. (HSOD.)

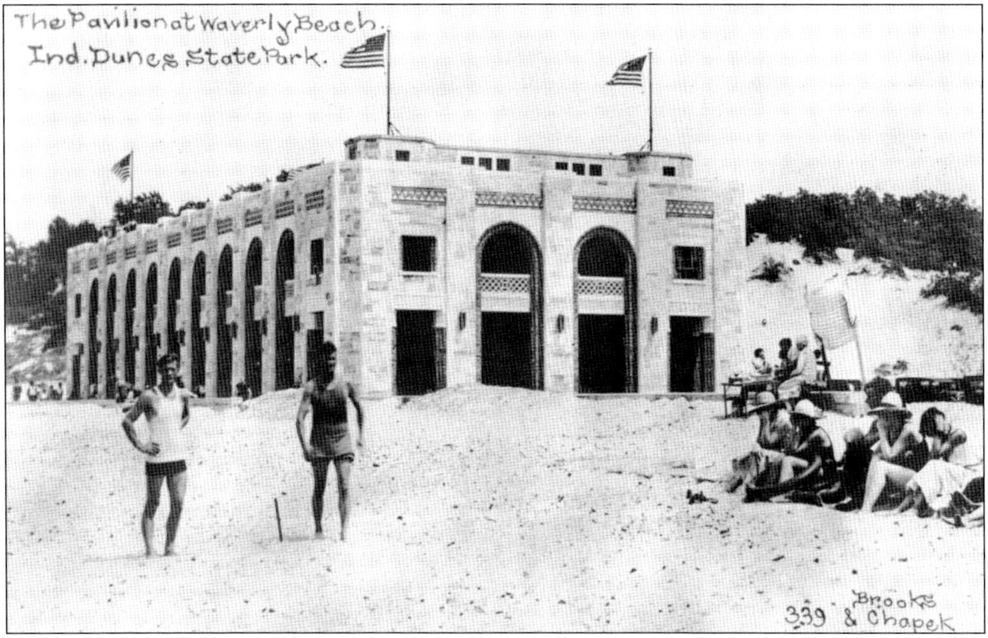

Indiana Dunes State Park Pavilion. After World War I, the movement to create a national park did not regain its momentum. Instead, supporters endorsed the creation of an Indiana Dunes State Park. In 1925, the state approved the establishment of a park of over 2,000 acres in the area where the Prairie Club had its lease, north of Chesterton. This led some members of the Prairie Club, and others who had cottages at Waverly Beach, to relocate to Ogden Dunes. Among these were the Tracht family and Sue Mechtersheimer. (WTHM.)

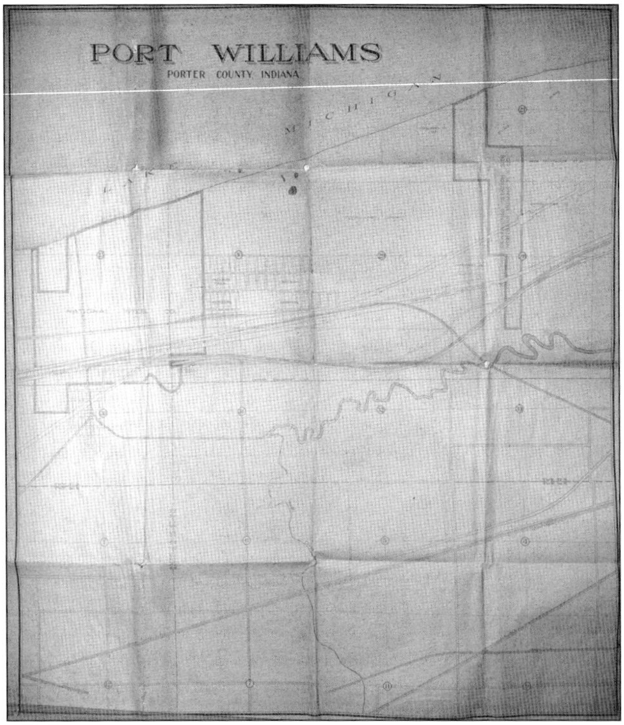

Port Williams, 1929. This map shows the proposed Port Williams, a deepwater port, a steel mill, and a new city. National Steel, headquartered in Pittsburgh, announced that its subsidiary, Midwest Steel, would build a large complex just east of Ogden Dunes. Indiana politicians supported this project, while advocates of a national park and the steel companies in Lake County opposed it. (Photograph by Emilie Cardoso-Seerup; HSOD.)

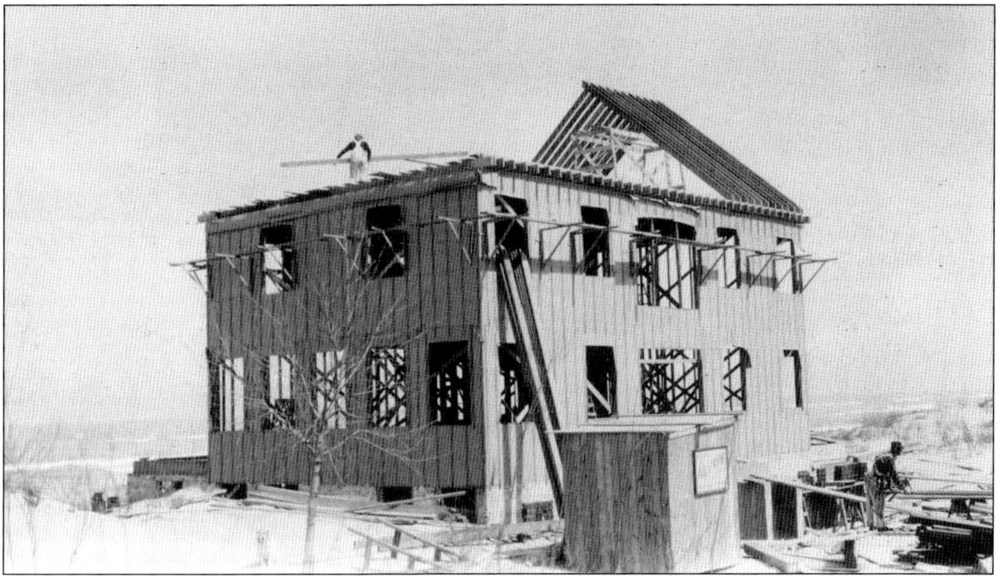

Kratz Home Construction. Ed Kratz (1891–1981) and his wife, Marion (1896–1988), built the first home on the beach, just north of the Reck and Glover homes. On February 4, 1930, the Valparaiso *Vidette-Messenger* reported, "the construction of a new $50,000 residence overlooking Lake Michigan . . . will be a seventeen-room English colonial . . . embodying a number of unique ideas." A.L. Cash, a Gary contractor, was the builder. (HSOD.)

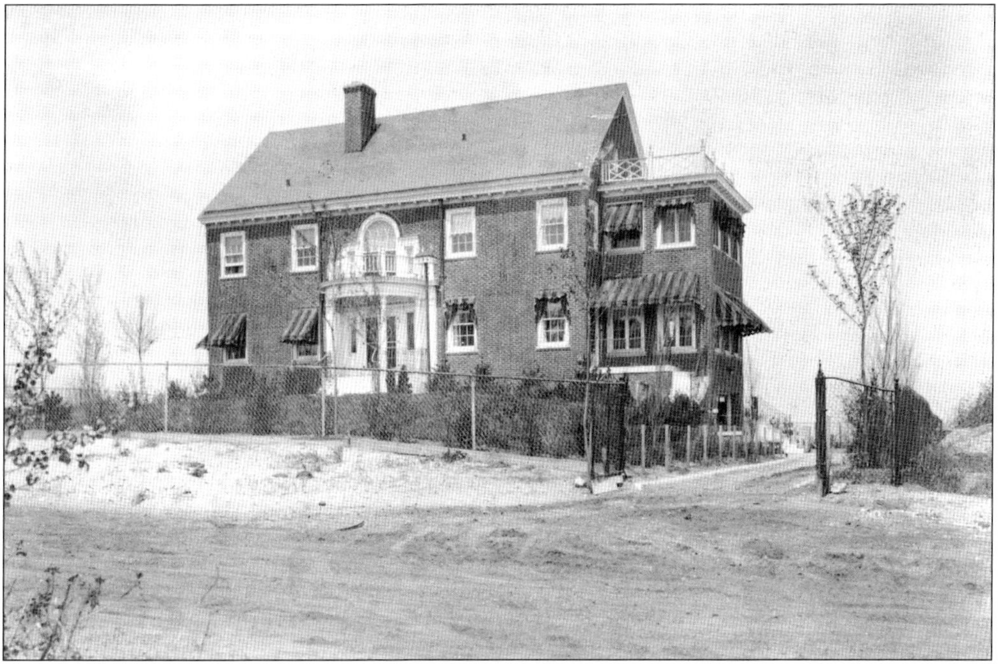

Kratz Home, 50 Shore Drive. Ed Kratz, a manufacturer, became a leader in the community. He served on the town board from 1935 to 1957 and as president during most of this period. The board held its summer meetings at Kratz's boathouse during most of these years. In 1976, the town recognized Kratz's contributions by naming the park that had been the open space for the ski jump Kratz Field. (HSOD.)

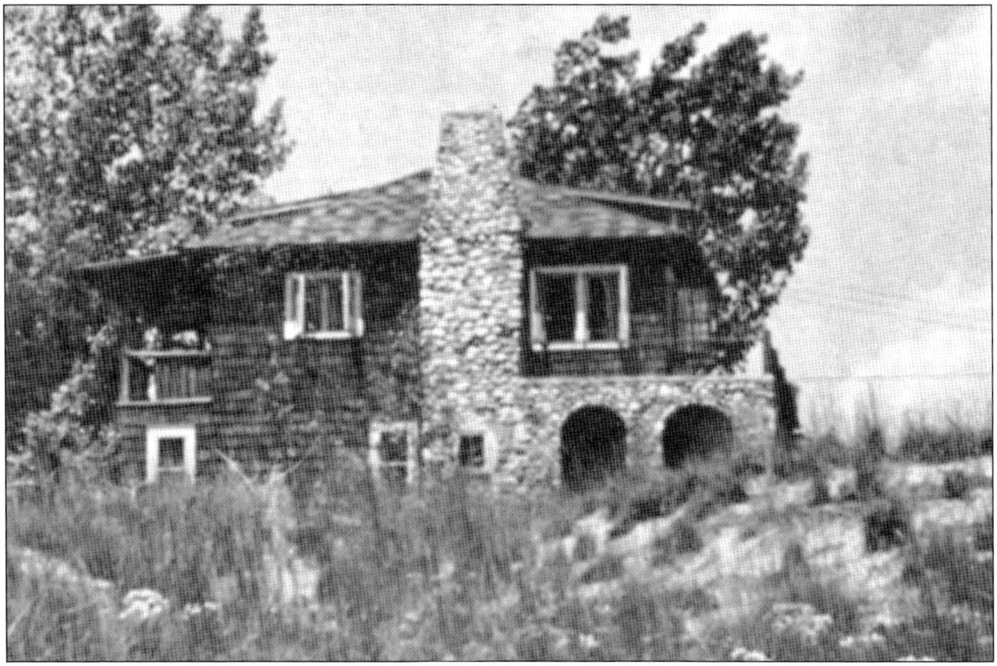

Tracht Cottage, 16 Hillcrest. In the 1920s, the Tracht family had a small cottage in Waverly Beach. Fred (1874–1952) and Nora Sloan (1879–1973) had two sons, Vernon (1915–2003) and Mel (1920–2000). Fred managed the University of Chicago bookstore. In 1930, after Waverly Beach became part of the state park, the family moved their cottage, in pieces, to a lot owned by in-laws in Ogden Dunes. (Courtesy of Mildred Tracht.)

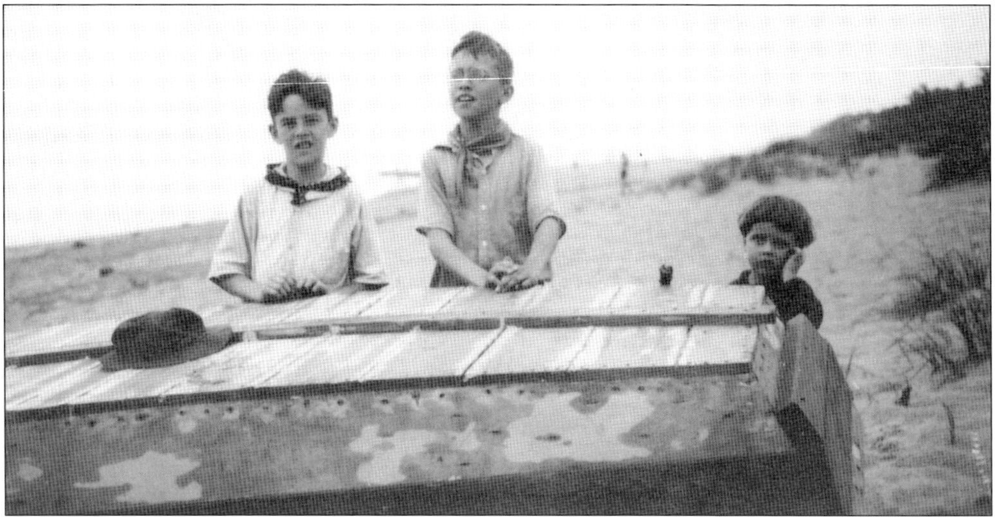

Mel and Vernon Tracht. The two brothers spent many summers on the beach, first at Waverly Beach near the Prairie Club and then in Ogden Dunes. In the late 1930s, both were rafters. Vernon (center), the older brother, received a PhD in psychology and became a national advocate for the disabled. Mel (left), following his marriage to Mildred Janousek in 1946, moved to the family's Hillcrest cottage. He spent his career in university administration, retiring as vice president of business at the Illinois Institute of Technology. The boy at right is an unidentified friend. (Courtesy of Mildred Tracht.)

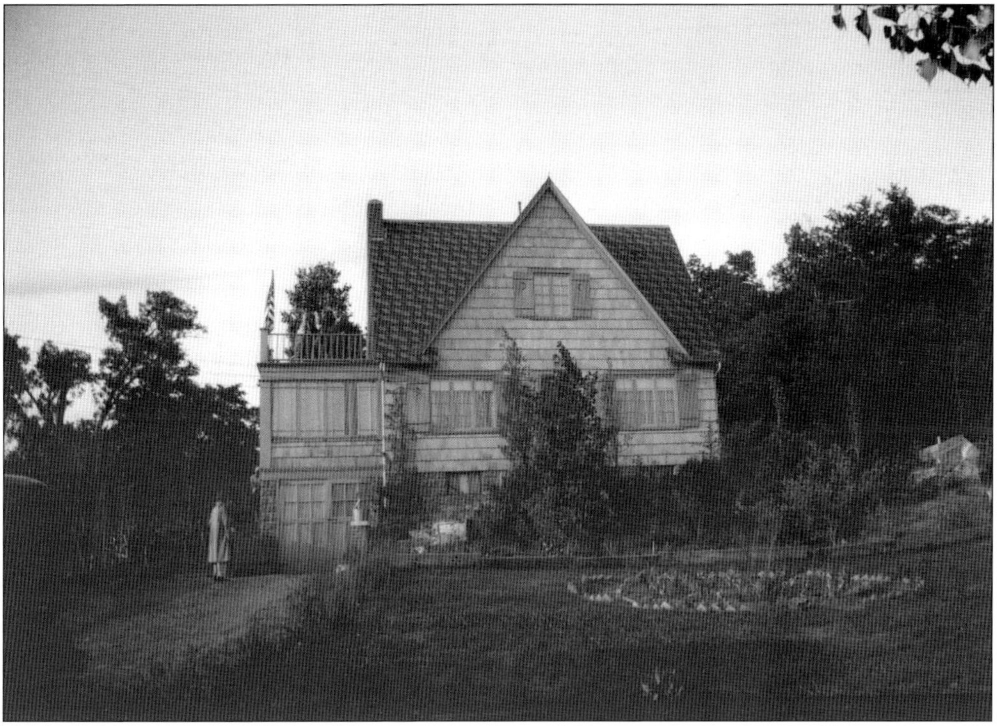

Linnberg Home, 4 Hillcrest Road. After Ogden Dunes Realty claimed ownership to the land containing the Linnbergs' cottage, the Linnberg family bought a lot from Ogden Dunes Realty and built a family home on Hillcrest Road. Their grandson, Dave Larson, and his wife now own the home. (Courtesy of Dave Larson.)

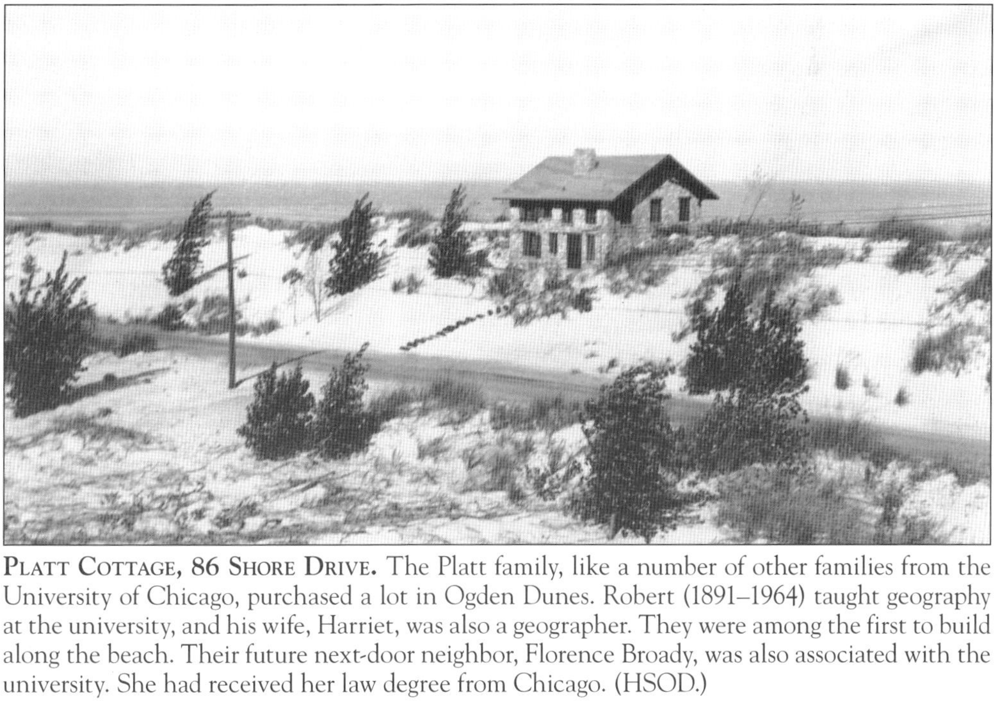

Platt Cottage, 86 Shore Drive. The Platt family, like a number of other families from the University of Chicago, purchased a lot in Ogden Dunes. Robert (1891–1964) taught geography at the university, and his wife, Harriet, was also a geographer. They were among the first to build along the beach. Their future next-door neighbor, Florence Broady, was also associated with the university. She had received her law degree from Chicago. (HSOD.)

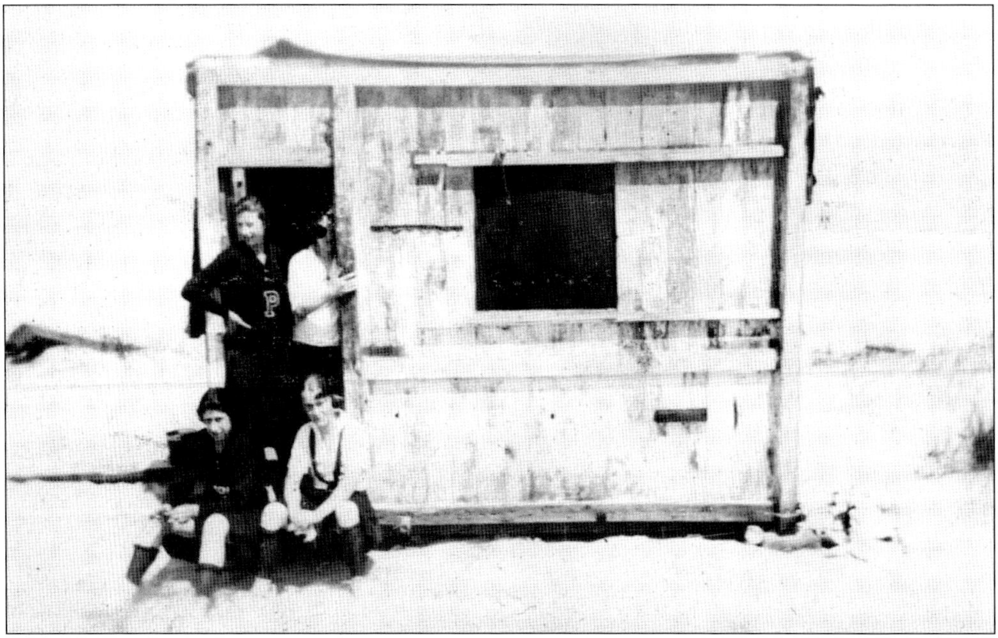

Sue Mechtersheimer's Cabin. Mechtersheimer, who grew up in a working-class family on Chicago's South Side, had a love for nature and the outdoors. As a young woman, she and two friends built a cabin near Waverly Beach. Like the Tracht family, she salvaged part of the cabin after the state park was established and rebuilt it in Ogden Dunes, near the north end of Diana Road. (HSOD, Mechtersheimer.)

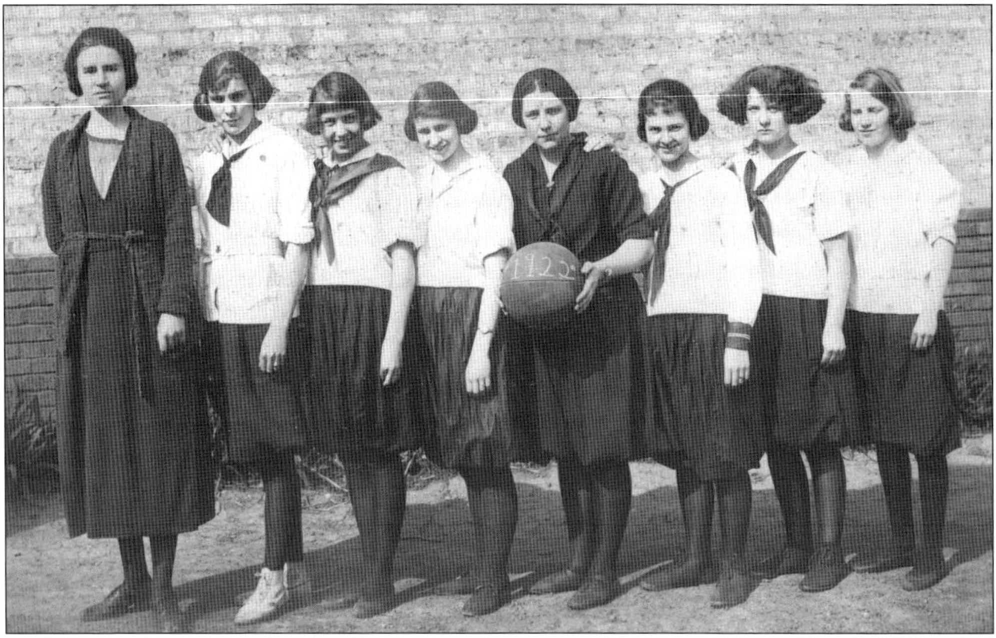

Sue Mechtersheimer and Friends. Following her graduation from Chicago Teachers College, Mechtersheimer (holding ball) taught and then became an administrator in the Chicago Public Schools. She was also an entrepreneur, becoming a real-estate salesperson for Ogden Dunes Realty. (HSOD, Mechtersheimer.)

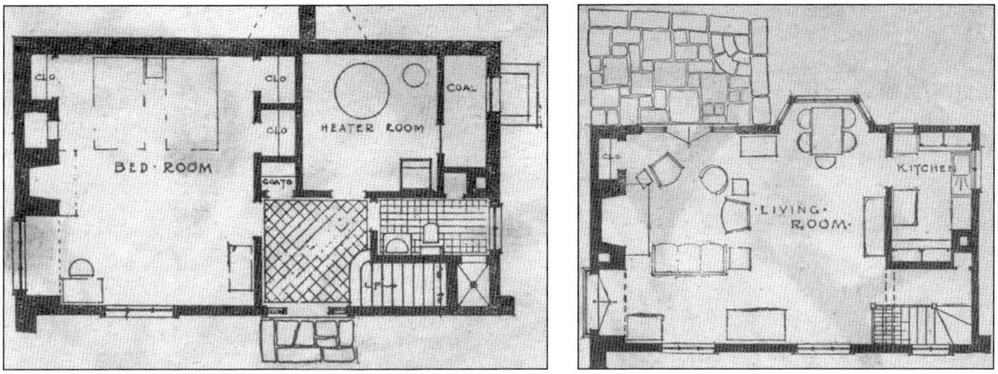

House Plans, 11 Ski Hill Road. On the eve of the Great Depression, the Second Subdivision was developed in the ski jump area. Among the cottages built there was that of Clifton Tidholm and Elwood Koch. They hired Henry Howe Bentley, a professor of architecture, to design a cottage on Skade (later Ski Hill) Road. The floor plans appeared in the *Architectural Record* in 1930 and in the *New York Herald Tribune* in 1931. (HSOD.)

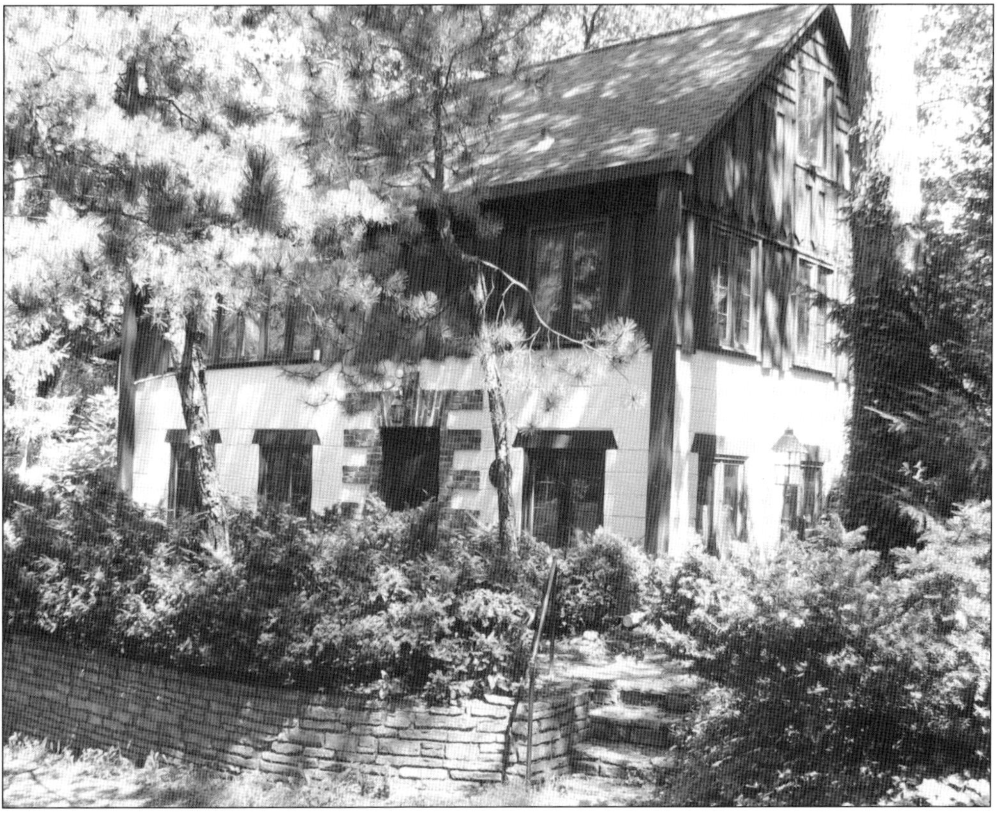

17 Ski Hill Road, 1933. On Ski Hill Road, a number of cement-block cottages were built. These generally followed the layout of the plans shown above. The only bedroom was on the lower level, and a great room with a small kitchen was on the upper level. The cottages featured many windows and a large fireplace. This one was built by the local contractor, R.B. "Pete" Nicholson. (HSOD.)

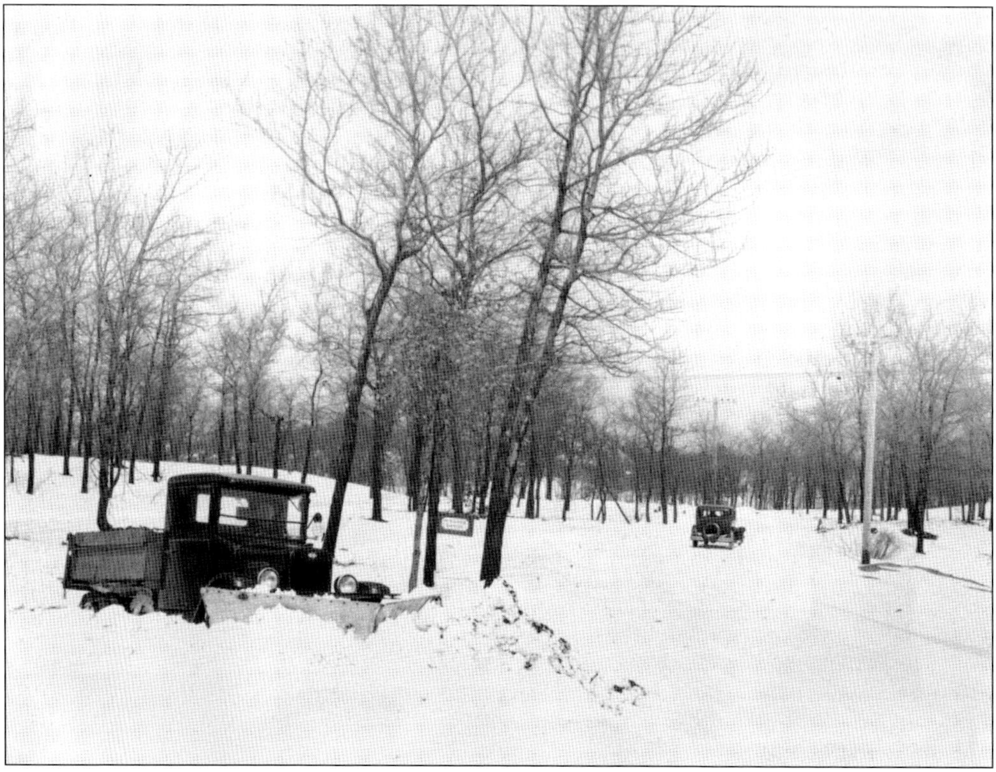

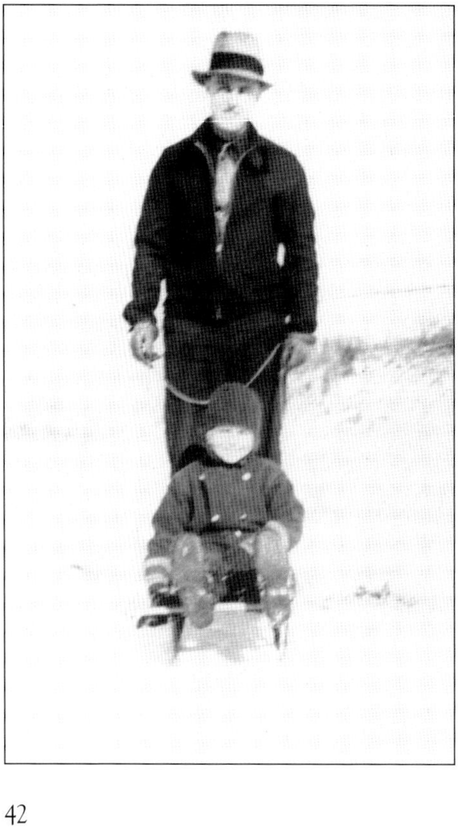

The Great Depression. This rather bleak photograph shows a crew attempting to remove snow at the entrance in 1930. (HSOD.)

Ogden and Mary Lou Nickerson. Ogden, like many skilled tradesmen, had irregular work during the Depression. His wife, Louise, remembers, "During the Depression we cut down trees and for two winters we heated our house by burning nothing but wood." (HSOD, Nickerson.)

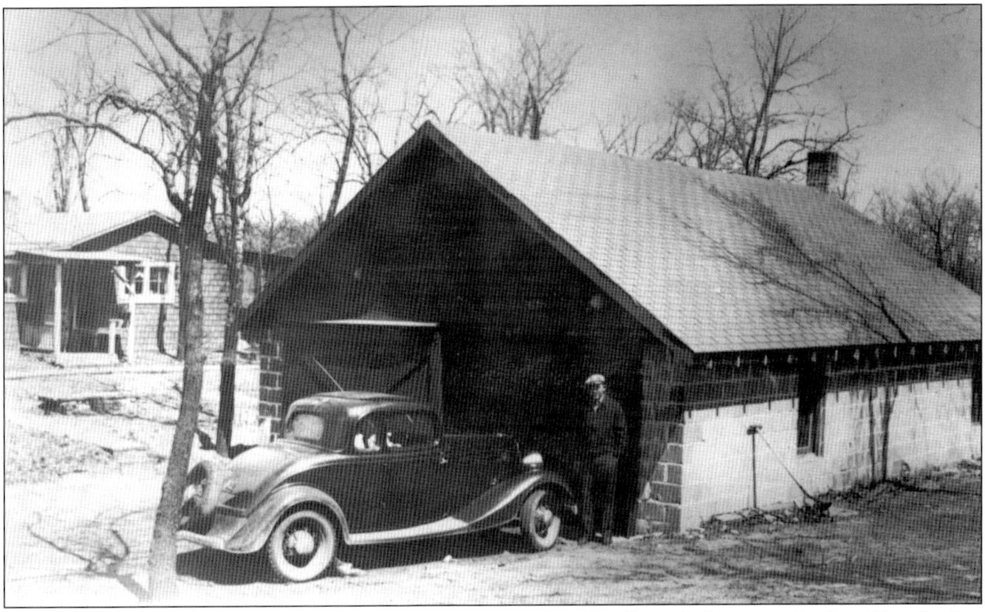

Town Garage. The condition of the town garage in 1935 reflected the struggle faced by Ogden Dunes Realty. Nelson Reck took over the business in the early 1930s, when his father retired to Florida. He wrote his dad in 1936, "though we have closed more deals than in any other spring for several years . . . we just barely were able to pay our taxes and ever since that time we have had a rather serious money shortage." (HSOD.)

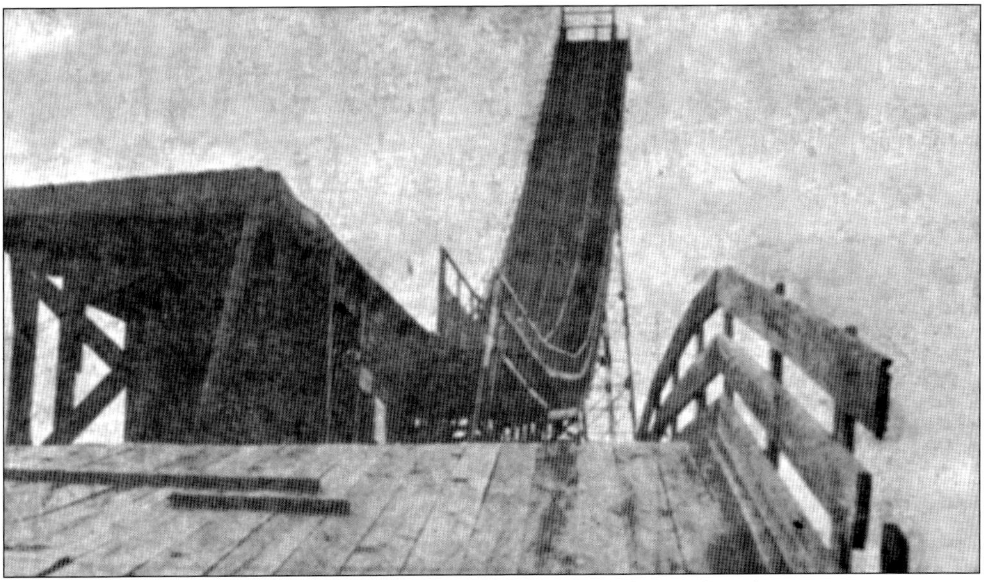

Closure of Ski Jump. The Ogden Dunes Ski Club closed down after the 1932 competitions, due to lack of funds and lack of snow. As a result, the jump was abandoned. By 1935, the steel structure had been sold, removed, and rebuilt near Rockford, Illinois. Ogden Dunes Realty platted new lots and renamed some of the streets at the site of the jump. (HSOD.)

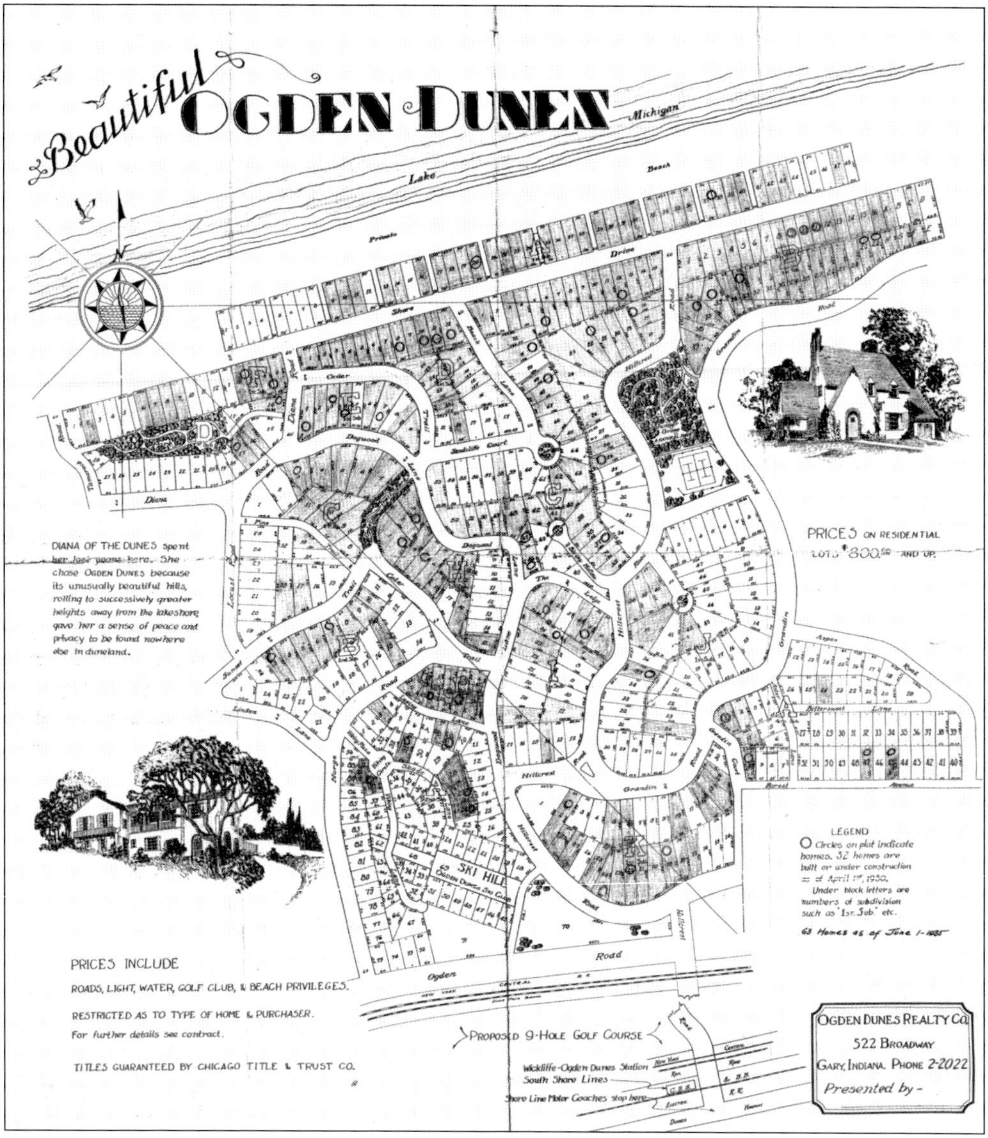

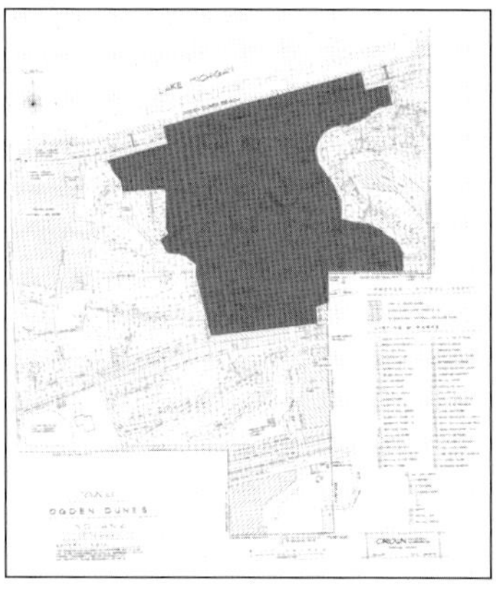

1935 MAP. The map above shows 63 homes and cottages, a significant increase from 1930, despite the Great Depression. The sales material still promised a golf course. The 1935 map at left shows the First and Second Subdivisions within the 1994 boundaries of Ogden Dunes, which remain the same today. (Both, HSOD.)

Four

Revival and Recovery 1935–1939

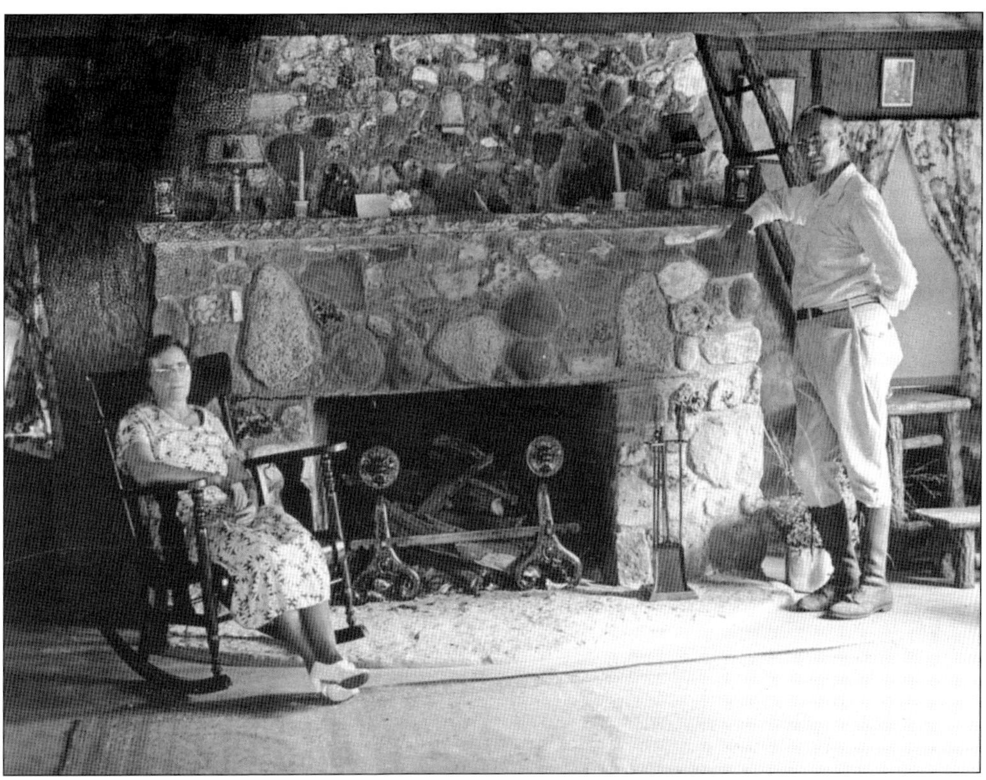

Friendship Fireplace. During their travels, O.D. (1879–1963) and Tillie Frank (1878–1960) collected rocks and fossils. He was a member of the Prairie Club and taught biology at the Laboratory School of the University of Chicago. As a result, their friends and students also contributed to their collection. Over 1,200 reminders of friends and travels were built into their "friendship fireplace" and their home. These items were numbered and indexed. (HSOD, Frank.)

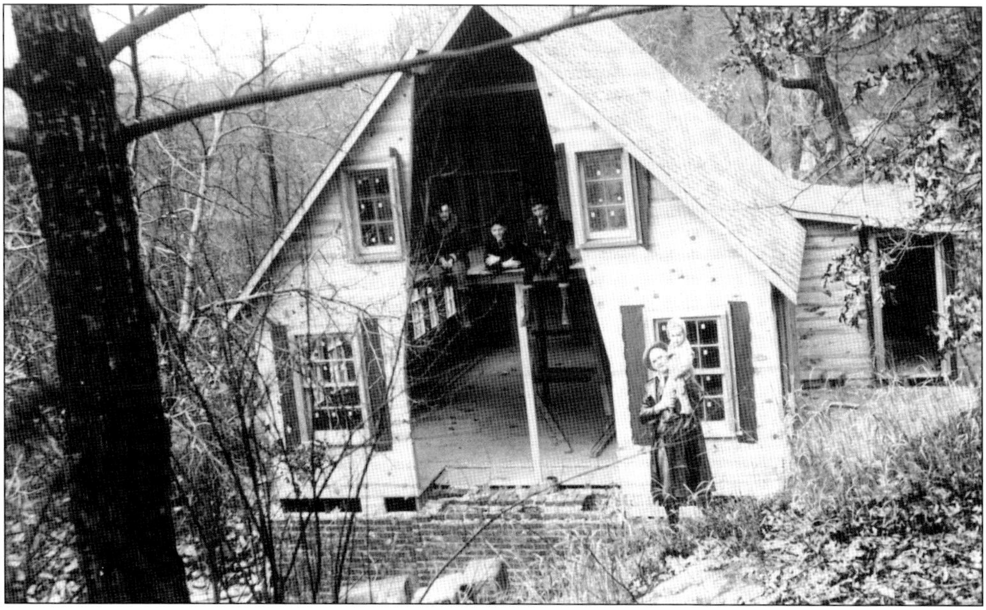

Hour Glass Cottage, 8 Lupine Lane. Sue Mechtersheimer, a teacher and real estate agent, took a summer course from O.D. Frank at the University of Chicago. She encouraged him and Tillie to build a cottage in Ogden Dunes. She also arranged, in 1933, for Pete Nicholson to do the construction. The cottage is seen here prior to the addition of the double fireplace on the upper level and the loft. (HSOD, Frank.)

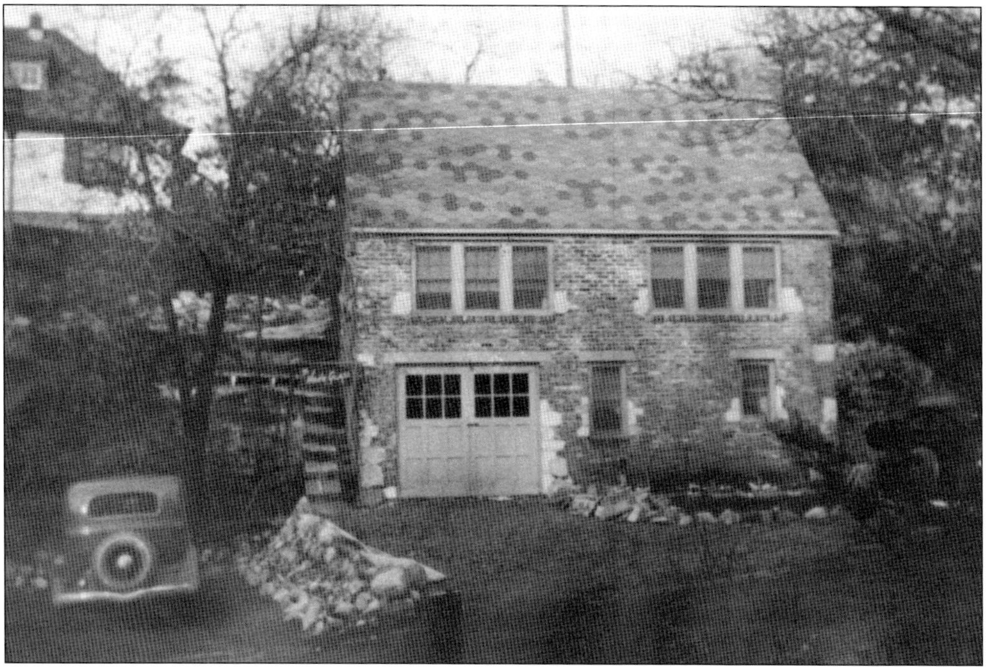

Hour Glass Completed. Like many others, the Franks' cottage had one bedroom, a bathroom, and a garage on the lower level. The upper level had one large, open room built around the fireplace. Above half of this room was a loft for guests. In planning for O.D.'s retirement, the Franks expanded the cottage, and it became their permanent residence in 1944. (HSOD, Frank.)

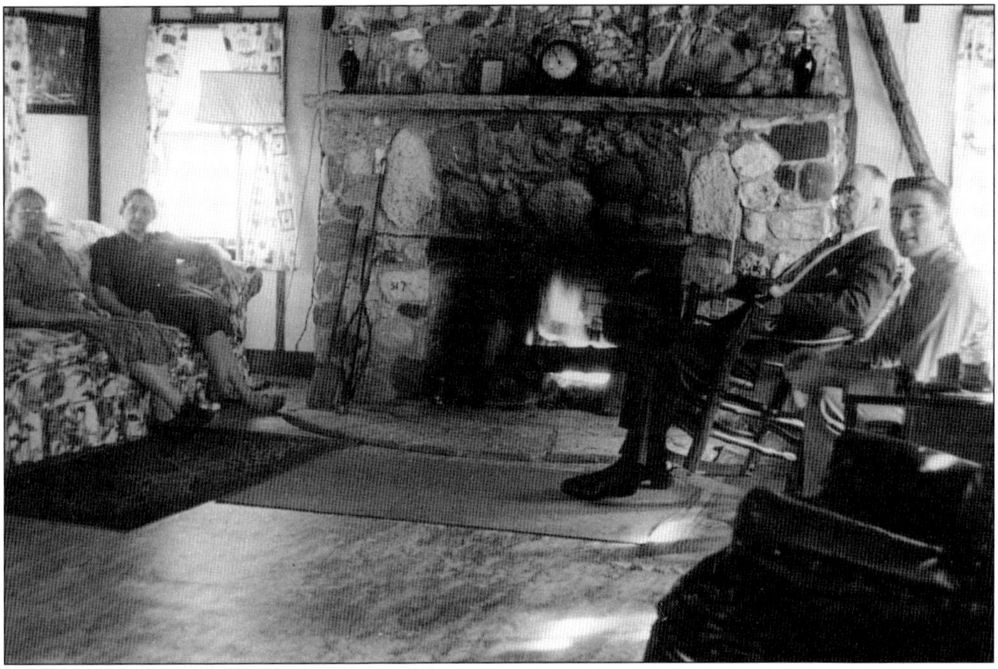

O.D. and Tillie Frank with Guests. O.D., a great naturalist, spent summers and weekends in the dunes, entertaining friends and students. He gave many nature talks around the fireplace and led countless hikes for the younger generation. He was honored with the title First Citizen of Ogden Dunes at the first annual meeting of the Ogden Dunes Home Association in 1959. (HSOD, Frank.)

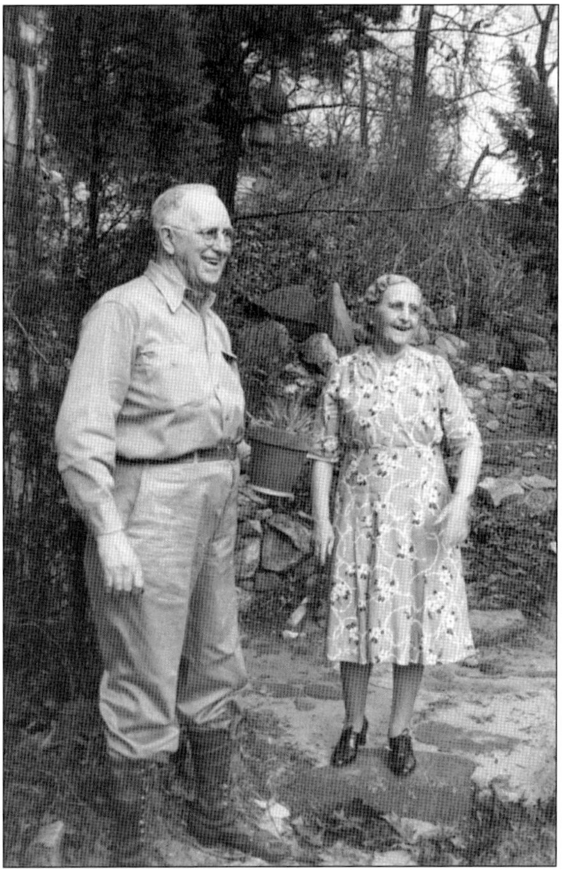

O.D. and Tillie Frank. O.D. gave his beloved wife, Martha Belle Gano, a pet name, "Tillie the Toiler." In June 1957, the Franks celebrated their 50th anniversary at the Quadrangle Club of the University of Chicago. More than 300 guests attended. (HSOD, Frank.)

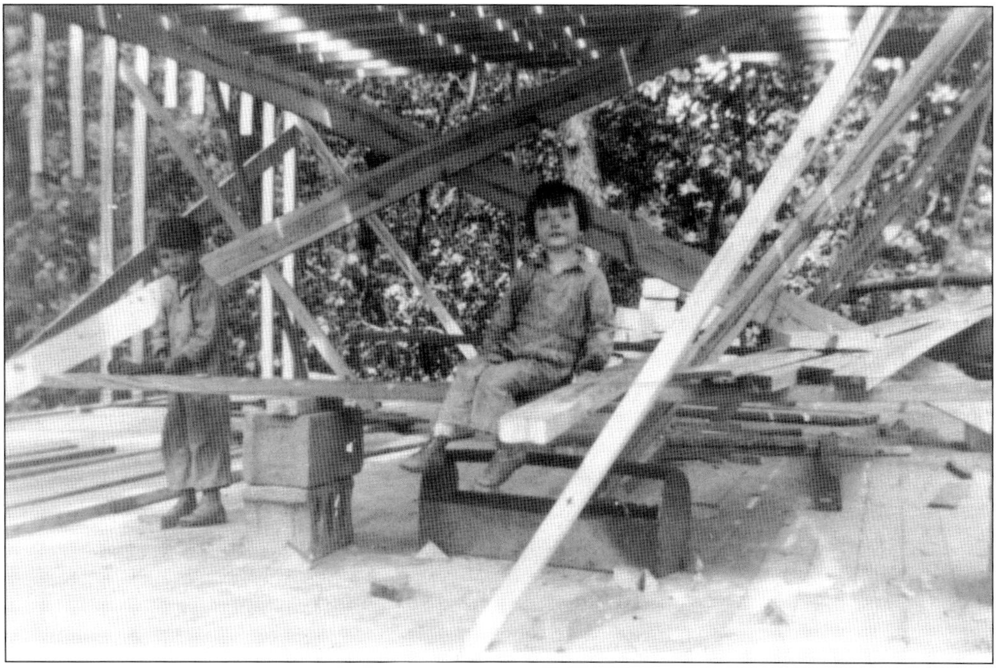

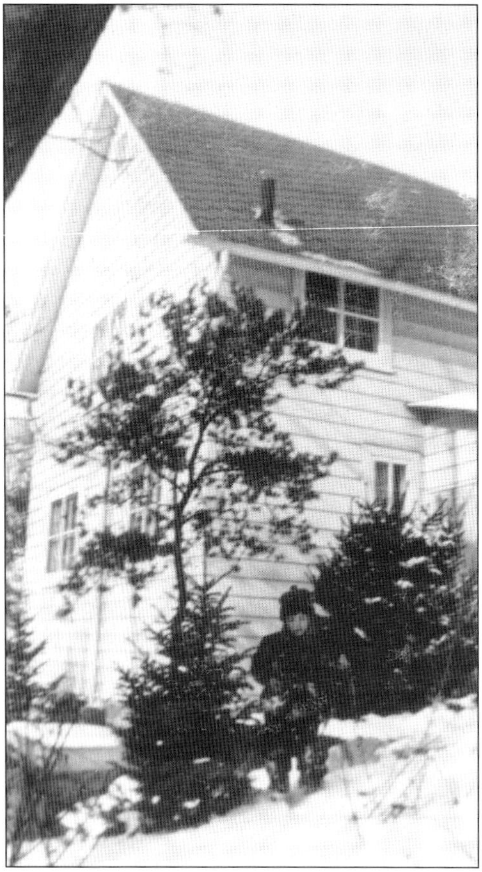

Mahoney Children. Joe Mahoney, who worked in advertising, and his wife, Ella, a writer, moved their family of three young children, Joe and twins Jerry (left) and Joella (right), to a cottage on Woodland Trail in 1936. Joe and his father-in-law built most of the home. They called their new residence Dune Ridge. (HSOD, Mahoney.)

Dune Ridge, 11 Woodland Trail. Joe and Ella Mahoney were very active in community affairs during their seven years in the dunes. Ella wrote poetry and contributed stories to the local newsletter. Their daughter, Joella Jean Mahoney, a well-known artist, continually refers to the influence her childhood in the dunes had on her art, especially her large canvases of the Southwest. (HSOD, Mahoney.)

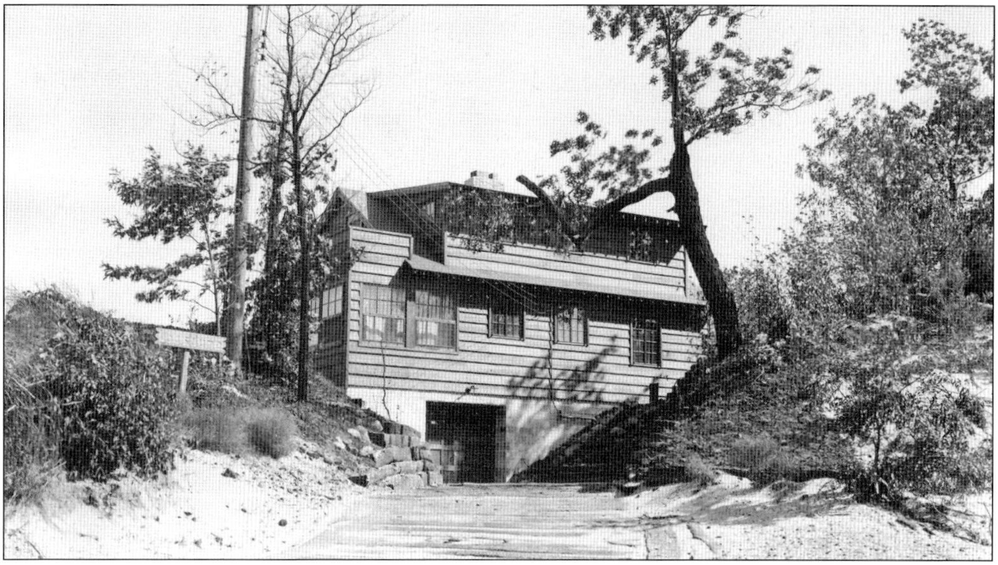

Logsdune, 49 Cedar Trail. In 1935, another University of Chicago professor, Mayme Logsdon (1881–1967), built a cottage in the dunes. Logsdon, who had been widowed not long after her marriage, became an older student in mathematics at the University of Chicago. After completing her PhD in 1921, she joined the faculty and became the first woman to receive tenure in mathematics. After she retired in 1946, she moved to the University of Miami and taught 15 more years. (HSOD.)

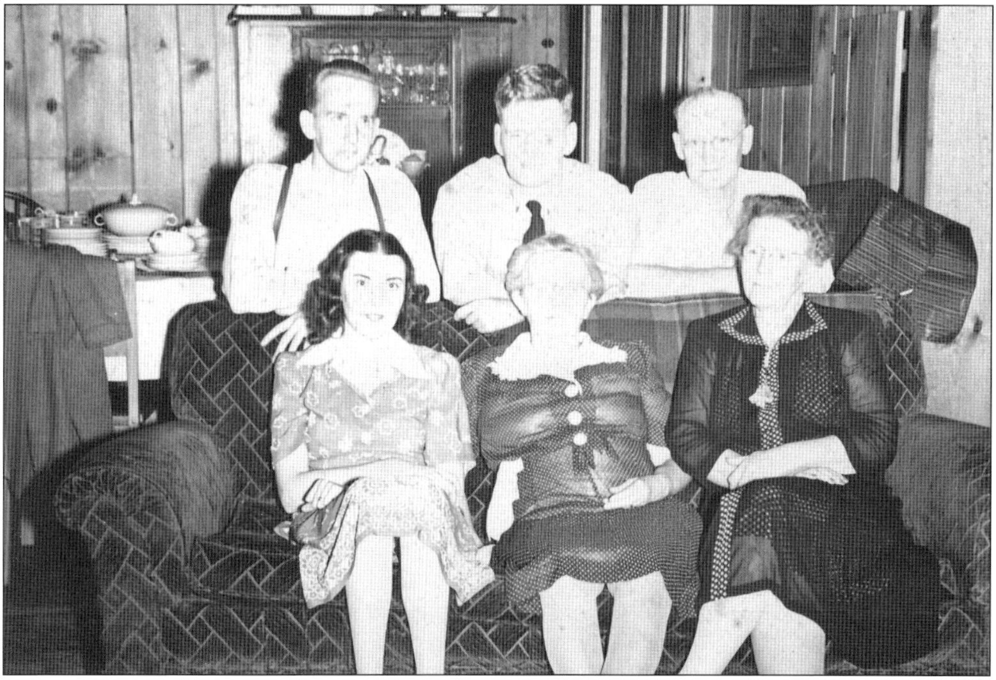

Mayme Logsdon with Cash Family. Logsdon became close friends with the Cash family. Shown here are, from left to right, (seated) Muriel (Mitchell Cash's future wife), Dess Cash, and Mayme Logsdon; (kneeling) Webster Cash, Mitchell Cash, and A.L. Cash. (Courtesy of Laura Cash Mitchell.)

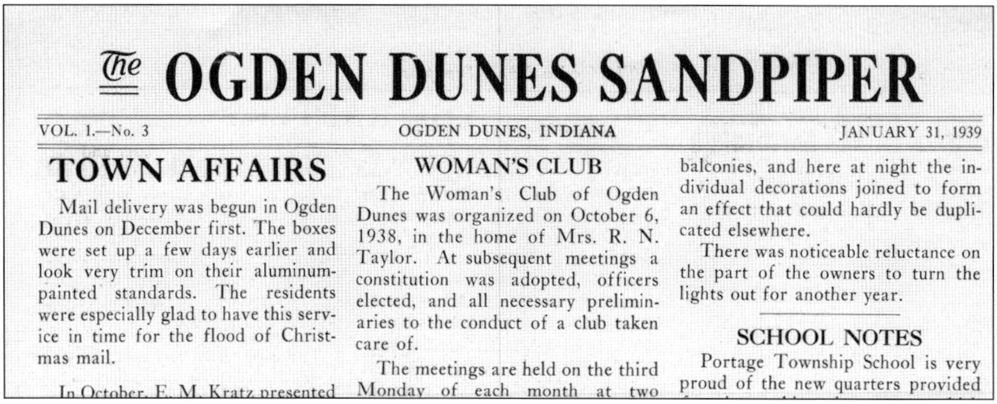

The OGDEN DUNES SANDPIPER

VOL. 1.—No. 3 OGDEN DUNES, INDIANA JANUARY 31, 1939

TOWN AFFAIRS

Mail delivery was begun in Ogden Dunes on December first. The boxes were set up a few days earlier and look very trim on their aluminum-painted standards. The residents were especially glad to have this service in time for the flood of Christmas mail.

In October, E. M. Kratz presented

WOMAN'S CLUB

The Woman's Club of Ogden Dunes was organized on October 6, 1938, in the home of Mrs. R. N. Taylor. At subsequent meetings a constitution was adopted, officers elected, and all necessary preliminaries to the conduct of a club taken care of.

The meetings are held on the third Monday of each month at two

balconies, and here at night the individual decorations joined to form an effect that could hardly be duplicated elsewhere.

There was noticeable reluctance on the part of the owners to turn the lights out for another year.

SCHOOL NOTES

Portage Township School is very proud of the new quarters provided

OGDEN DUNES SANDPIPER. This periodic newsletter is an invaluable source of information about the history of the community. Ogden Dunes Realty published the newsletter; Helen Reck, a Gary teacher and the wife of Nelson Reck, edited it. The third issue contained information on the newly established Woman's Club. (HSOD.)

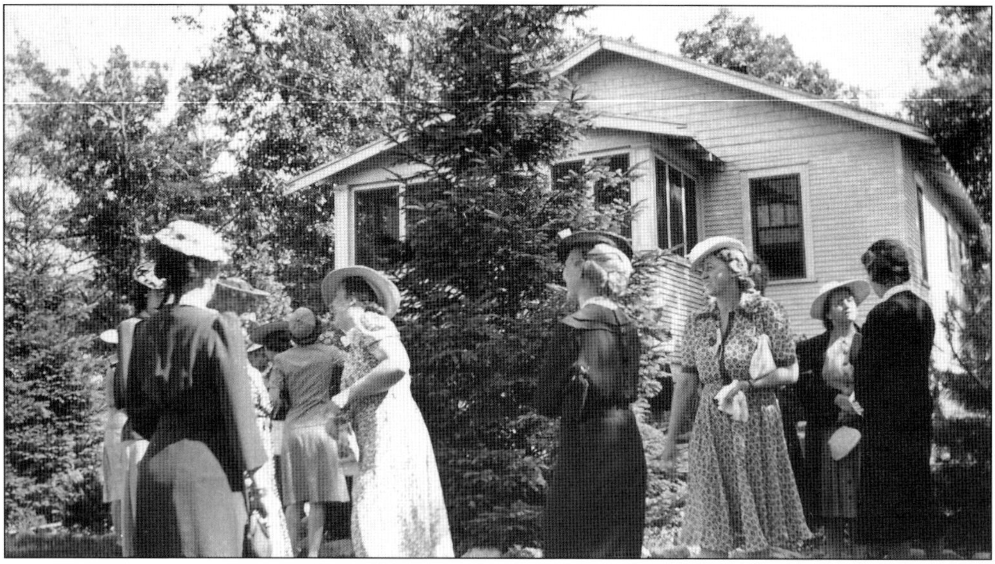

WOMAN'S CLUB LUNCHEON, 1940. In 1938, two major events occurred that encouraged the development of community: the publication of the *Sandpiper*, and the founding of the Woman's Club. The first planning meeting was attended by 17 women, who agreed to establish the Woman's Club. At that time, Ogden Dunes had neither street signs nor mailboxes. These became the club's first community projects. In 1940, the women held their first annual luncheon at Stuga's Restaurant on Stage Coach Road, just south of Ogden Dunes. (HSOD.)

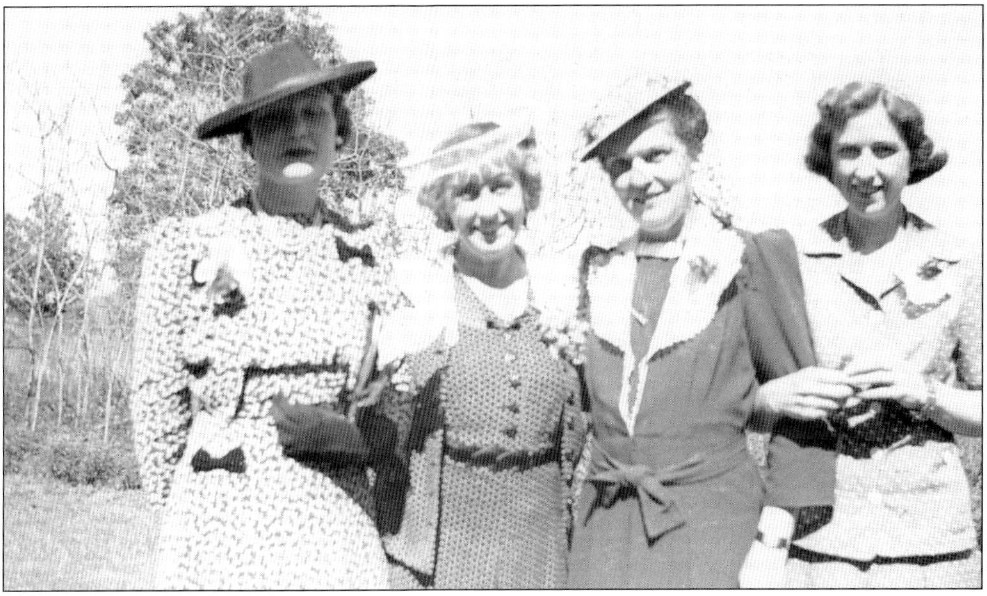

Woman's Club Members. By 1940, membership had risen to over 50. Because money was scarce, the women opted to hold the luncheon at the small restaurant near Ogden Dunes. The Woman's Club did not change its name to Women's Club until 1980. (HSOD.)

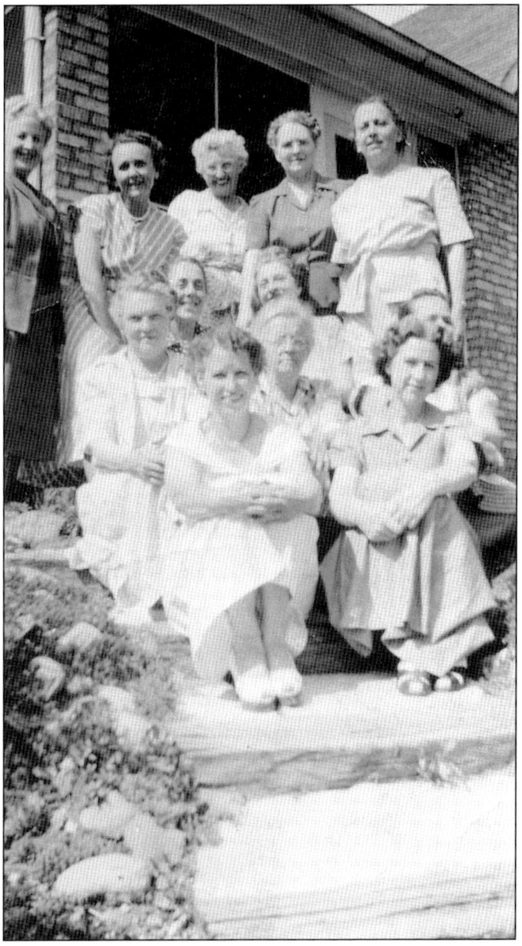

Active in the Community. These 12 women were among the most active members of the club and the community. They are, from left to right, (first row) Alene Stevens and Neva Tittle; (second row) Edna Harris, Dess Cash, and Louisa Nickerson; (third row) Helen Cates and Erna Semerau; (fourth row) Marj Dorman, Betty Mullin, Flo Thorpe, Lois Kidwell, and Flora Fogarty. (HSOD.)

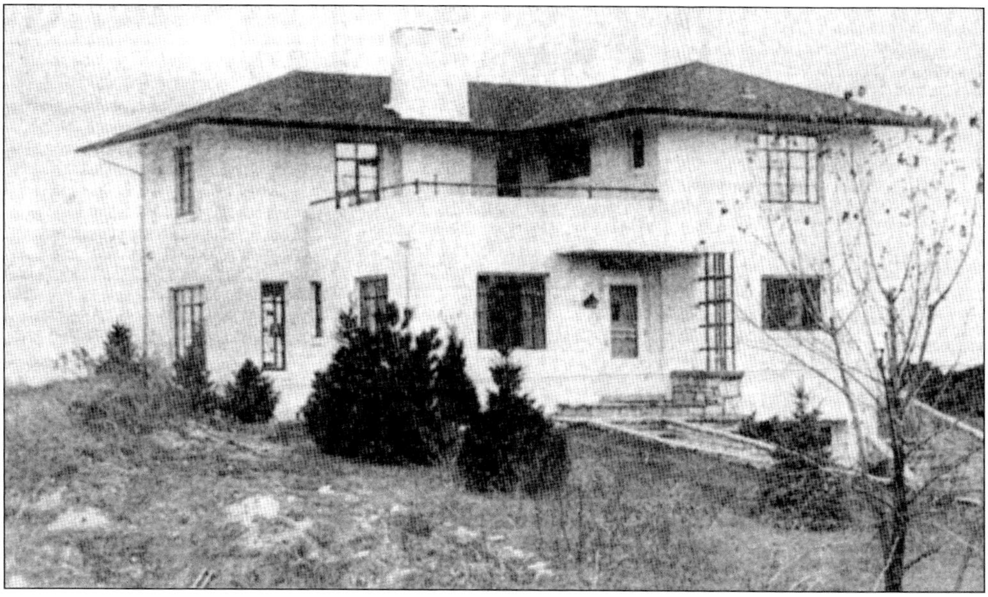

DORMAN HOME, 94 SHORE DRIVE. During the late 1930s, a number of large, new homes were built in Ogden Dunes, especially along Shore Drive. In 1939, Willard (1899–1960) and Marjorie Dorman (1904–1986) moved into their new home. They built in Ogden Dunes because of their love of the water and their membership in the Gary Boat Club. Willard managed Fifth Avenue Motors. This firm had been established in 1912 by his older brother, John C. Dorman (1893–c. 1928) and his partners William and Ralph Sykes. John C. later married Edith Sykes (1891–1983), his partners' daughter and sister. (HSOD.)

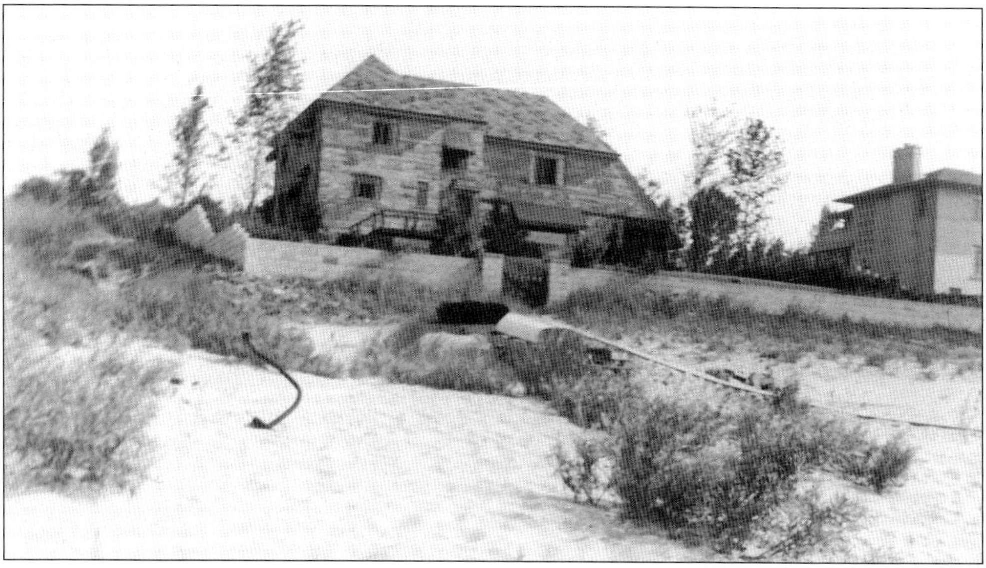

SYKES HOME, 114 SHORE DRIVE. The Ralph Sykes family's beautiful sandstone home on Shore Drive was built in 1940. Ralph Sykes (1889–1964) had married Alice Blodgett (1892–1975). Their daughter Marion (1914–2002) married Howard Stinson and moved to Shore Drive in 1950. Their son William (1916–1999) bought the family home in 1957. Alice's brother, Frank Blodgett (1898–1970), who was also associated with the family businesses, Fifth Avenue Buick and Monarch Oil, built a large home on Shore Drive in 1939. (HSOD.)

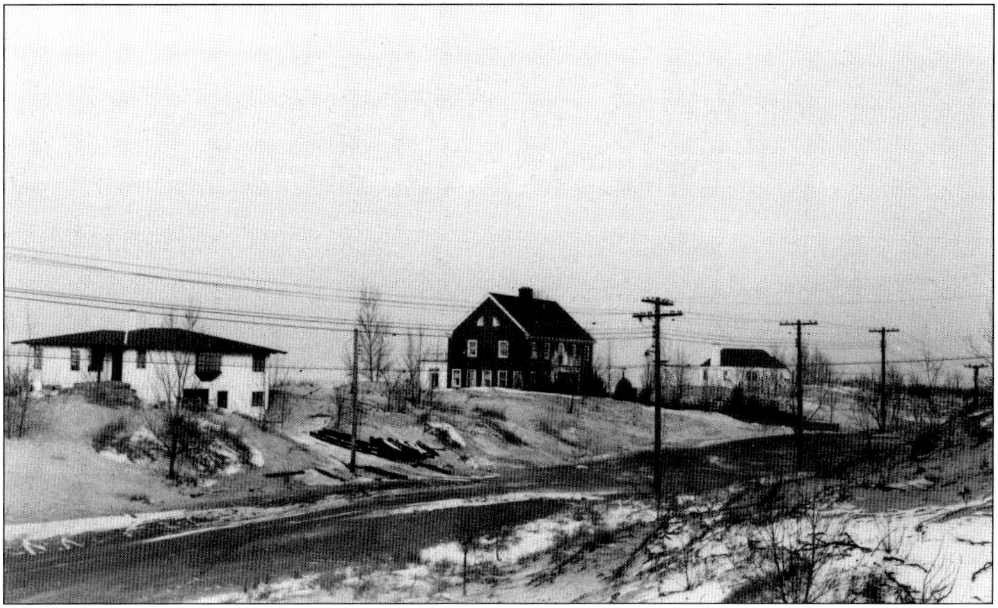

Nelson Reck Home, 58 Shore Drive. Nelson and Helen Reck built their home in 1939, pictured here at left. The other two are the Kratz home, at 50 Shore Drive, and the Glen Jones home, at 44 Shore Drive, both built before 1938. The Reck home, designed by Keck and Keck, a highly respected Chicago architectural firm, represents the economic recovery of Ogden Dunes Realty and of the Ogden Dunes area. (HSOD.)

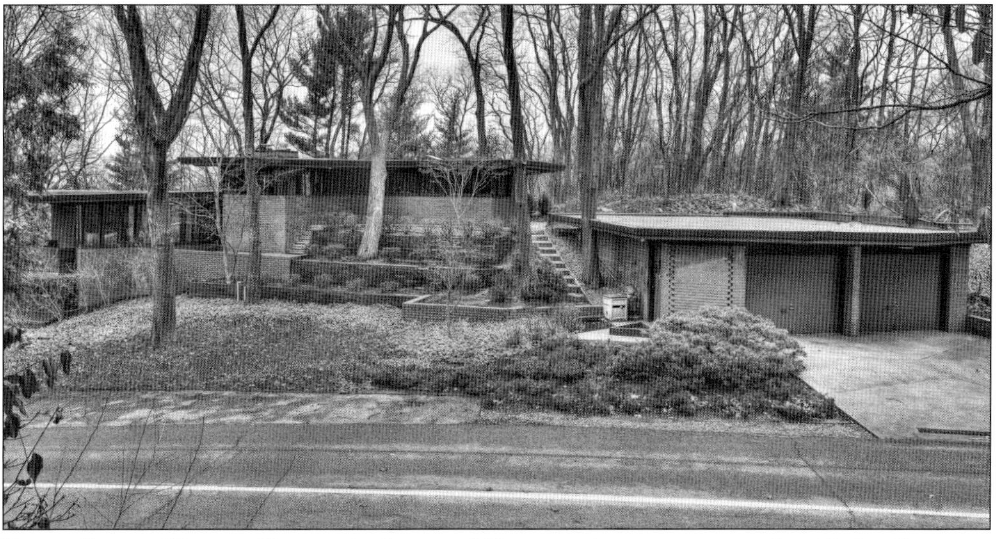

Frank Lloyd Wright House. Andrew and Florence Armstrong moved to Ogden Dunes in 1939 from New England. He worked for a major advertising firm in Chicago. They rented a house while arranging for Frank Lloyd Wright to design a home for their wooded lot on Cedar Trail. Wright's plans included an innovative heating system of hot-water pipes laid in the cement floor. However, the Armstrongs soon replaced the system because Wright's innovation failed to work. (Courtesy of John Peterson.)

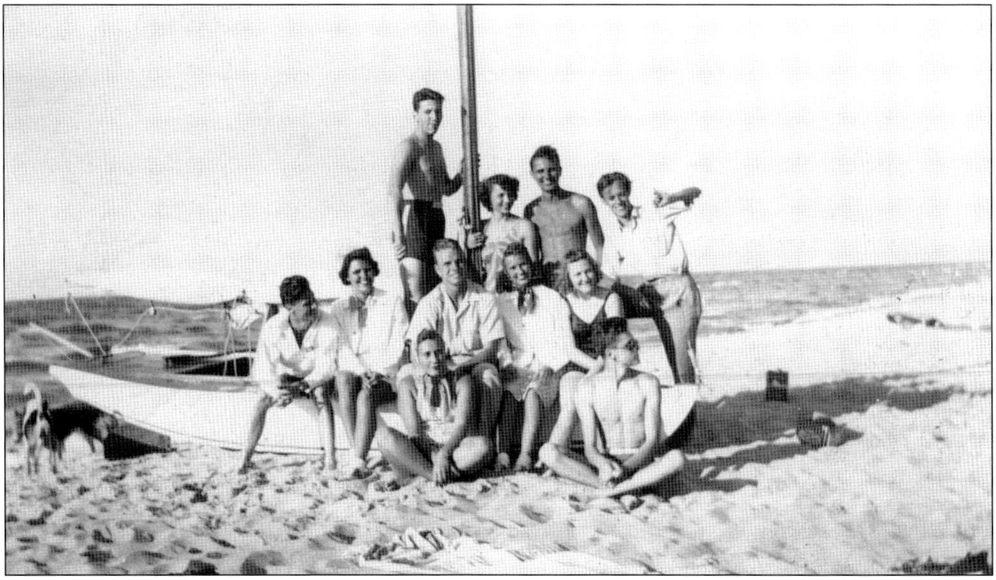

The Rafters. During the summers of the late 1930s, 20 or more teenagers and college students created a close-knit community. They became known as the rafters. This photograph of them was taken on the Thompson family's sailboat in 1939. It provides a glimpse into a time of innocence, a few years before Pearl Harbor. The William D. and Helen Thompson family was from St. Louis and spent its summers in the dunes. The family's children were Bill, Joan, and Mary Jean. Shown here are, from left to right, (first row) unidentified and Mel Tracht; (second row) Fred Collins, Mary Jean Thompson, Charles Berkley, Joan Thompson, and unidentified; (third row) unidentified, Margaret "Mike" Breed, Bill Thompson, and Howie Marten. (HSOD, Thompson.)

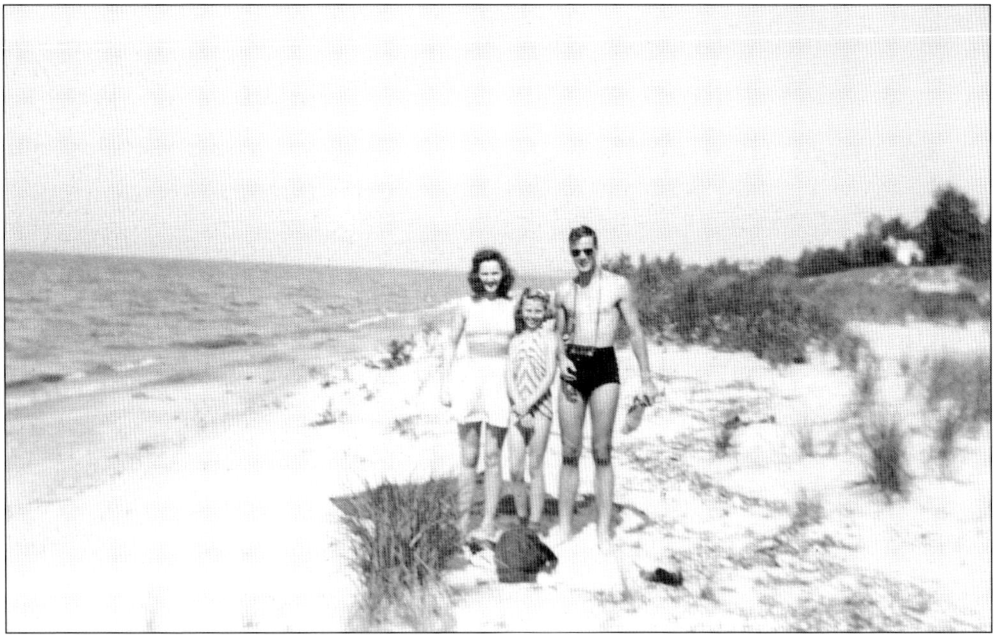

Beach Scene. In this photograph is a young girl, Barbara Funkey (center), with family friends. Her parents built a home on the south side of Shore Drive in the early 1940s. (HSOD.)

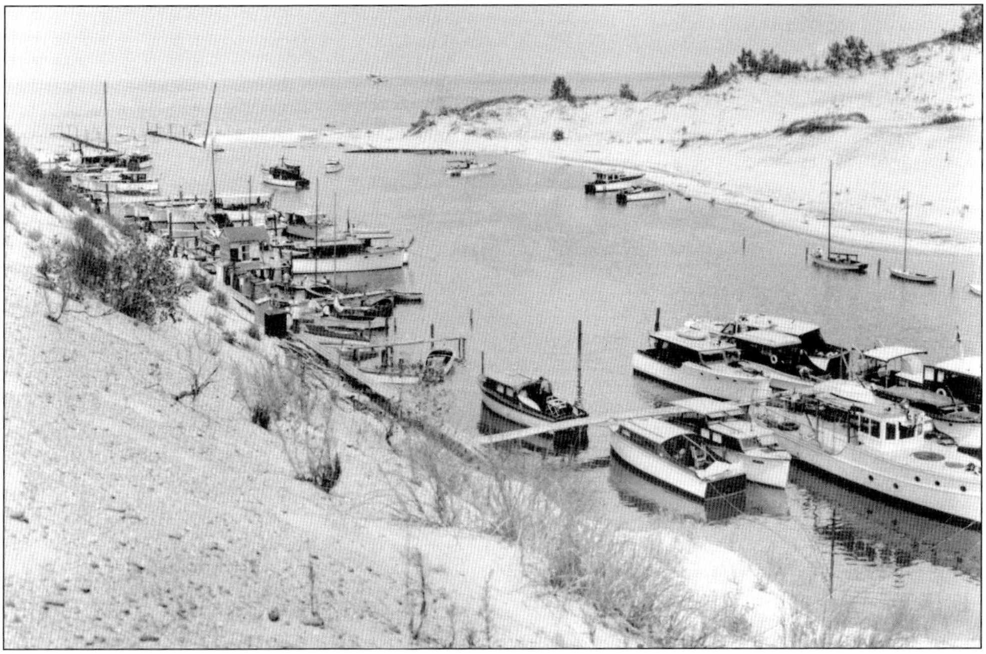

Gary Boat Club. Although Samuel Reck's dream of a yacht club was dashed by the Great Depression, a group of avid sailors, including a few from Ogden Dunes, formed the Gary Boat Club in 1936. The club leased land near the mouth of the Burns Ditch for a clubhouse and docks. To provide access, Ogden Dunes agreed to build Boat Club Road, just to the east of the old ski jump. A number of the club's members moved from Gary and built homes in Ogden Dunes, including the Tittle, Dorman, Sykes, and Blodgett families. The above photograph was taken from the west bank. Below, the boat club is seen from the east bank. (Above, courtesy of Tom Tittle; below, courtesy of Richard Hallman.)

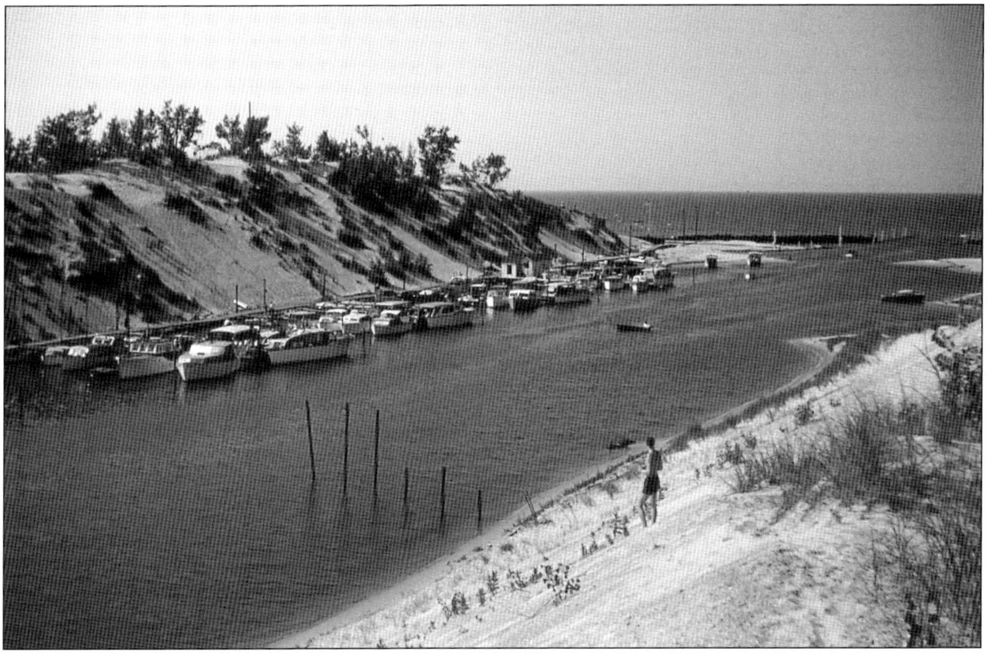

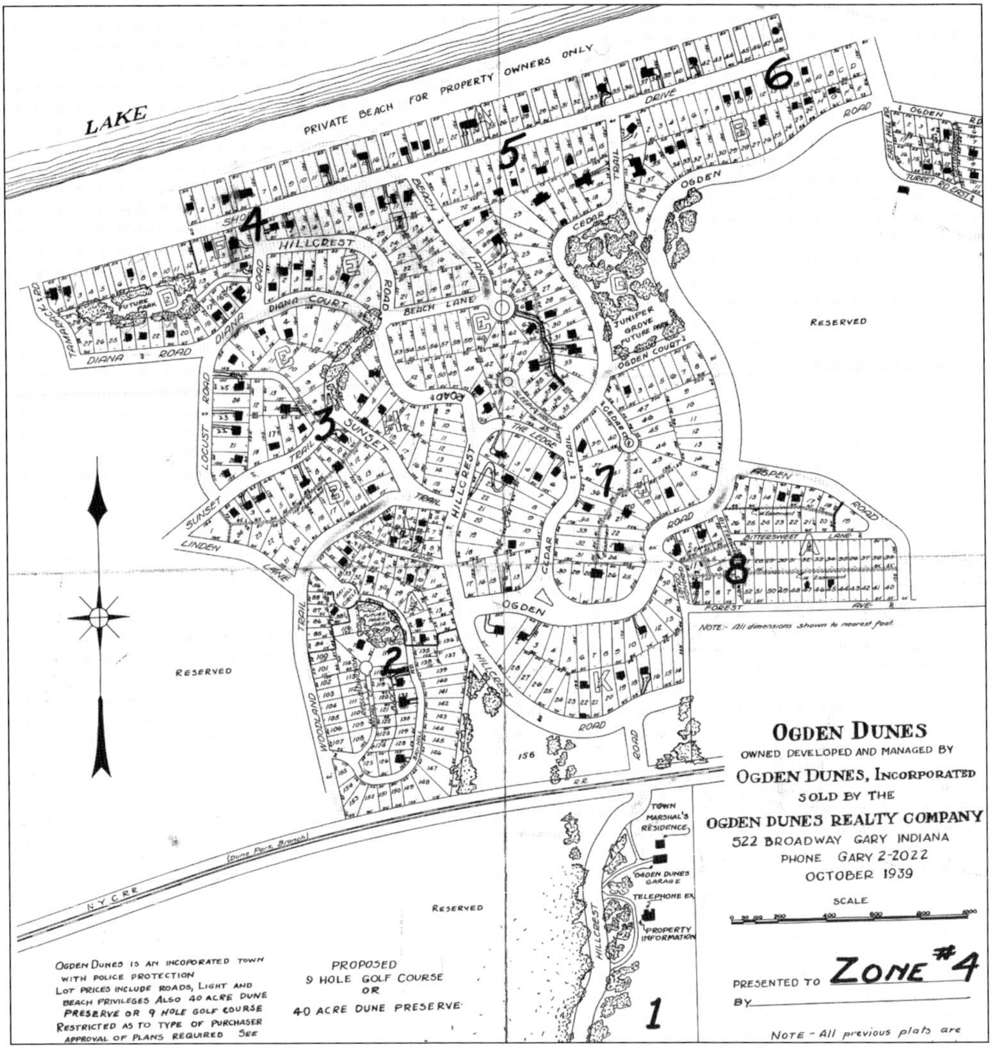

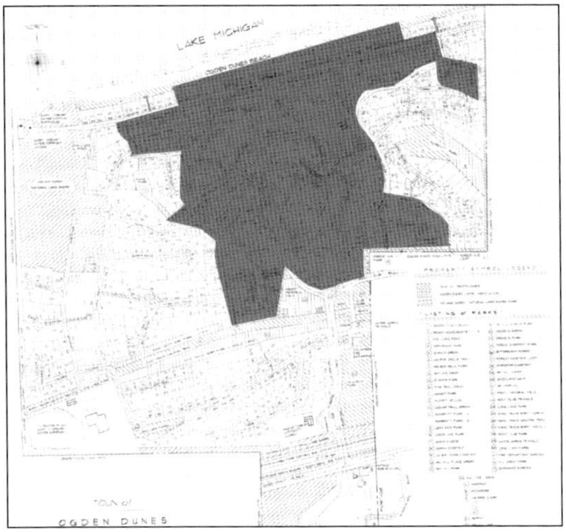

1939 Map. The map above shows a small addition on the east side of town and the new lots and renamed streets in the Second Subdivision following the closure of the ski jump. Included here are 132 homes and cottages, almost double the number from five years earlier. Most of the owners were summer residents. The 1940 census lists 43 families and 144 individuals as full-time residents of Ogden Dunes. The *Ogden Dunes Sandpiper* newsletter of October 5, 1940, lists 21 Ogden Dunes students attending Crisman (Portage Township) School. The 1939 map at left shows the town within the 1994 boundaries of Ogden Dunes, which remain the same today. (Both, HSOD.)

Five

War and After
1940s

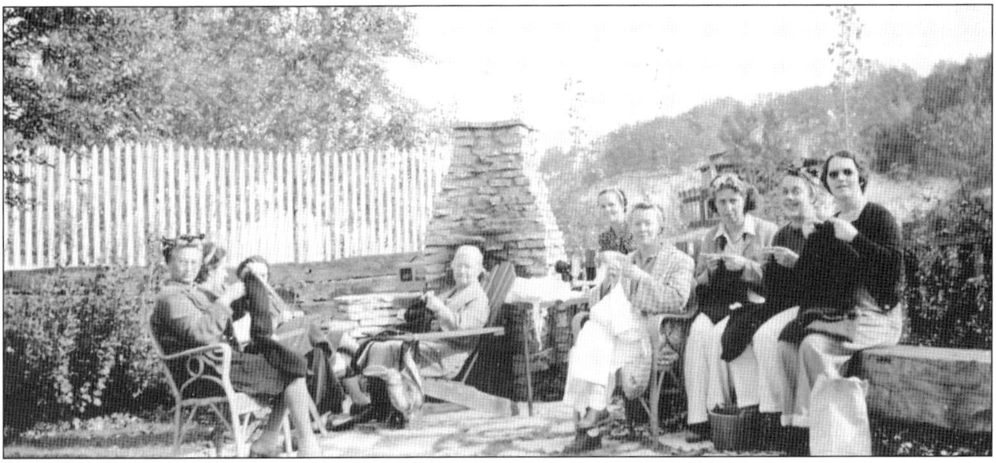

Red Cross Volunteers. With the outbreak of World War II in 1939, the Woman's Club formed a group of Red Cross volunteers. They met every two weeks to sew and knit as well as to support one another. Most soon had sons or relatives serving in the military. Among their gathering spots was Jane Thompson's patio on Shore Drive, shown here. (HSOD.)

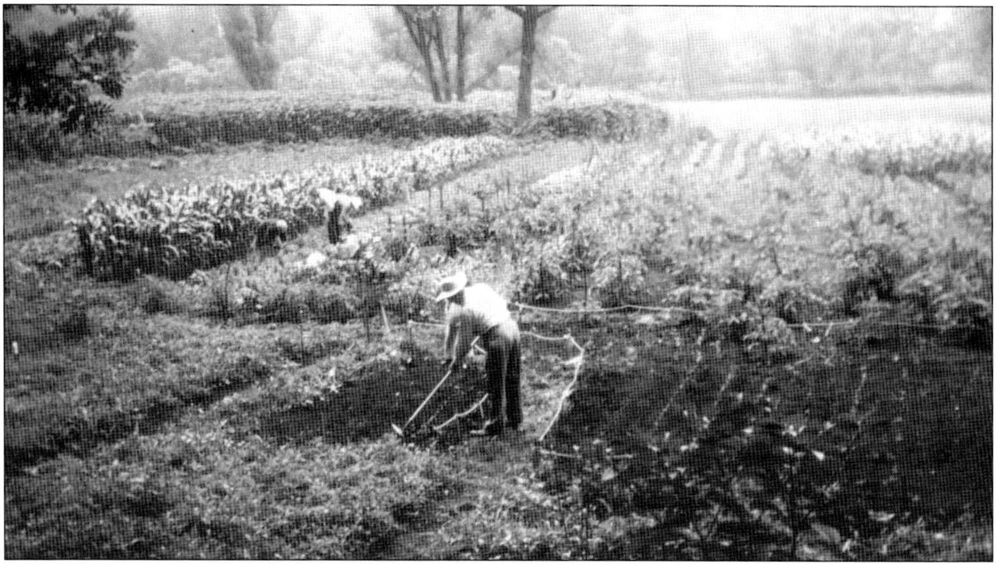

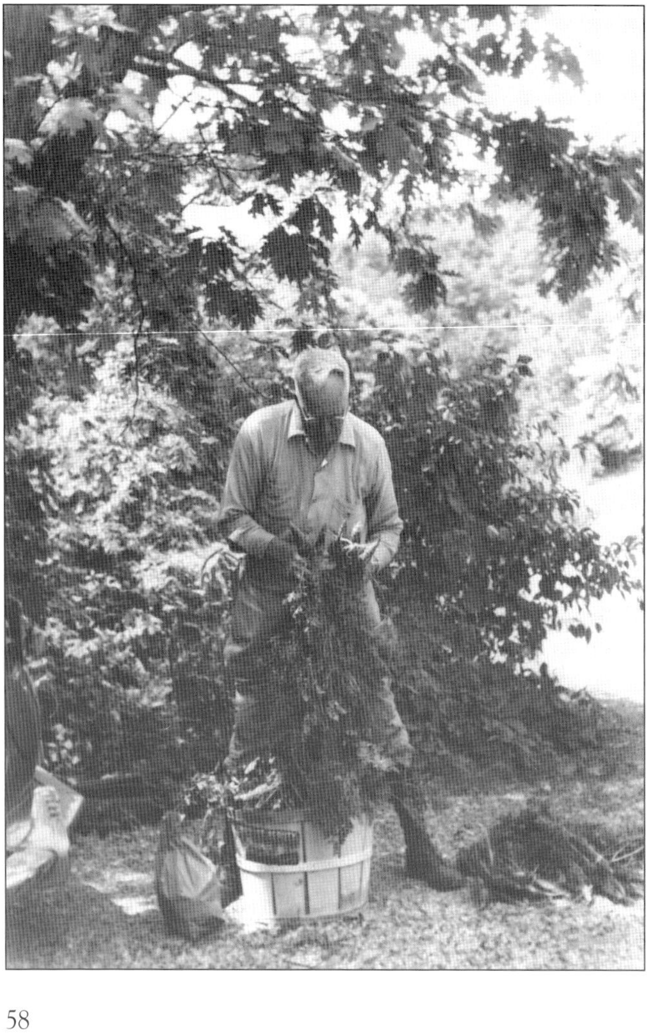

Victory Gardens. The community organized a local civil defense corps, with Ed Kratz and Dess Cash serving as coordinators. The community established two Victory Gardens. One was in the open area that once served the ski jump, and the other was on fertile, drained land just south of US 12. Here, O.D. Frank and others are at work in the garden. (HSOD.)

O.D. Frank's Vegetable Stand. It was natural that O.D. Frank took the lead in doing gardening. During the war, he had a garden and a vegetable and fruit stand on Lupine Lane to serve his neighbors. (HSOD, Frank.)

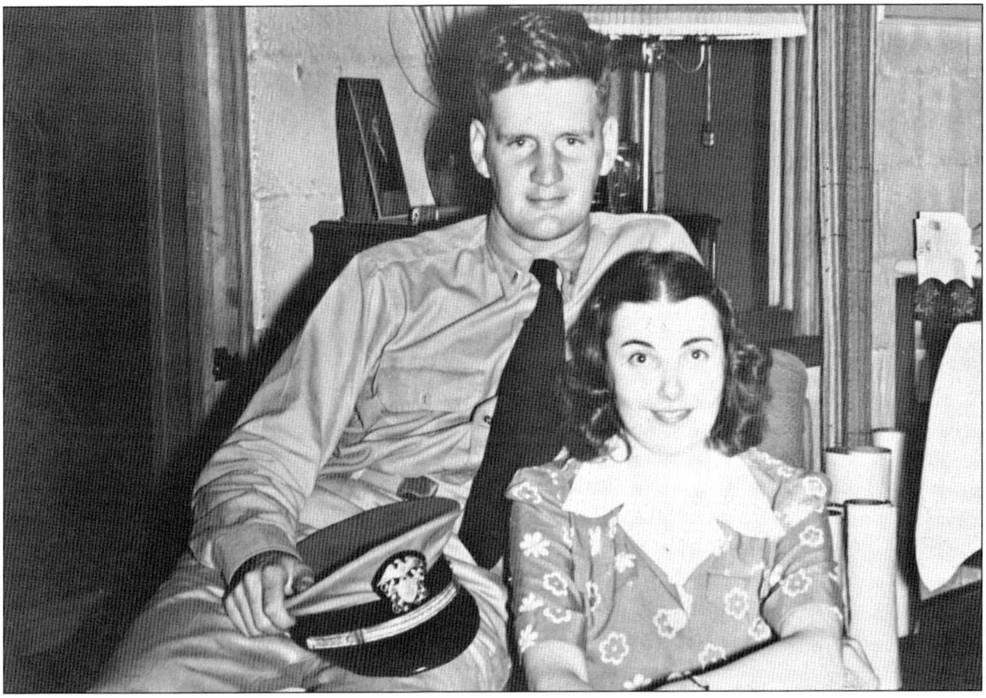

Mitchell and Muriel Cash. Mitchell Cash (1918–2011), the oldest son of A.L. and Dess Cash, graduated from Purdue University with an engineering degree in June 1941. Following graduation, he immediately entered the US Navy as an officer. On August 21, 1941, he married Muriel Smith (1918–1993) of South Bend. At the outbreak of the Korean War, he was recalled to service and went on to have a distinguished naval career. Mitchell was among over 30 young servicemen who lived in or had connections with Ogden Dunes. (Courtesy of Laura Mitchell Cash.)

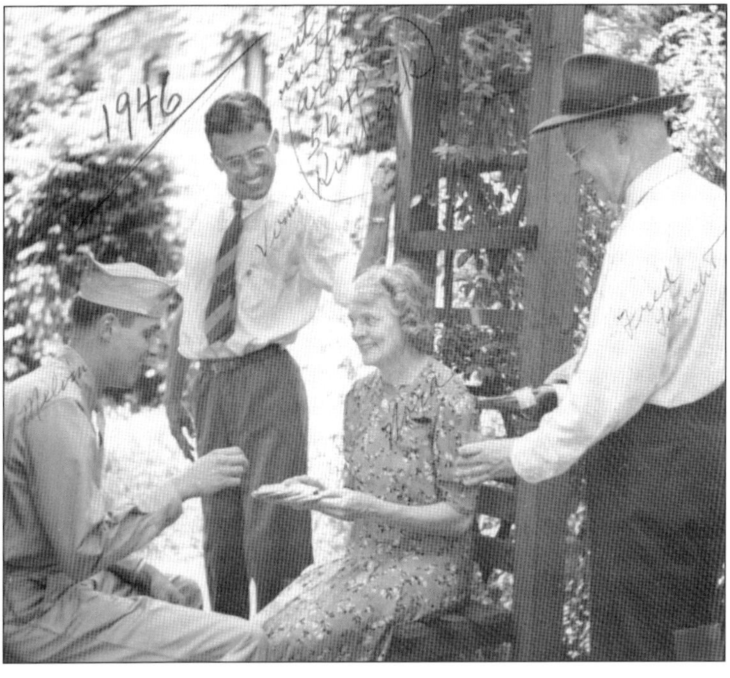

Mel Tracht and Family. After graduating from the University of Chicago in 1941, Mel Tracht worked in the business department of the Illinois Institute of Technology. He enlisted in the US Army and served from 1943 to 1945. Here, Mel (left) visits with his parents, Fred and Nora, and his brother Vernon (second from left). (Courtesy of Mildred Tracht.)

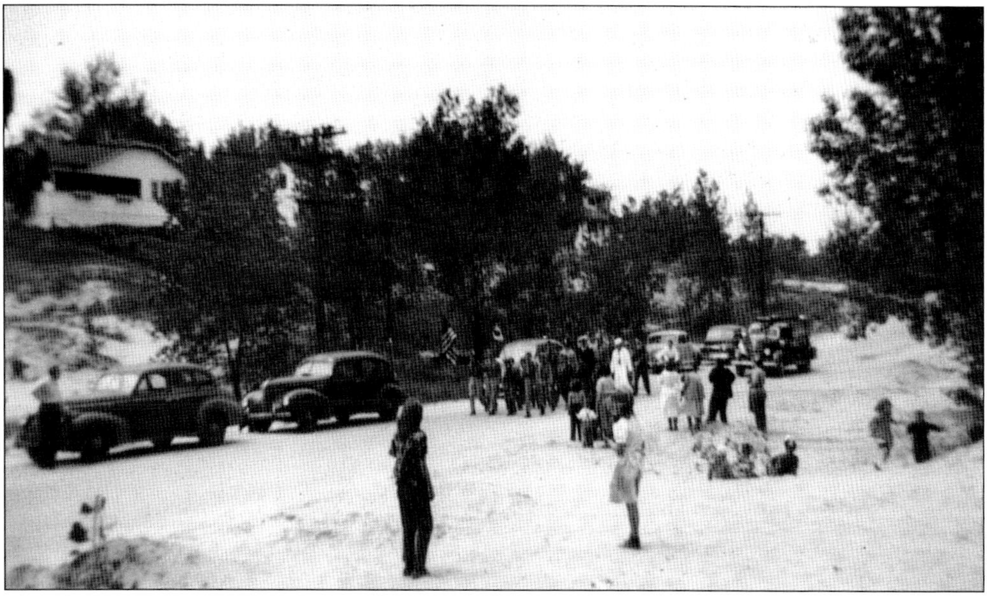

MEMORIAL DAY, 1948. On Memorial Day 1947, the newly established American Legion Post 132 in Ogden Dunes sponsored a parade down Shore Drive to the beach, at the end of Cedar Trail. It was a great success and soon became the most important community day of the year. The 1948 Memorial Day observance repeated the parade and picnic, which took place at the easement to the beach by Cedar Trail. In the background are the participants in the parade, including Scouts. Also visible is the Dalby cottage, high on the dune. (HSOD.)

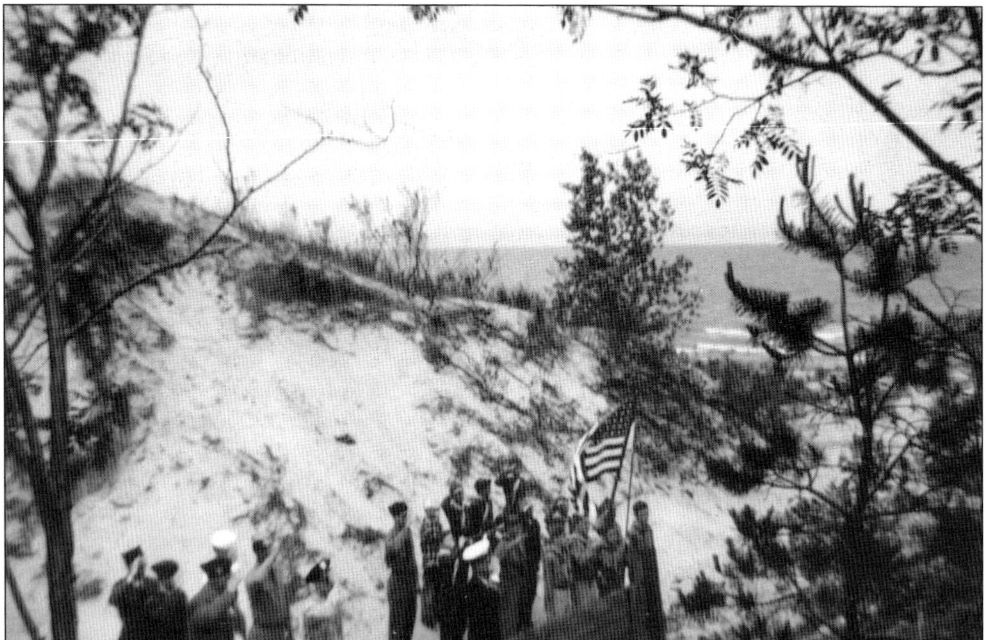

AMERICAN LEGION POST 132. The American flag is presented before the flagpole that was erected on the easement to the beach, just west of Nelson Reck's home on Shore Drive. This photograph was taken in 1948. (HSOD.)

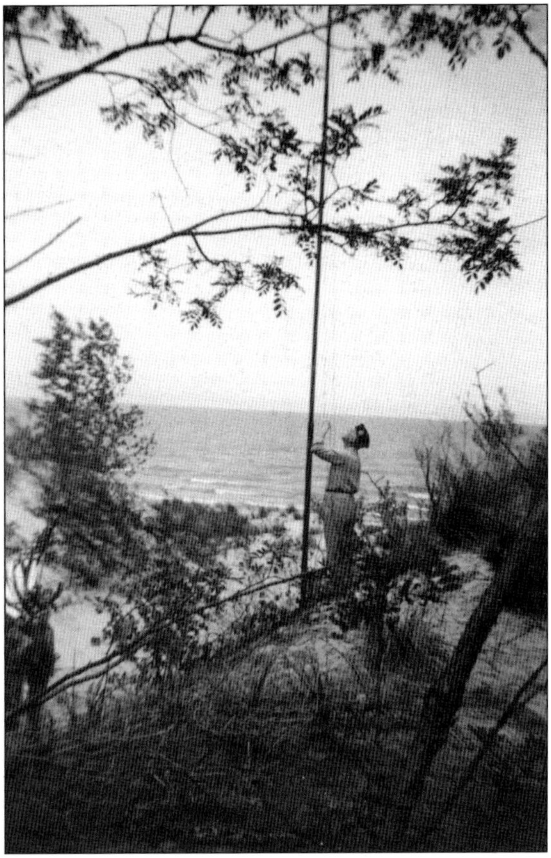

Raising the Flag. The post was formed in April 1946, with 22 residents, veterans of World Wars I and II. Dennis Harvey became the first commander. Also holding offices were three former rafters, Mitchell Cash (vice commander), George Semerau (second vice commander), and Leonard Whelpley (service officer). (HSOD.)

Children Watching. Among those enjoying sodas and, later, hot dogs, were Mike and Laura Cash, Mitch and Muriel's children. They watched the flag ceremony in awe. (HSOD.)

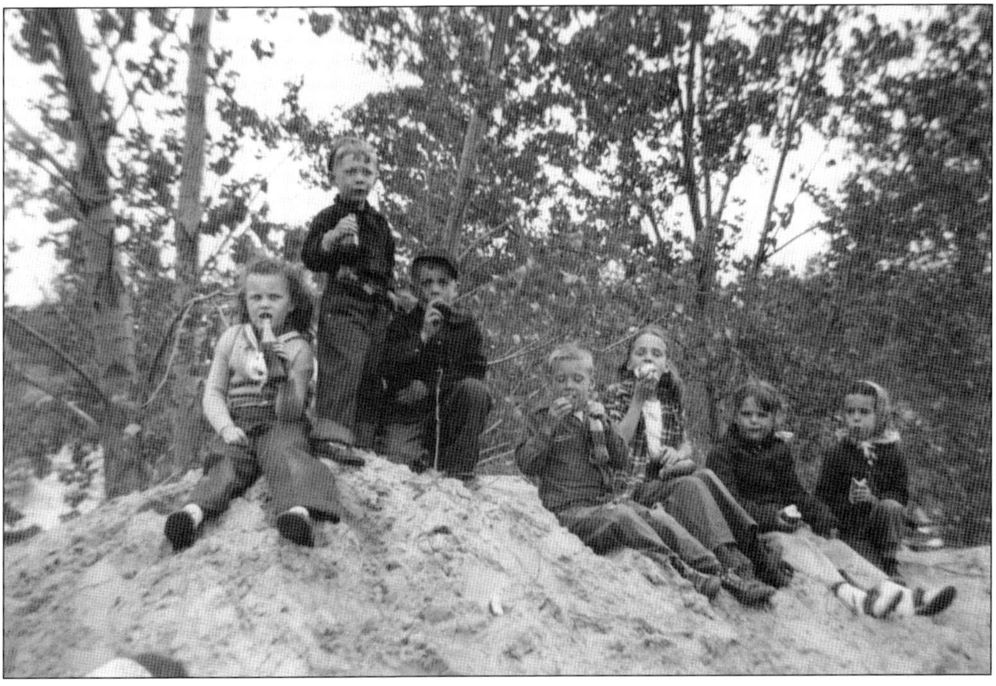

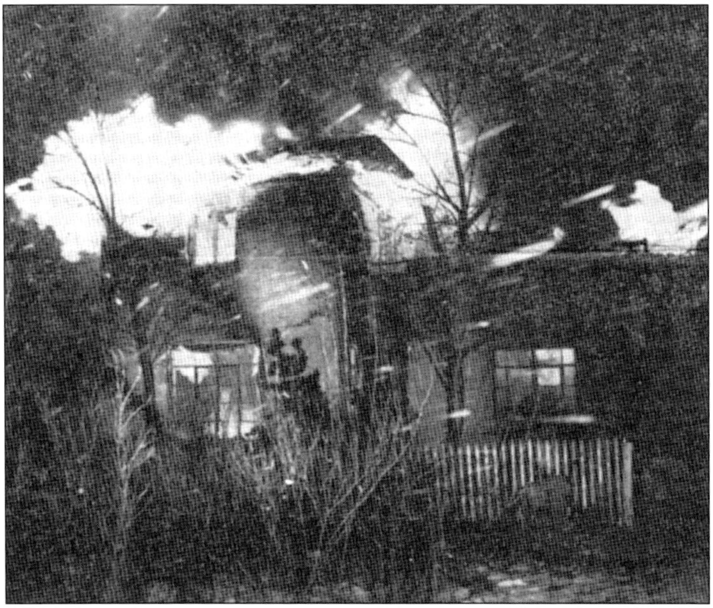

Dorman Home Fire. Newspaper headlines shocked the community in 1948. On January 15 of that year, a fire destroyed Willard and Marjorie Dorman's home at 94 Shore Drive. The Dormans had hosted many community activities at their residence (see page 52). It was this fire that mobilized the community to establish a volunteer fire department. (HSOD.)

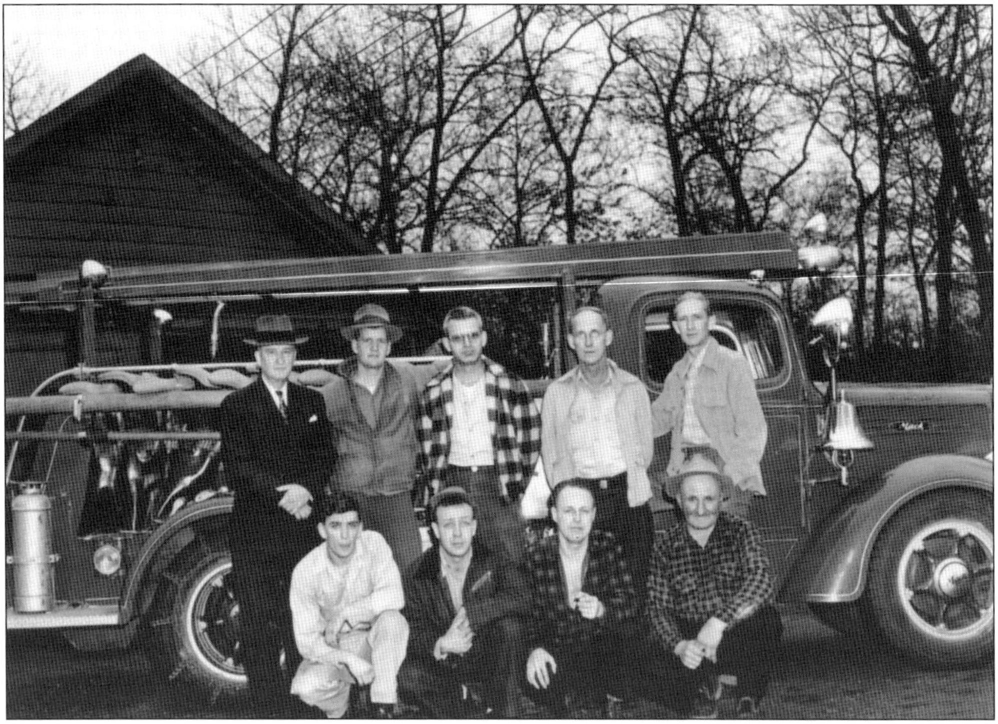

Volunteer Fire Department, 1948. No fire in Ogden Dunes had as much of an effect on the community as the Dorman blaze. And, by 1948, there were a sufficient number of young men to support an all-volunteer fire department. Each household was asked to give $50 to purchase fire equipment. The initial department comprised 18 volunteers; Mitch Cash became the first fire chief. Posing with the recently purchased used fire truck are, from left to right, (first row) Ron Stevens, Paul Hake, Ogden Nickerson, and Gus Lawson; (second row) Ed Kratz, Mitch Cash, Roger Willis, Ted Borg, and Ed Pittet. (HSOD, Stevens.)

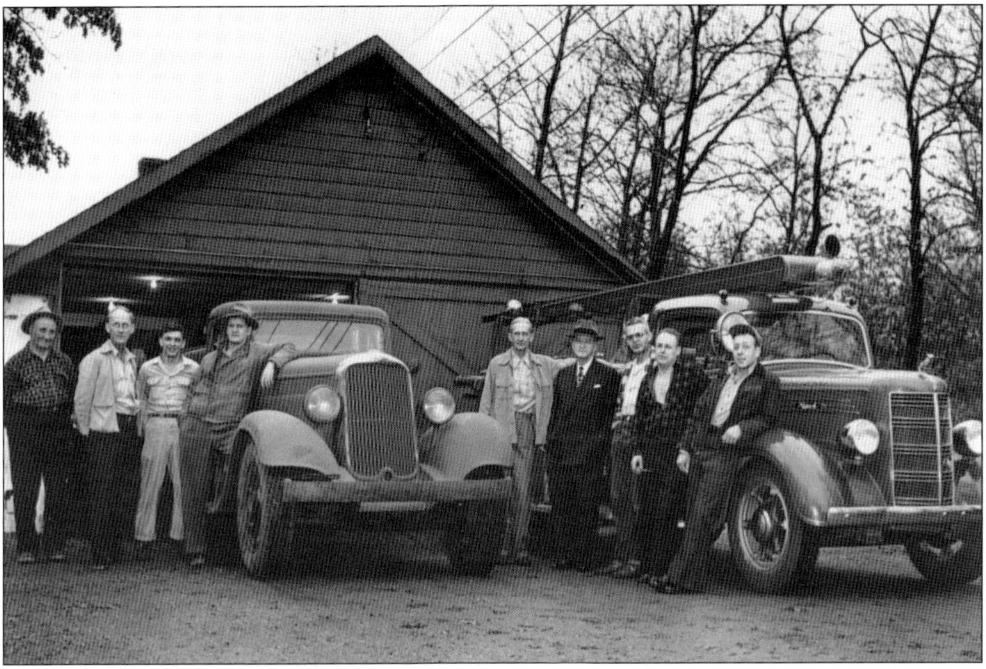

Fire Equipment. Ogden Dunes Realty made its garage available to house the used equipment prior to the construction of a fire station. The men standing by the 1935 Dodge Tanker (left) and 1942 Mack Pumper (right) are, from left to right, Gus Lawson, Ted Borg, Ron Stevens, Chief Mitch Cash, Ed Pittet, Ed Kratz, Roger Willis, Ogden Nickerson, and Paul Hake. (HSOD, Stevens.)

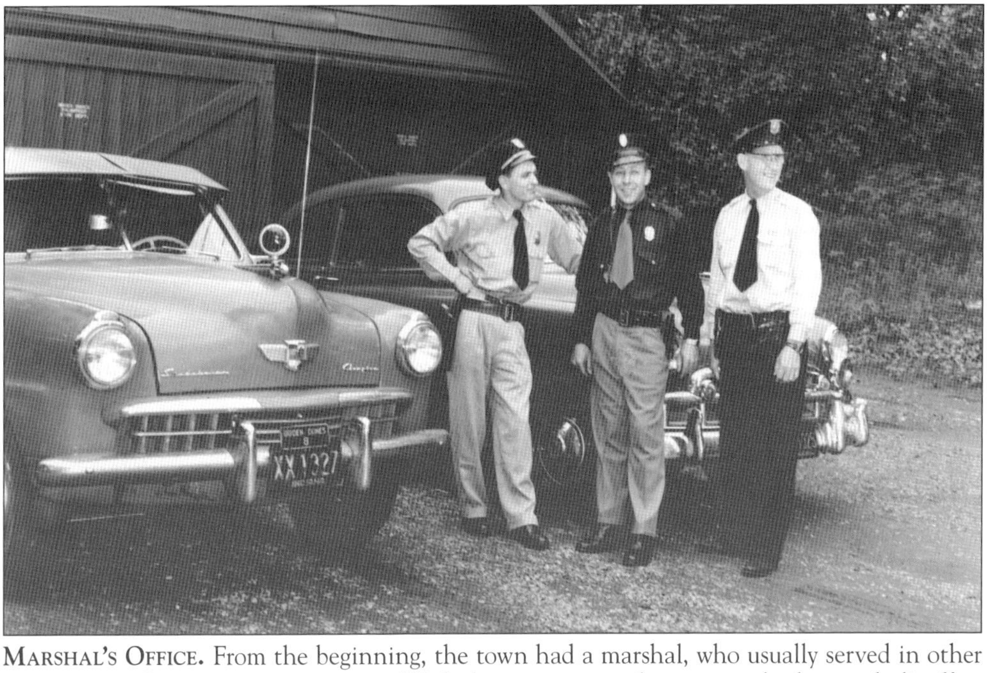

Marshal's Office. From the beginning, the town had a marshal, who usually served in other capacities, such as street commissioner. With the postwar population growth, the marshal's office hired part-time deputy marshals. Shown here from left to right are Ron Stevens, Paul Hake, and Marshal Ted Borg. (HSOD, Stevens.)

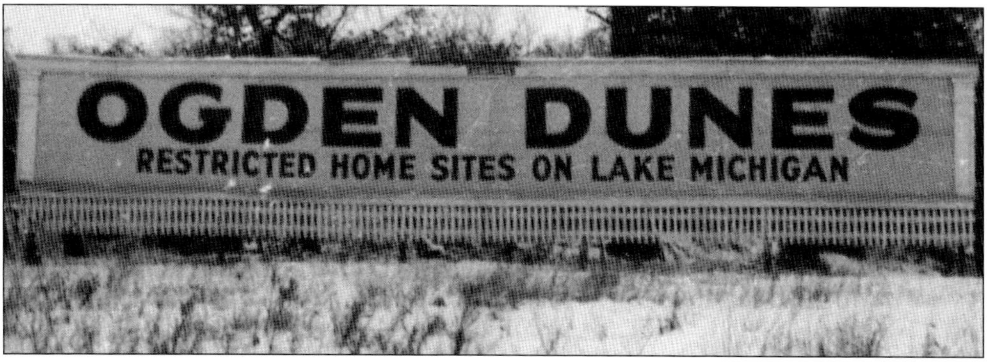

OGDEN DUNES ENTRANCE SIGN. Until 1948, this sign proclaimed Ogden Dunes a highly restricted community. Nonwhites and non-Gentiles were prohibited from buying or being sold land in Ogden Dunes. In 1948, in *Shelley vs. Kraemer*, the Supreme Court declared these restrictions unconstitutional. Such restrictions were common in planned communities and in many urban neighborhoods. Today, it is difficult to understand society's lack of sensitivity, especially in the aftermath of World War II. (HSOD.)

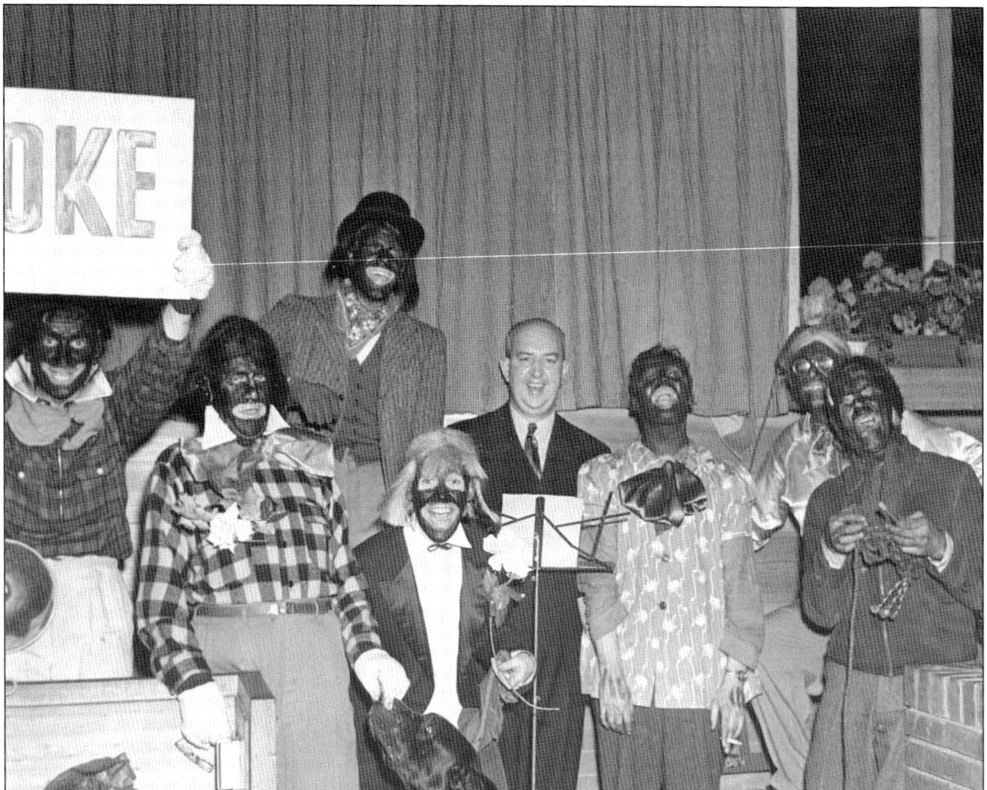

MINSTREL SHOW, 1941. Another example of a lack of sensitivity was the amateur production of minstrel shows that were common in American society. This one, a fundraiser, was sponsored by the men of Ogden Dunes in 1941. (HSOD.)

George Svihla Jr. After World War II, Ogden Dunes Realty sold lots in the Fourth Subdivision. This subdivision was south of Ogden Road, primarily along the large dune running parallel with Ogden and the new and extended streets to the east: Skyline Drive, Aspen Road, and Bittersweet Lane. Here, George Svihla Jr. prepares to ski the sloping dune behind his home at 49 Ogden Road. His parents, George (1915–2002), a scientist at Argonne Laboratories, and Beth Svihla, literally built their environmentally friendly home in 1947. (Courtesy of George Svihla.)

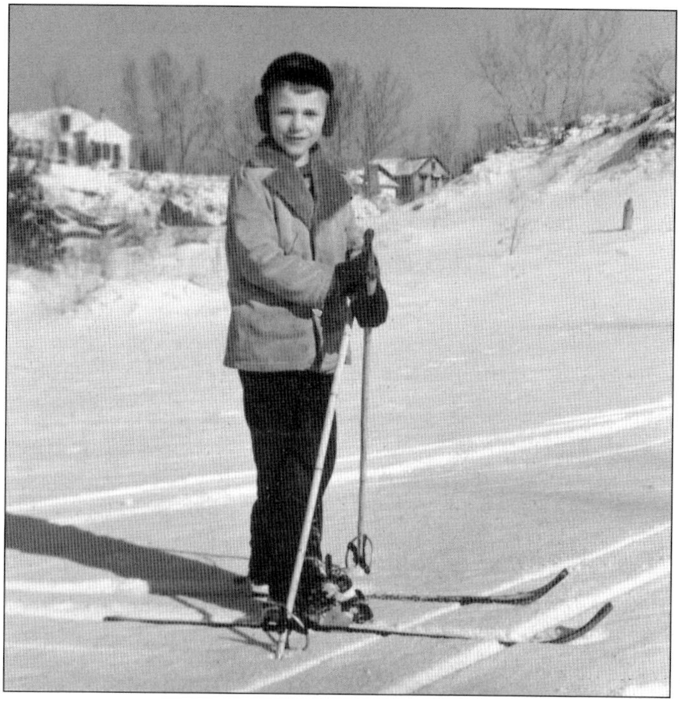

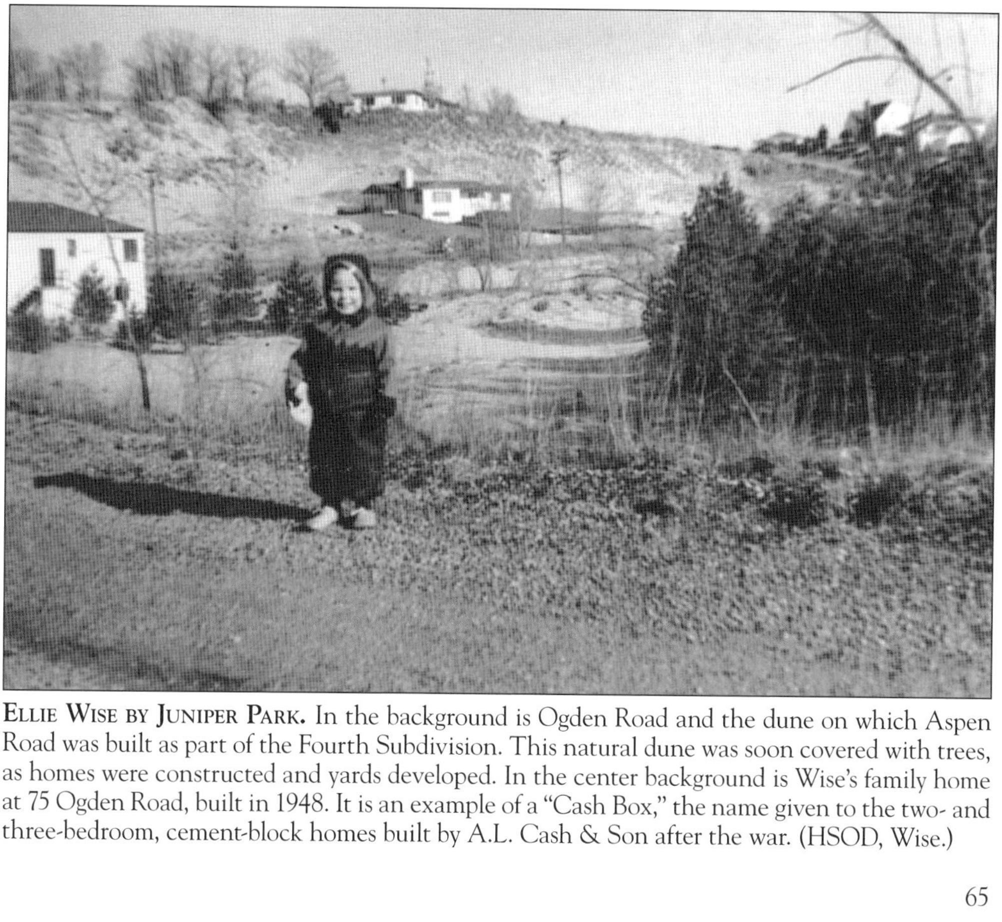

Ellie Wise by Juniper Park. In the background is Ogden Road and the dune on which Aspen Road was built as part of the Fourth Subdivision. This natural dune was soon covered with trees, as homes were constructed and yards developed. In the center background is Wise's family home at 75 Ogden Road, built in 1948. It is an example of a "Cash Box," the name given to the two- and three-bedroom, cement-block homes built by A.L. Cash & Son after the war. (HSOD, Wise.)

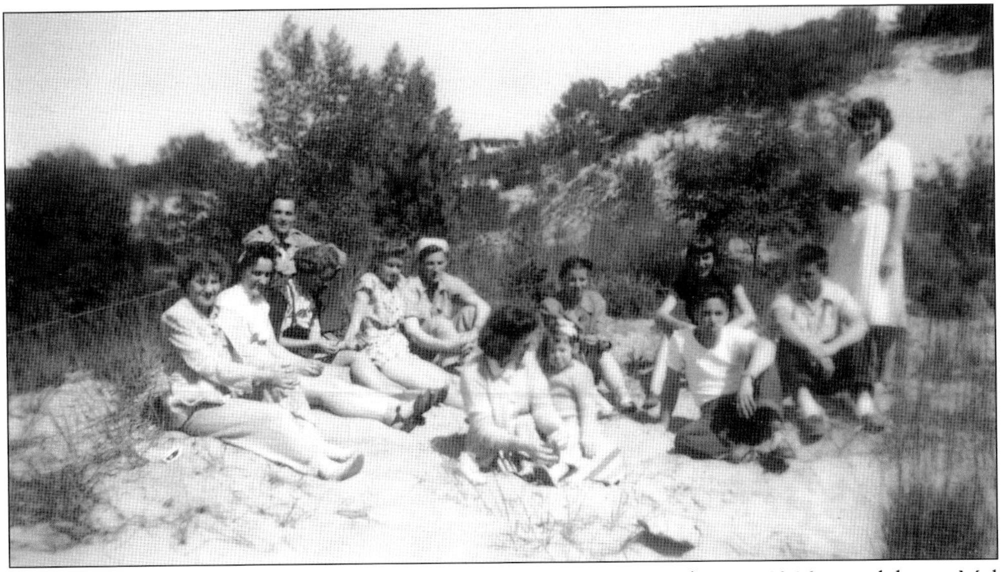

Tracht Celebration. Friends and family members came together in 1946 to celebrate Mel and Millie's marriage and to enjoy the outdoors. The beach was a block north of the Trachts' Hillcrest Road cottage. (Courtesy of Mildred Tracht.)

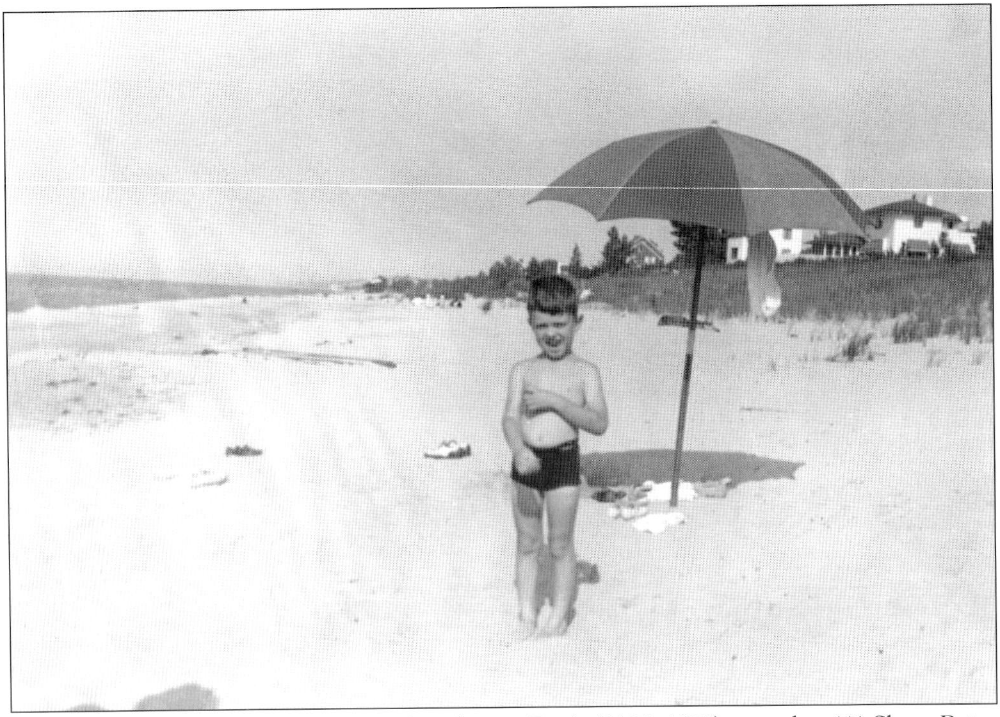

Tom Tittle, 1942. Walter (1907–1979) and Neva Tittle (1909–1979) moved to 111 Shore Drive in the late 1930s. Walter was a partner in the family's meat and grocery business in Gary. The family built in Ogden Dunes because of their involvement with the Gary Boat Club. Their son Tom is seen here on the beach, across the street from their home. (HSOD, Tittle.)

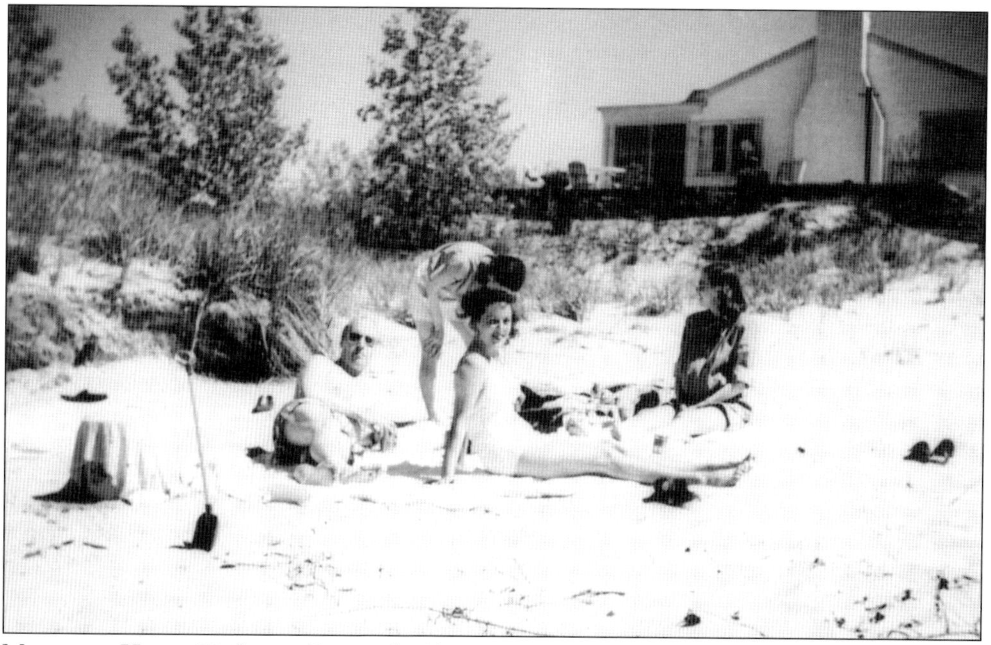

MONAHAN HOME, 70 SHORE DRIVE. In 1941, Marietta Monahan, an English teacher in Gary, and her mother, Anna, built a cement-block home on Shore Drive. Later, two of Marietta's sisters, Kathryn and Eleanor, would marry Fred Collins and Laurence LaTourette, respectively, and settle in Ogden Dunes. Shown here facing the camera are family friends Dr. Don Trinosky and his wife, Scott. (Courtesy of Rick Collins.)

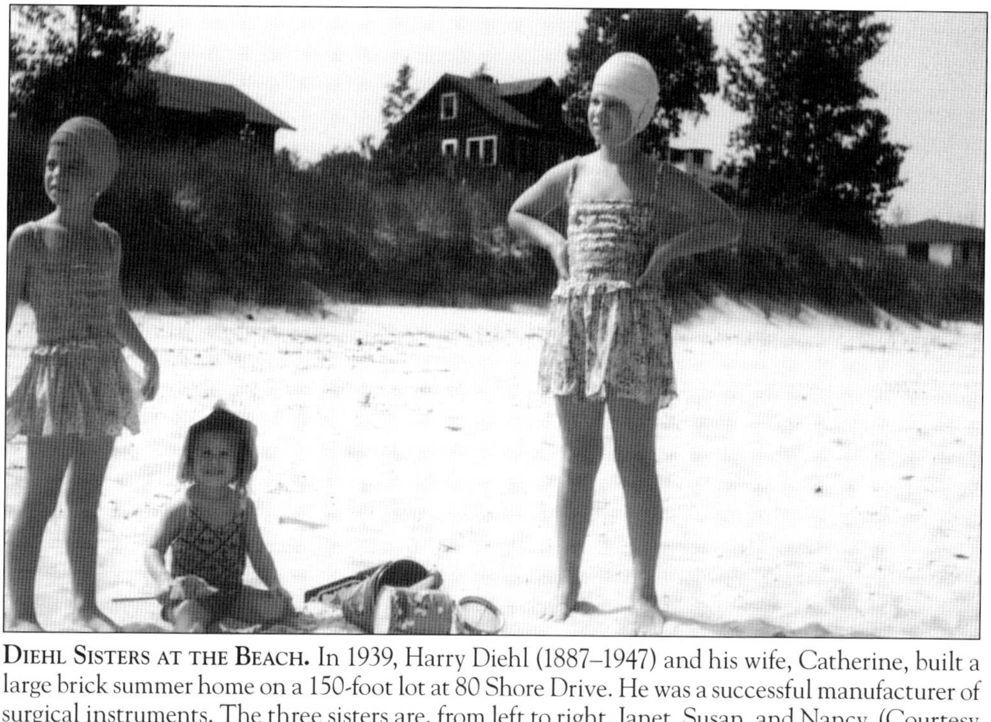

DIEHL SISTERS AT THE BEACH. In 1939, Harry Diehl (1887–1947) and his wife, Catherine, built a large brick summer home on a 150-foot lot at 80 Shore Drive. He was a successful manufacturer of surgical instruments. The three sisters are, from left to right, Janet, Susan, and Nancy. (Courtesy of Richard Hallman.)

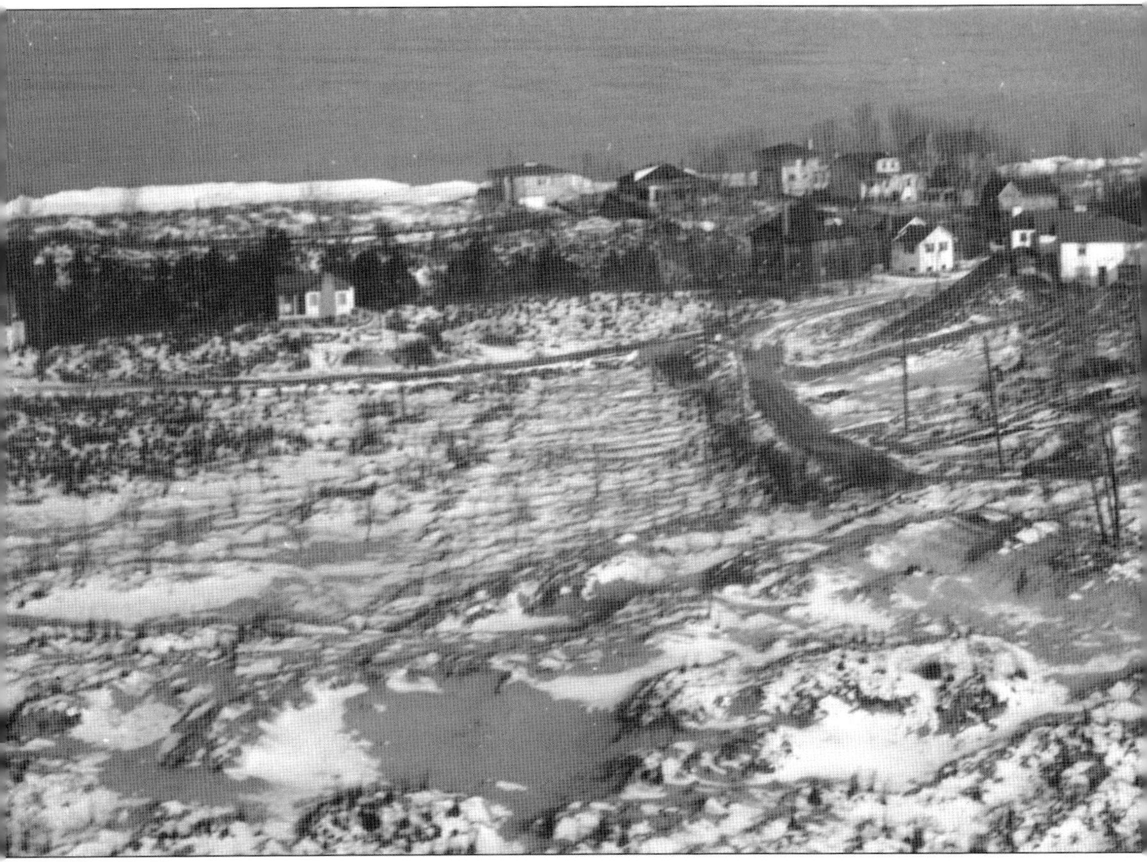

West End Panorama. In 1943, Frank Mullin, who had moved his family into a home at 37 Sunset Trail, took this photograph from the high dune behind his home. That dune was called Mount Everest; today, it is Summit Road. The photograph, a panorama of the west side of Ogden

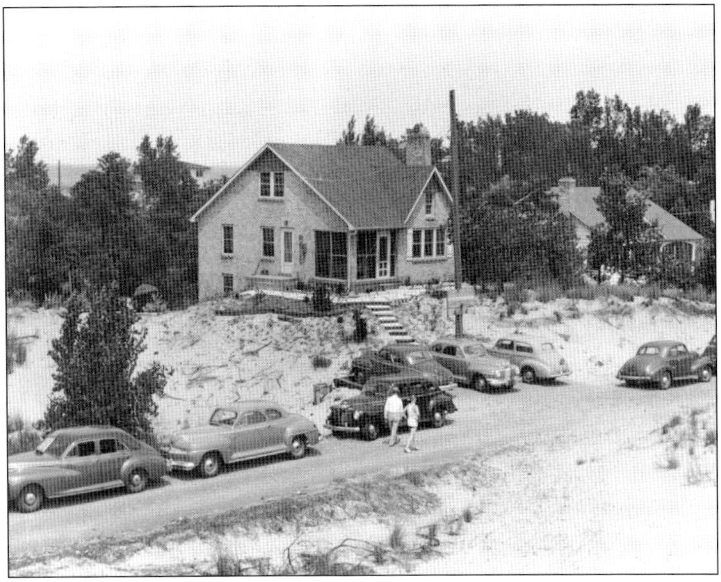

New Home, 24 Diana Road. Diana Road was extended south and then east in the 1950s and 1960s with the development of the Third and Fifth Subdivisions. (HSOD.)

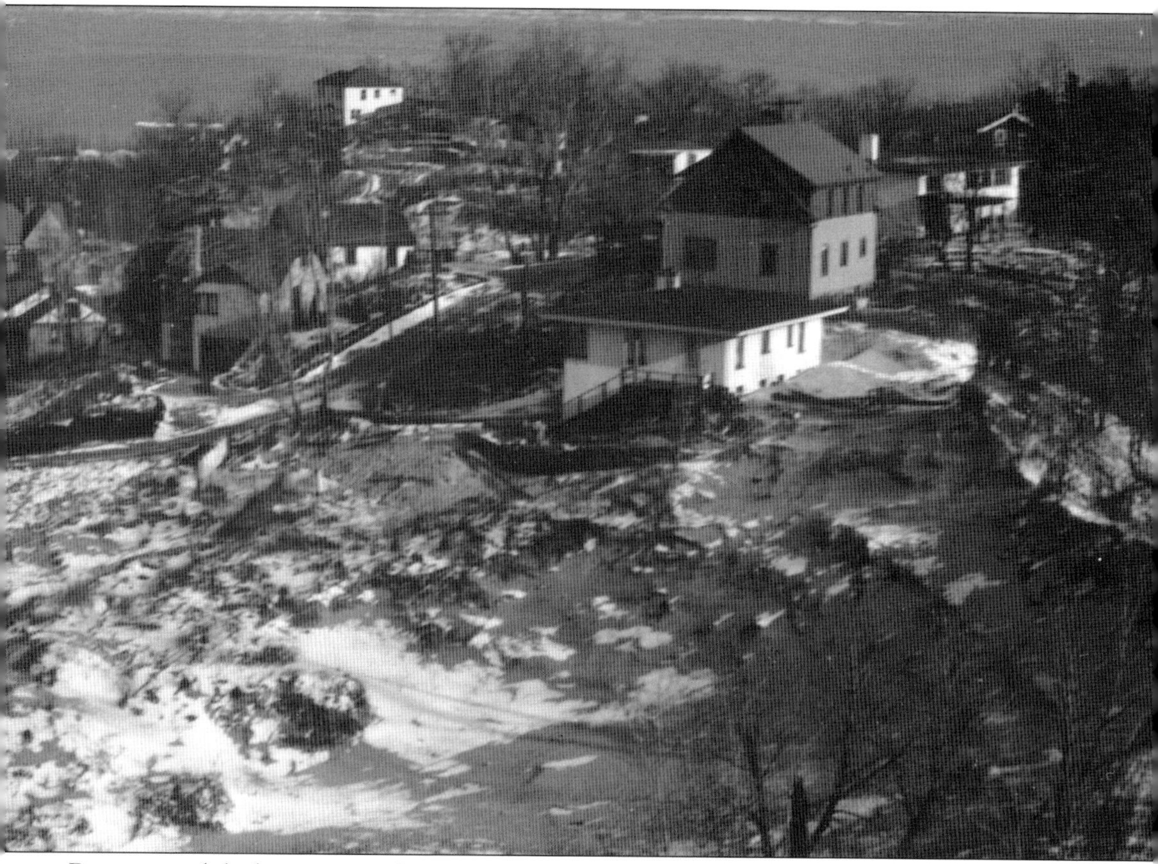

Dunes, reveals little vegetation. It was not until 1955 that much of this area was developed. Frank Mullin and his wife, Betty, were leaders in Ogden Dunes for many years. (HSOD, Mullin.)

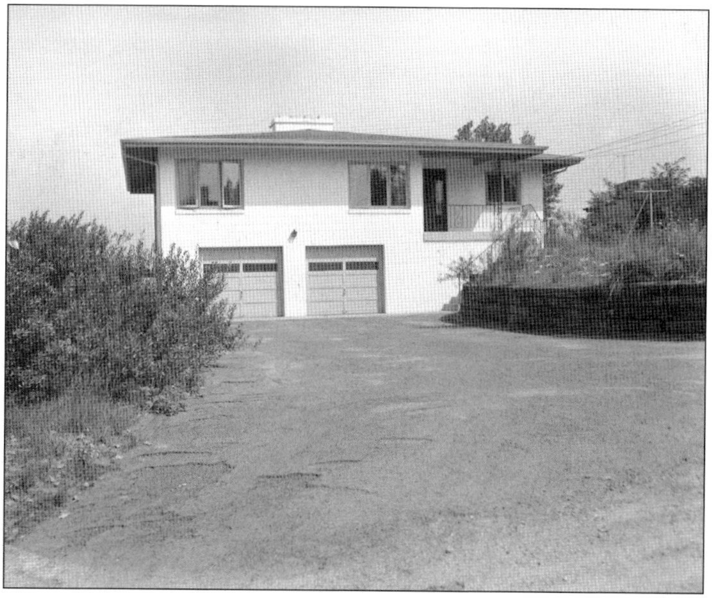

New Home, 10 Shore Drive. Much of the new construction along Shore Drive occurred west of Cedar Trail. However, a number of lakefront homes were built on the eastern end of Shore Drive after the war. This cement-block home near the east end was built by A.L. Cash & Son and designed by Fred Collins. (HSOD.)

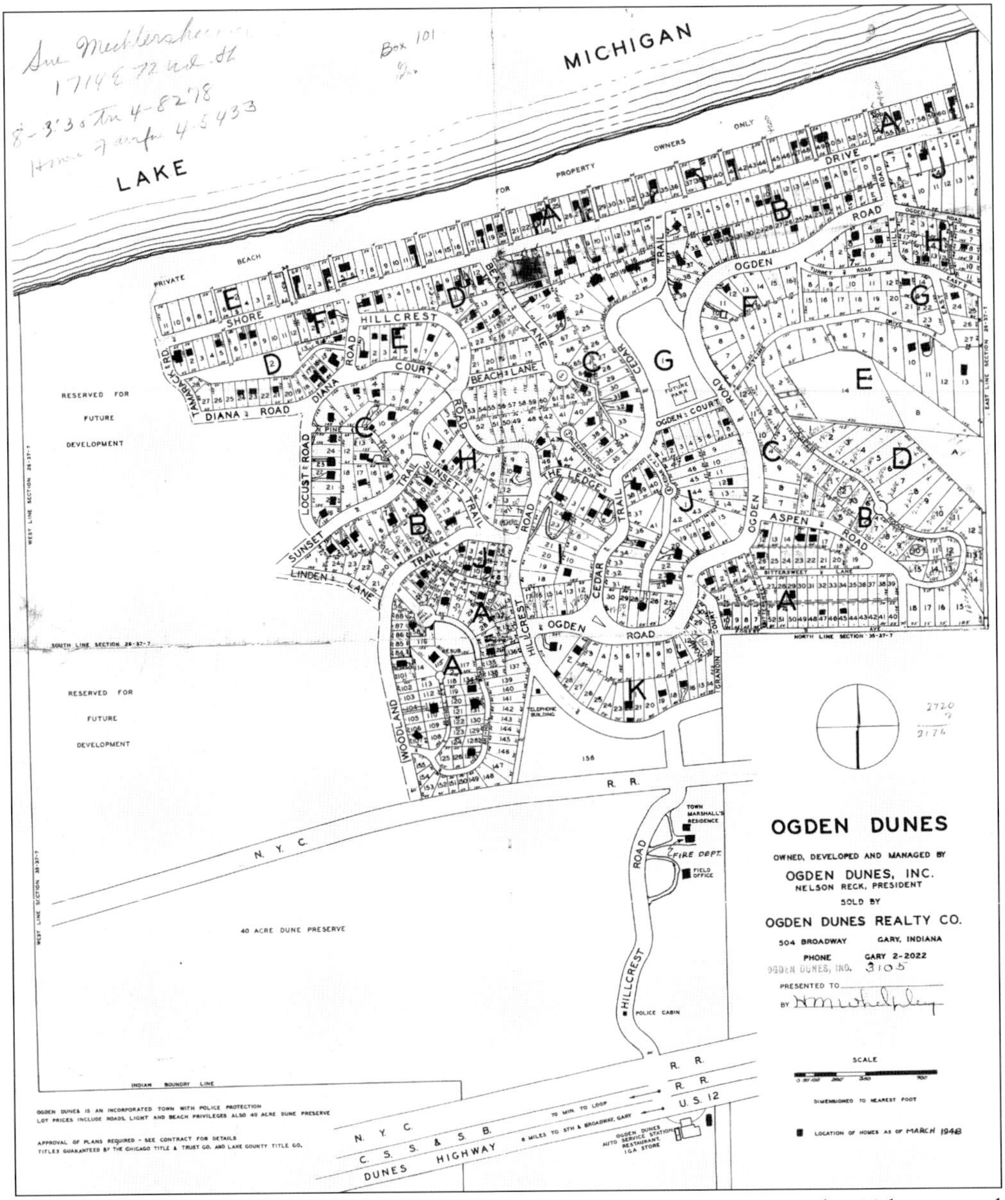

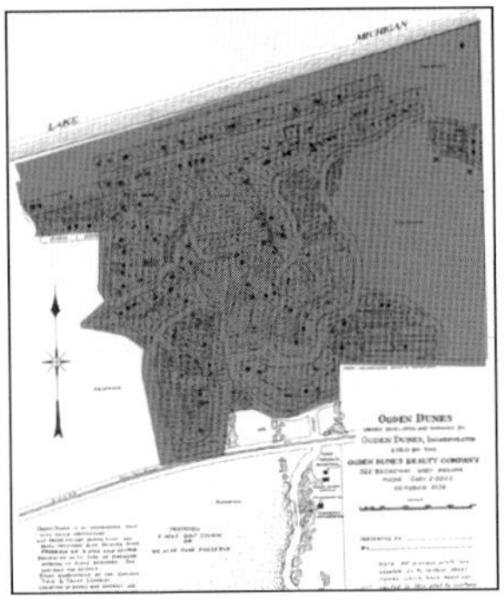

MAP, 1949. The map above shows approximately 180 homes and cottages. The addition of the Fourth Subdivision contributed to this growth. According to the 1950 census, the number of full-time residents increased from 144 in 1940 to 429. The *Ogden Dunes Sandpiper* of September 28, 1950, lists 81 students in the Portage Township Public Schools and 28 in college. The 1949 map at left shows the town within the 1994 boundaries of Ogden Dunes, which remain the same today. (Both, HSOD.)

Six

Threats and Responses 1950s

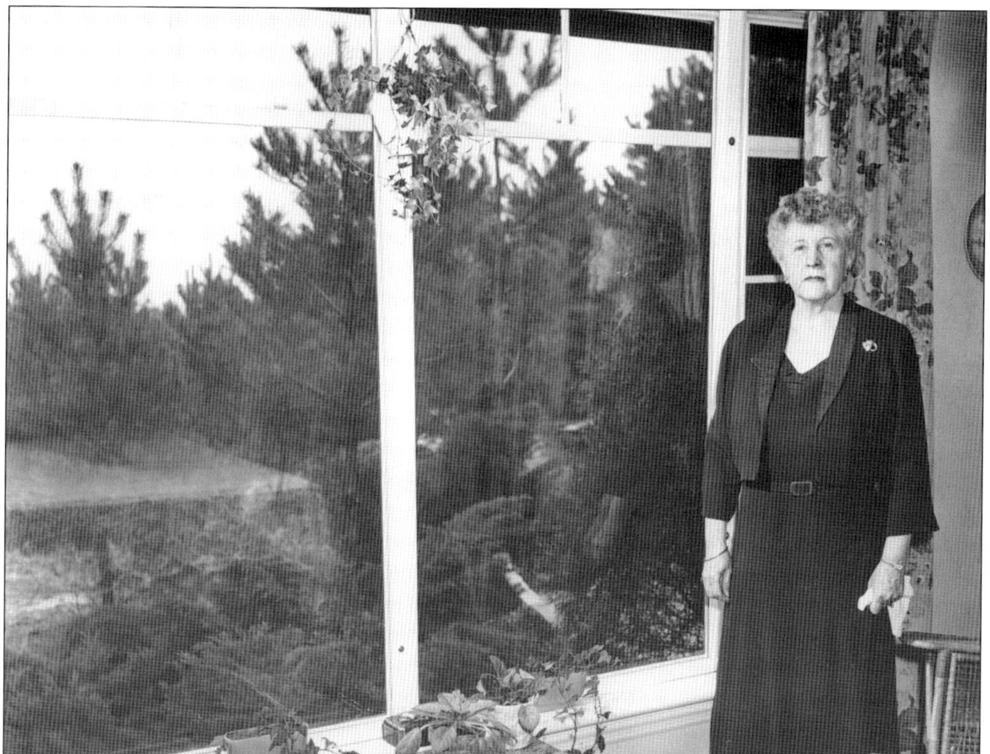

Dorothy Richardson Buell. Dorothy Richardson (1886–1977) was the youngest of three sisters, all of whom had a long association with Ogden Dunes. Her two older sisters, Olive and Elizabeth, both teachers, built a cottage at 39 Shore Drive in 1924. Dorothy, after her marriage in 1918 to James Hal Buell (1881–1970), an engineer, lived in a number of states before returning to the Chicago area. In 1941, they built a home at 17 Cedar Court. (CRAIUN.)

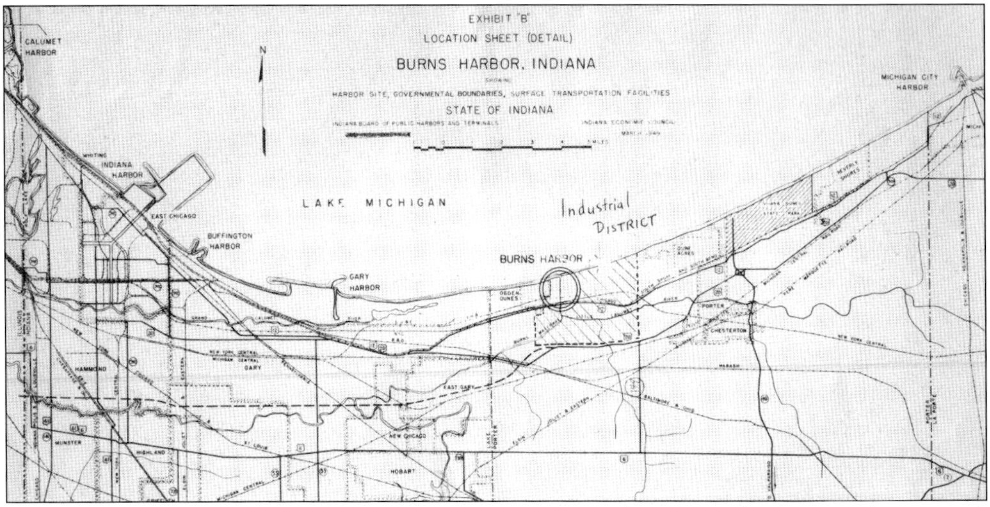

Proposed Steel Mill and Harbor, 1949. National Steel and its subsidiary, Midwest Steel, revived the 1929 plans to build a large mill and a deepwater port east of Burns Ditch. The rapid development of plans for industry for the five miles between Ogden Dunes and Dune Acres led to a revival of support for a national park in the dunes. It also caused Ogden Dunes Town Board to establish a planning commission to protect the dunes and to plan for the future. (HSOD.)

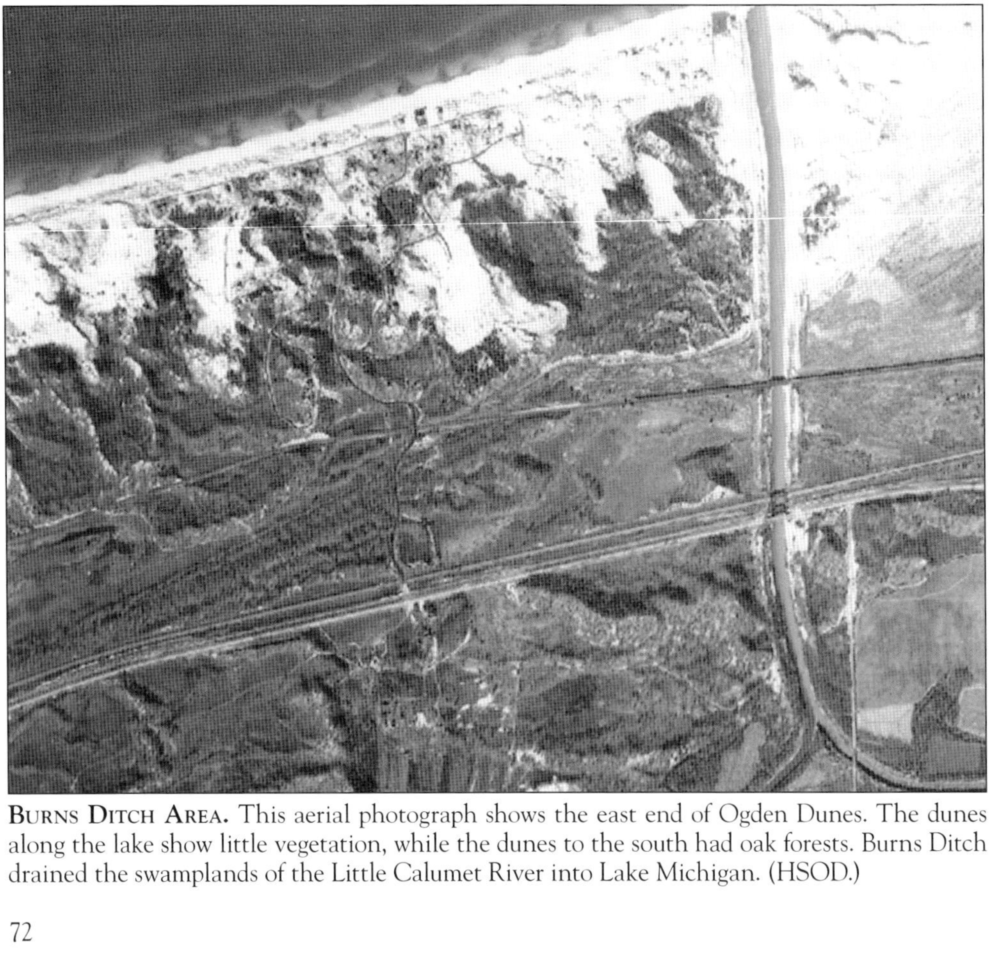

Burns Ditch Area. This aerial photograph shows the east end of Ogden Dunes. The dunes along the lake show little vegetation, while the dunes to the south had oak forests. Burns Ditch drained the swamplands of the Little Calumet River into Lake Michigan. (HSOD.)

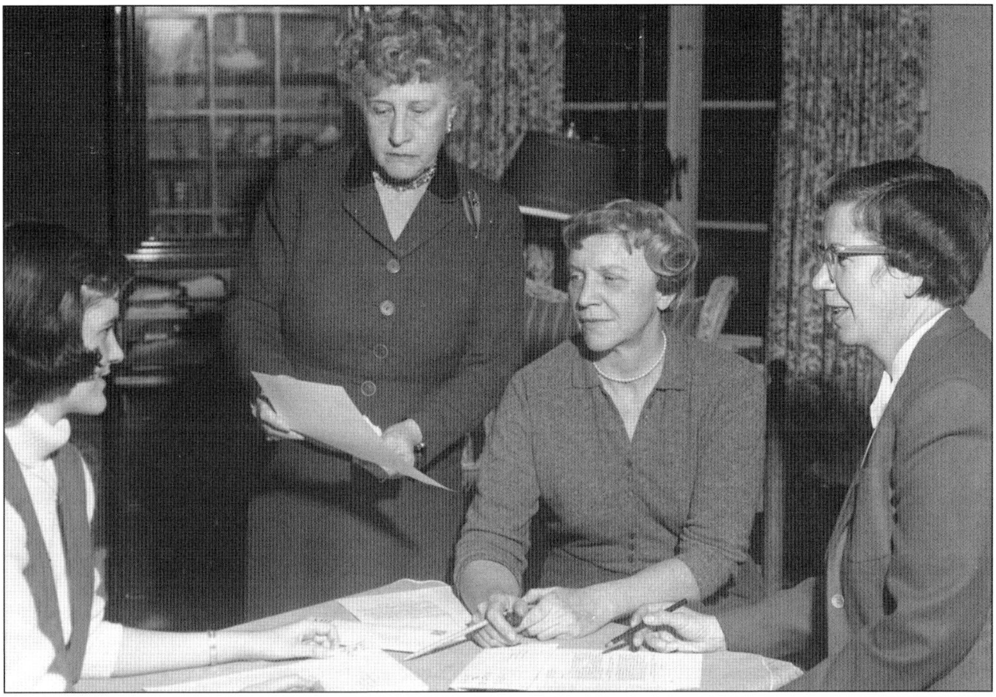

SAVE THE DUNES COUNCIL. In 1952, Dorothy Buell realized that new energy had to be brought to the movement to save the dunes. She invited nearly 30 women from Northwest Indiana to her home in June of that year. As a result of this meeting, the Save the Dunes Council was formally established in August. Shown here attending a council committee meeting at Buell's home are, from left to right, Suzie Butz (daughter of Hester), Buell, Florence Broady, and Hester Butz. All lived in Ogden Dunes. (CRAIUN.)

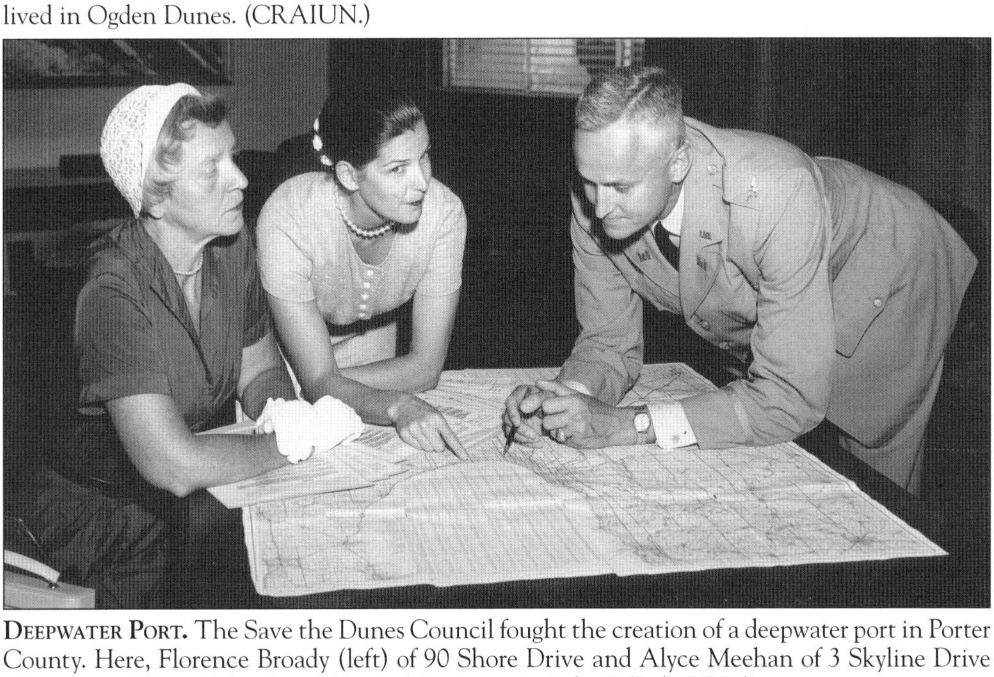

DEEPWATER PORT. The Save the Dunes Council fought the creation of a deepwater port in Porter County. Here, Florence Broady (left) of 90 Shore Drive and Alyce Meehan of 3 Skyline Drive take on an officer of the Army Corp of Engineers in July 1957. (HSOD.)

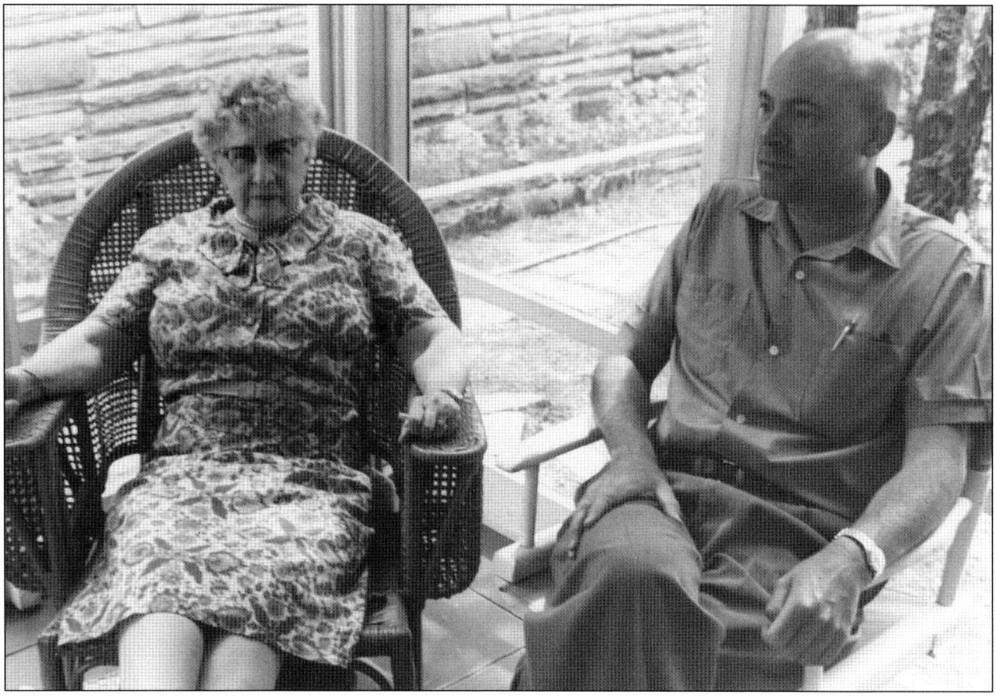

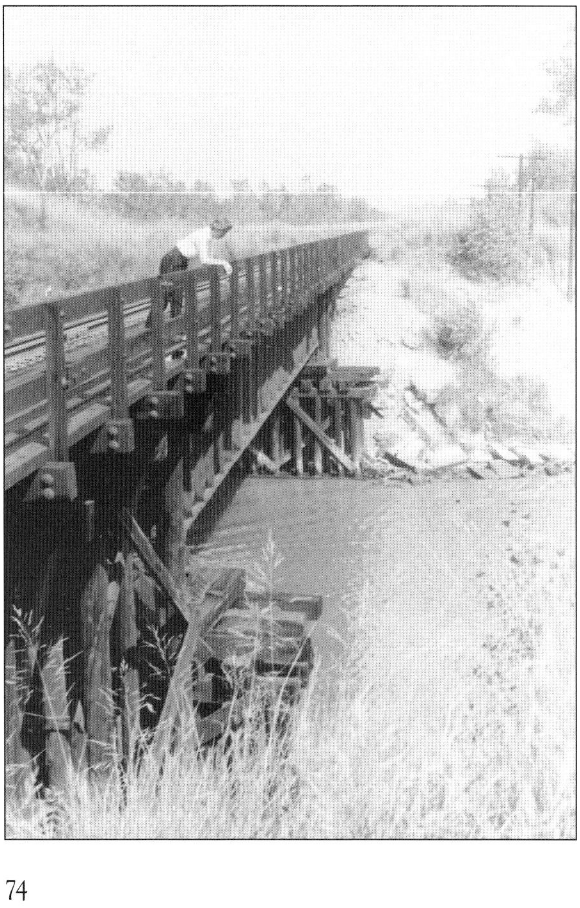

Dorothy Buell and Ed Osann. Buell and Osann represent two responses to the threatened industrialization of the dunes: the Save the Dunes Council, and land-use planning. Osann, a patent attorney in Chicago, moved to Ogden Dunes in 1953. He served in many capacities in the Save the Dunes Council and was a leader of the group that established the town's land-use plan and the planning commission. (HSOD.)

Trestle over Burns Ditch. The woman standing on the rarely used "sand track" railroad trestle over Burns Ditch represents the planning commission's vision in 1956 of controlling the development of unincorporated land within two miles of the town limits. A 1947 state law gave communities this power. The rail line, part of the Indiana Harbor Belt line, bisected Ogden Dunes until the town took it over in the late 1960s. (HSOD, Planning Commission.)

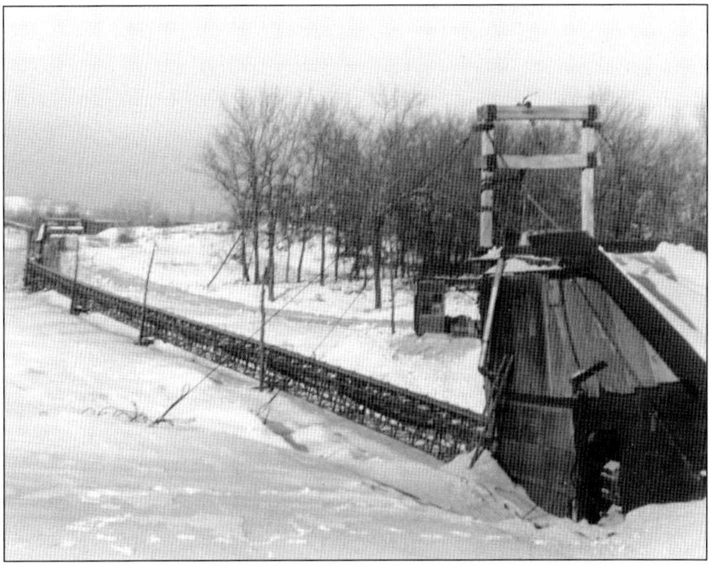

Sand Mining near Ogden Dunes. Sand mining again became a profitable enterprise with the building of the Indiana Toll Road and the demand for lake fill. Mining was also necessary to level the sand dunes for the planned steel mills and lake port. (HSOD, Planning Commission.)

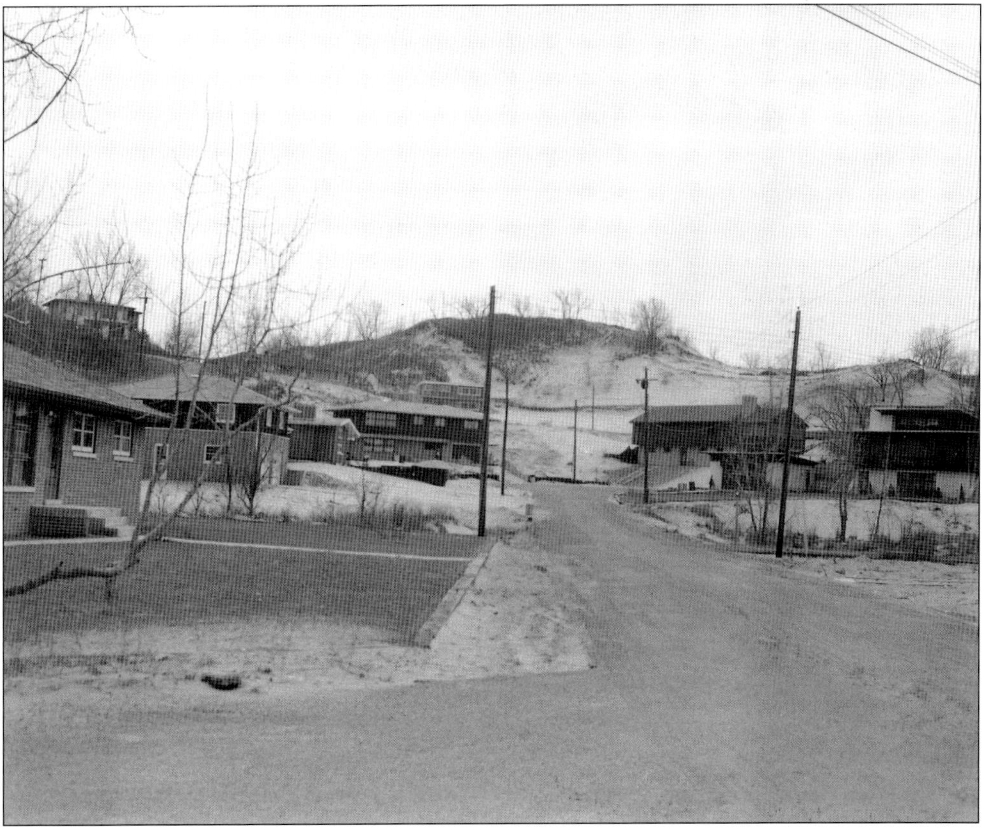

New Homes on Locust Place. Once established, the planning commission developed zoning laws and building codes for what occurred within the boundaries of Ogden Dunes. This photograph shows a new development in 1956, Locust Place. Smaller dunes were leveled to make room on this cul-de-sac for new homes. In the background is the undeveloped dune just below Mount Everest, the name given to the community's highest dune. (HSOD, Planning Commission.)

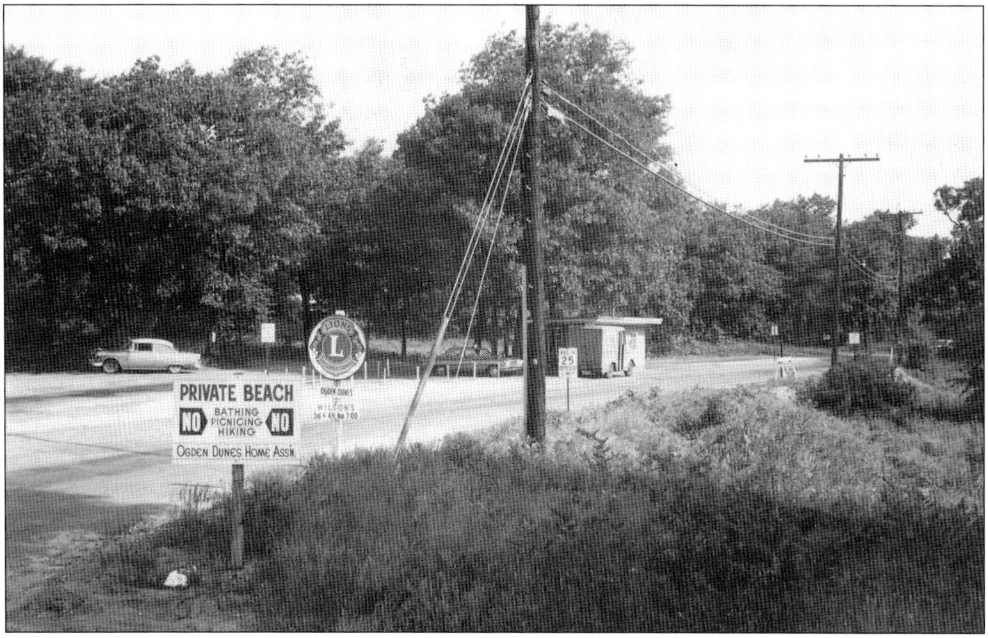

Community Entrance. The iconic images of Ogden Dunes are its understated entrance and Polliwog Pond. The entrance sign in 1959 was most unwelcoming, listing all of the "no's" to discourage visitors. On a positive note, Ogden Dunes supported a Lions Club, a service organization established in 1959. (HSOD.)

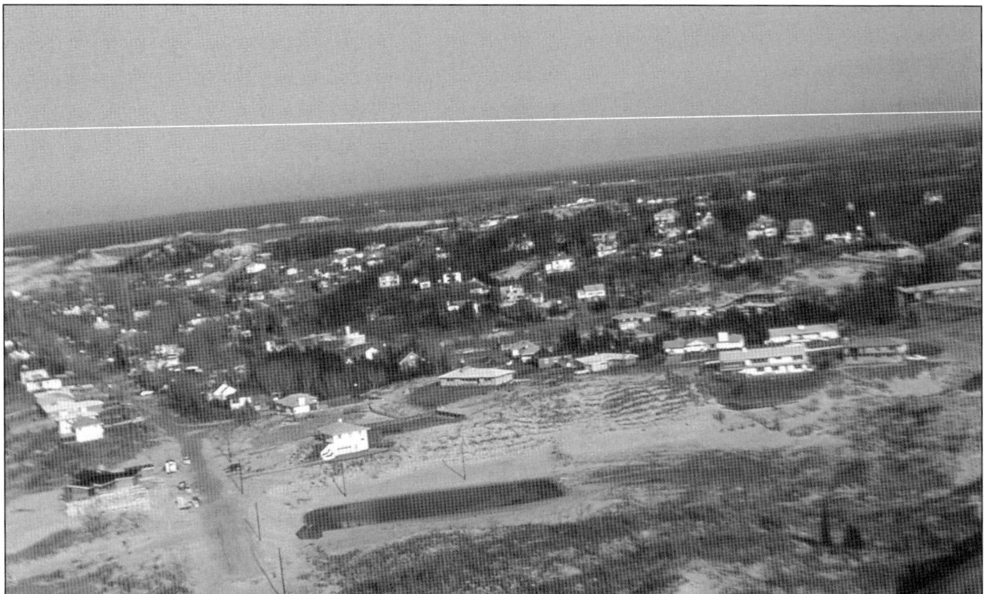

Polliwog Pond. Located in the northwest corner of the community, Polliwog Pond was separated by one ridge of dunes from Lake Michigan. It was a popular gathering place for skating in the winter and even swimming in the summer. This photograph shows some leveling of the dunes around the pond in order to create buildable lots along Diana Road and Shore Drive. (Courtesy of Richard Hallman.)

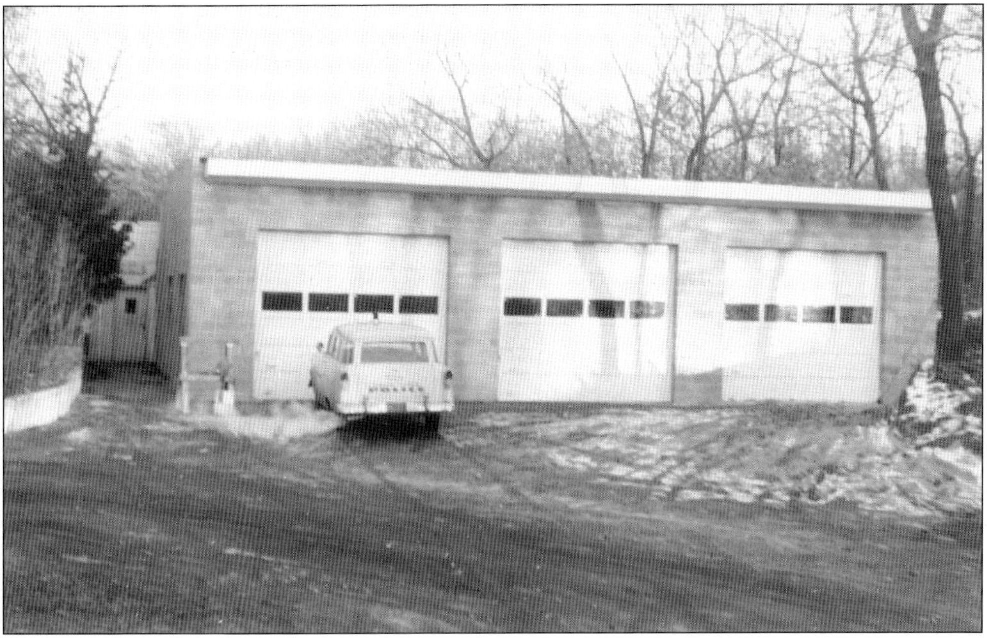

Town Firehouse. After the volunteer fire department was established in 1948, funds were raised and time was donated to build a department garage for the equipment. In 1952, the meeting space for firemen was expanded to include a community hall with a kitchen and other facilities. This photograph was taken in 1956. (HSOD, Planning Commission.)

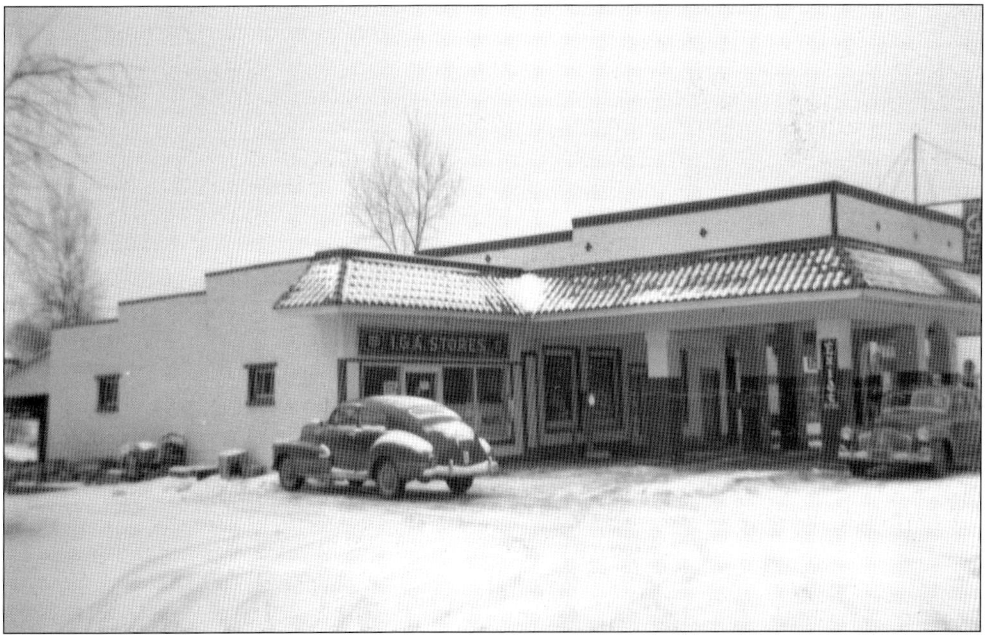

Gas Station and Grocery Store. Homer Lee and his son-in-law Gordon Engel operated the original garage and grocery store on US 12, across from the entrance to Ogden Dunes. Though they did not live in the dunes, Lee and Engel were highly respected and very much part of the community. In 1947, they sold to the Brady and Bluck families, who later built brick homes on the dune behind the station and grocery. They operated the businesses until the mid-1970s. (HSOD.)

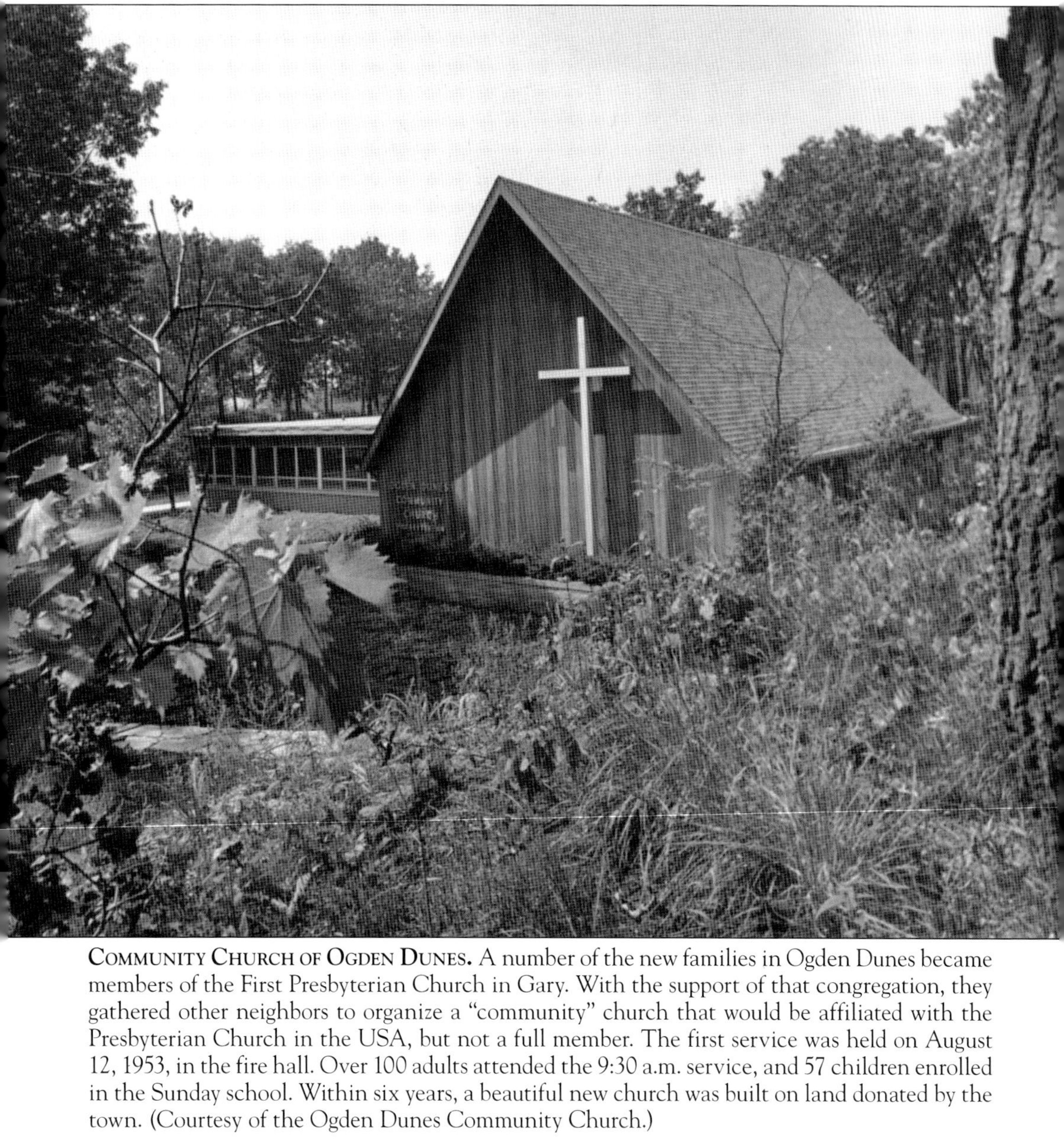

COMMUNITY CHURCH OF OGDEN DUNES. A number of the new families in Ogden Dunes became members of the First Presbyterian Church in Gary. With the support of that congregation, they gathered other neighbors to organize a "community" church that would be affiliated with the Presbyterian Church in the USA, but not a full member. The first service was held on August 12, 1953, in the fire hall. Over 100 adults attended the 9:30 a.m. service, and 57 children enrolled in the Sunday school. Within six years, a beautiful new church was built on land donated by the town. (Courtesy of the Ogden Dunes Community Church.)

Chapel. The chapel, with seating for 180, is a sacred space. Its warmth is provided by the beautiful woodwork and high ceiling. During the 1970s, the congregation sponsored and provided space for two new community activities, the Sandpiper Co-op Nursery School and the Prime Timers, which fostered community among retired members. (Courtesy of the Ogden Dunes Community Church.)

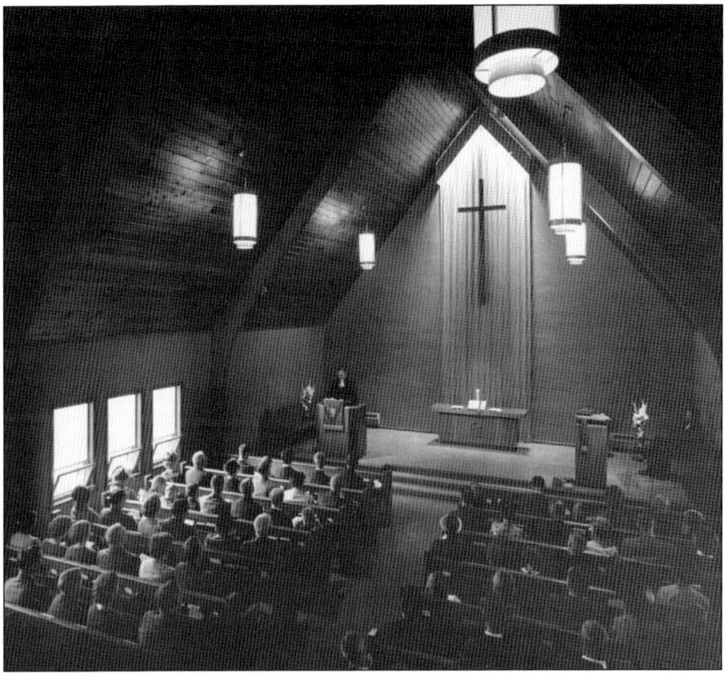

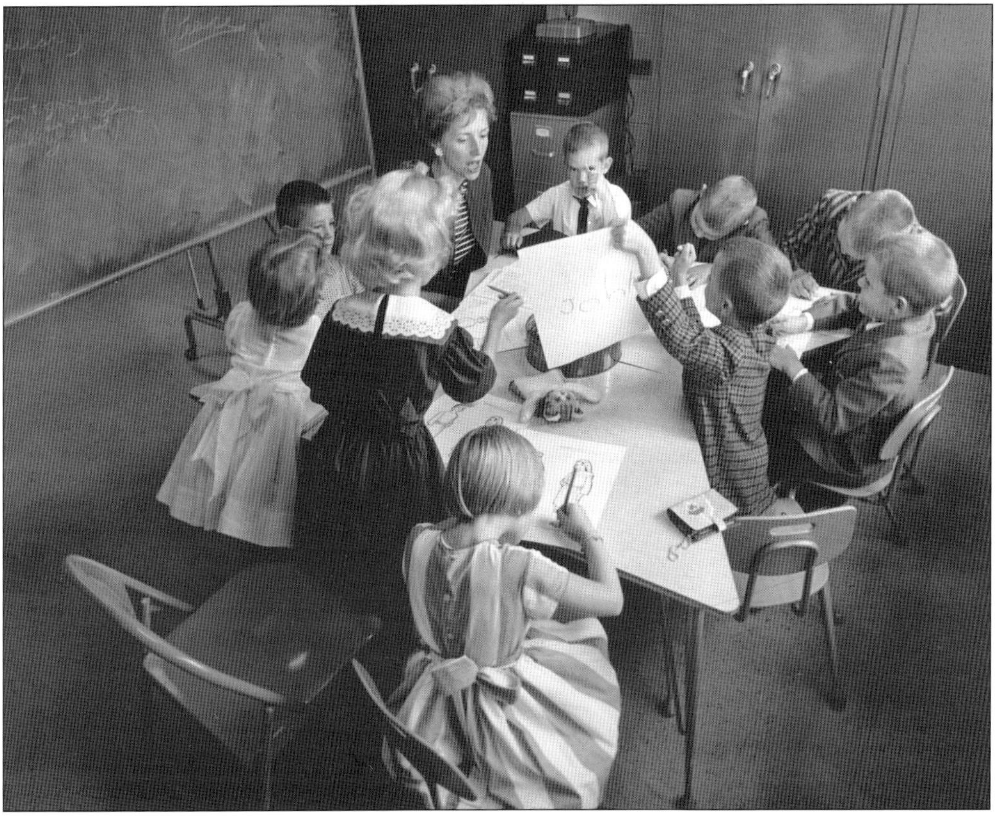

Sunday School. These young children and their teacher are deeply involved in a Sunday school lesson. (Courtesy of the Ogden Dunes Community Church.)

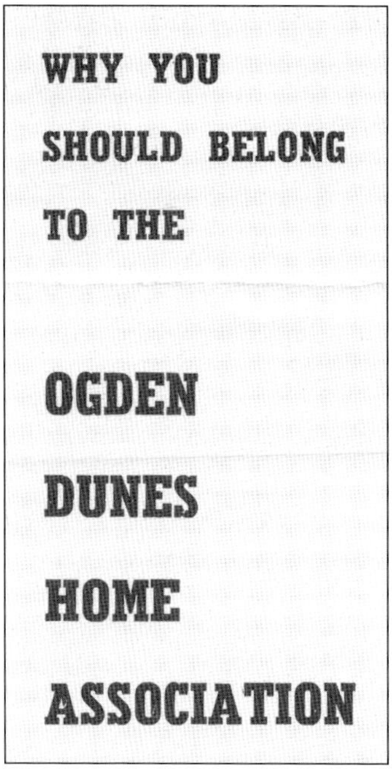

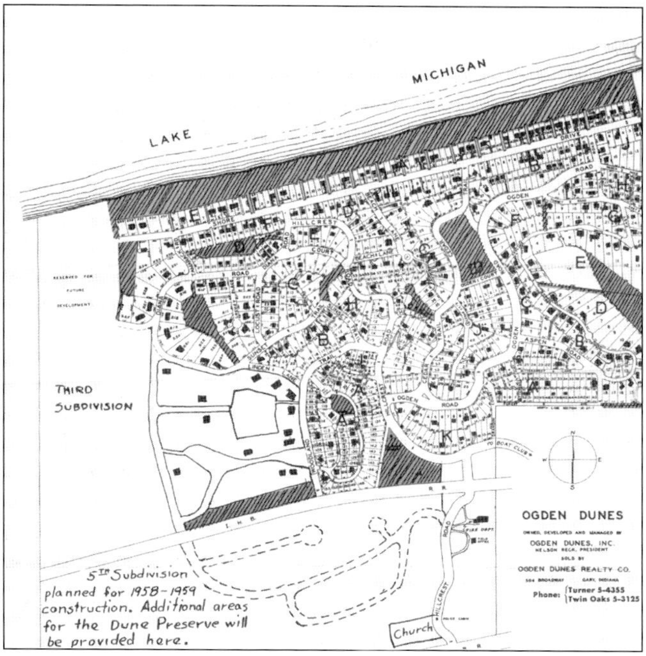

OGDEN DUNES HOME ASSOCIATION. In 1950, Nelson Reck, who had led the development of Ogden Dunes for more than 25 years, began to plan for the future. This included the creation of the planning commission and the transfer of ownership of the common lands (access points to the beach, parks, and nature preserves) to the Ogden Dunes Home Association in 1957. This brochure map from February 1958 shows the transferred land, as well as the development of the Third and Fifth Subdivision on the west and south sides. (HSOD.)

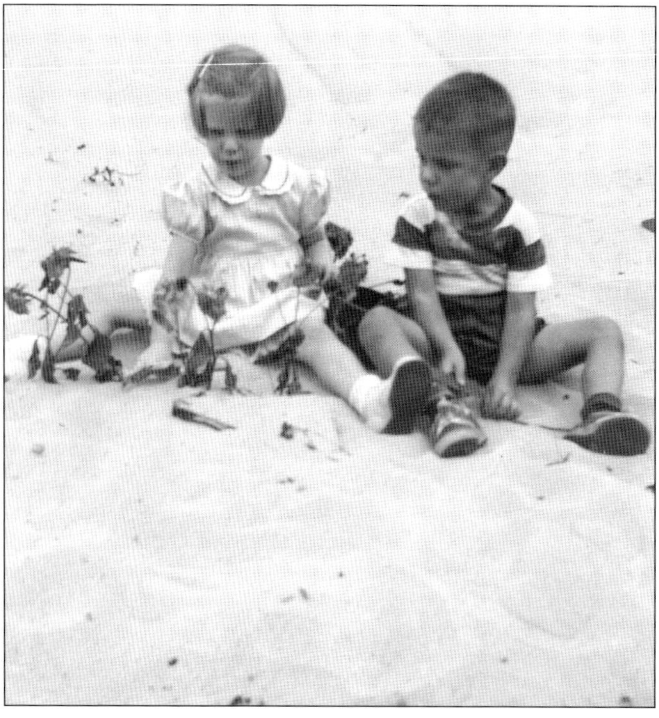

MONAHAN GRANDCHILDREN. The beauty of the lake and the sandy beach are enjoyed by all ages. It is a priceless part of living in Ogden Dunes. Here, Martha LaTourette and Johnny Collins enjoy the sand on an August day in 1951. (Courtesy of Rick Collins.)

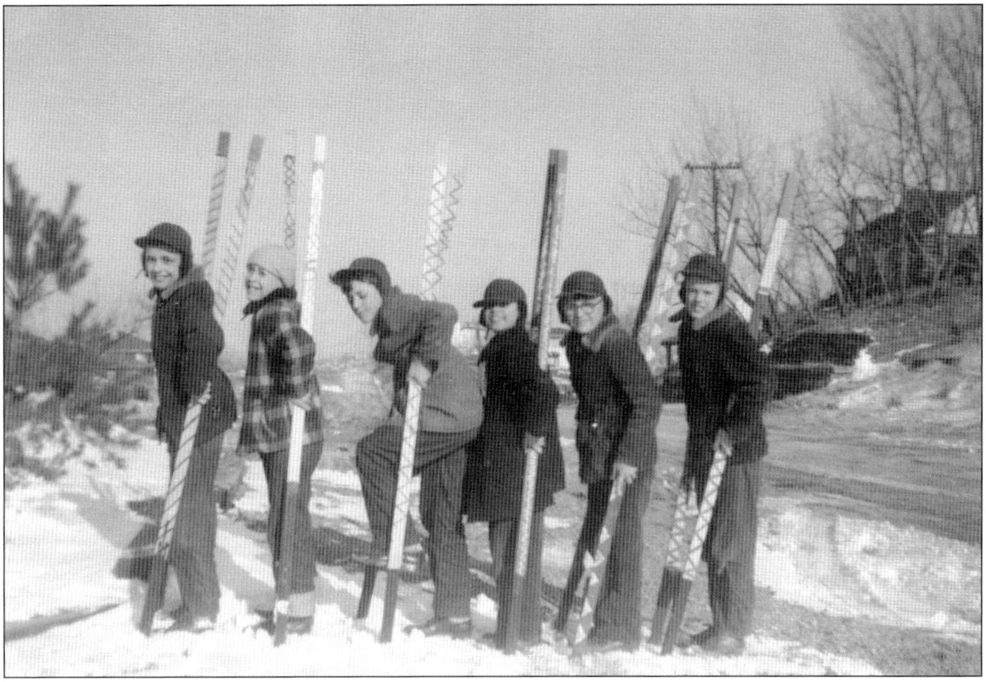

Cub Scouts on Stilts. In the winter of 1944, Ed Pittet and Ed Kidwell organized the first Boy Scout troop, with seven boys as charter members. The *Sandpiper* described the participation of the Scouts in the Memorial Day parade five years later. At that time, Beth Svihla was the den mother for the Cub Scouts, and Ken Hine was the scoutmaster. Posing in this March 3, 1954, photograph of Cub Scouts of Den 2 are, from left to right, Jon Deak, Ladd Svihla, Robbie Graves, James Baum, Jerry Cates, and Bob Messersmith. (Courtesy of Dave Larson.)

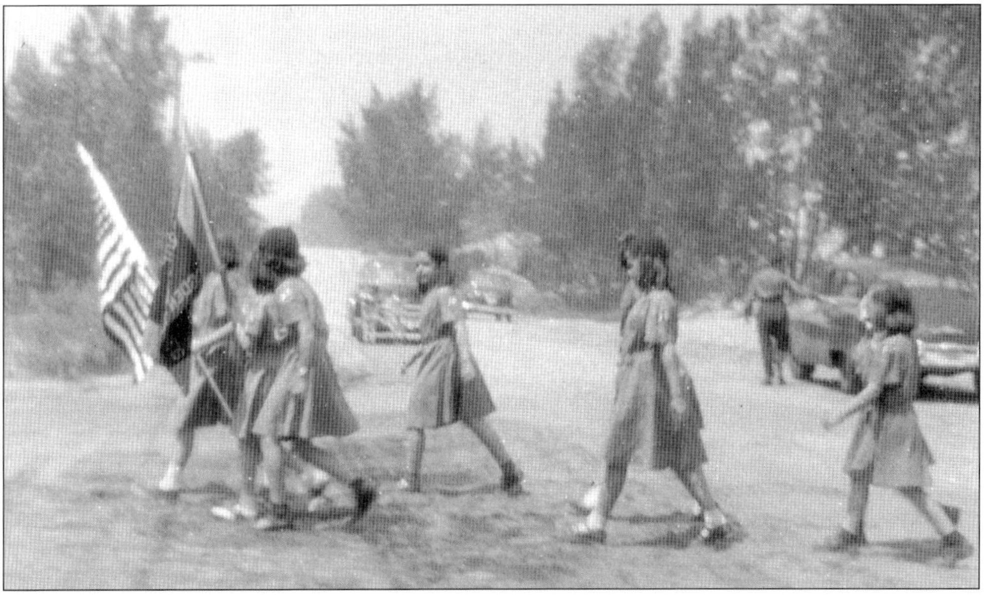

Girl Scouts, 1951. After the war, a Girl Scout troop was organized. In September 1950, two Brownie Patrols, as well as a new intermediate Girl Scout troop, were active. This 1951 photograph shows the Girl Scouts marching in the Memorial Day parade. (HSOD.)

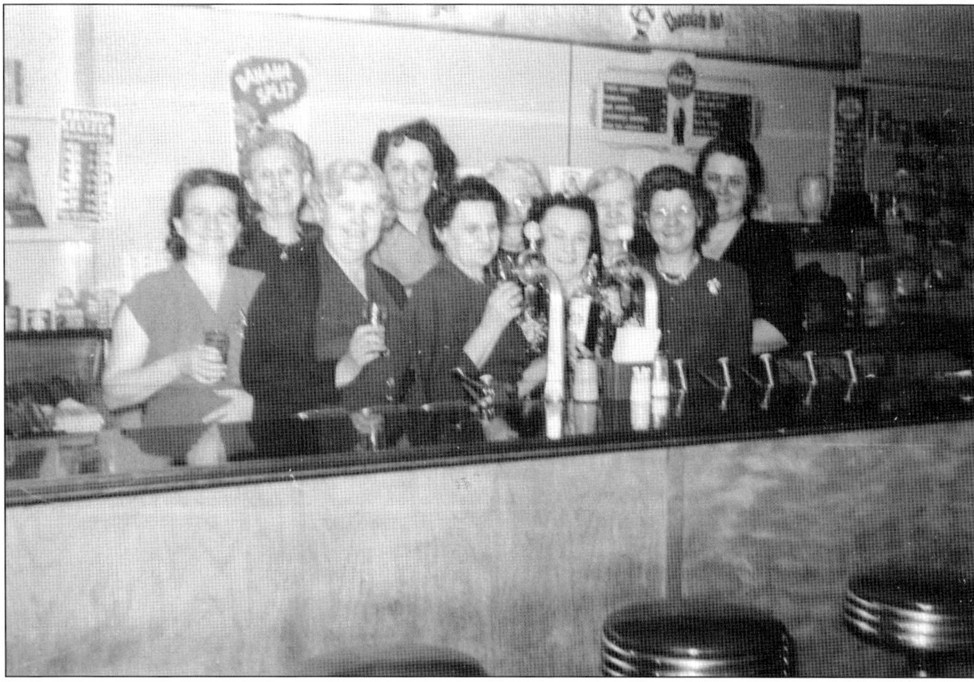

Waiting to Serve. The soda fountain was added to the grocery store at the entrance, and it became a favorite gathering place for the community in the postwar period. Here, a group of Ogden Dunes women are enjoying themselves at the fountain. (HSOD.)

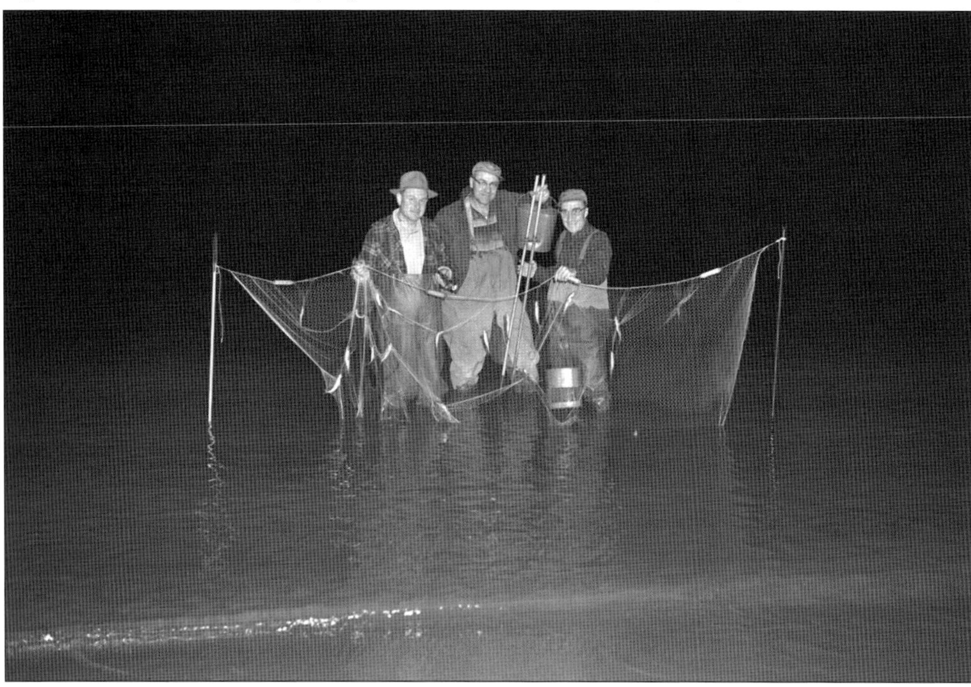

Smelt Fishing. Life in the dunes included, for some, the springtime ritual of netting smelt, which ran in shallow water along the shore. The tradition has long since disappeared, along with the smelt. (Courtesy of Steve Mark.)

George Svihla Jr. Bartending. Given the relatively small, tightly knit community in Ogden Dunes in the 1950s, the most common gatherings were large parties. One way to handle such a crowd was to hire a high school student to help out. In this case, George Jr. enjoys his role as bartender. (Courtesy of George Svihla.)

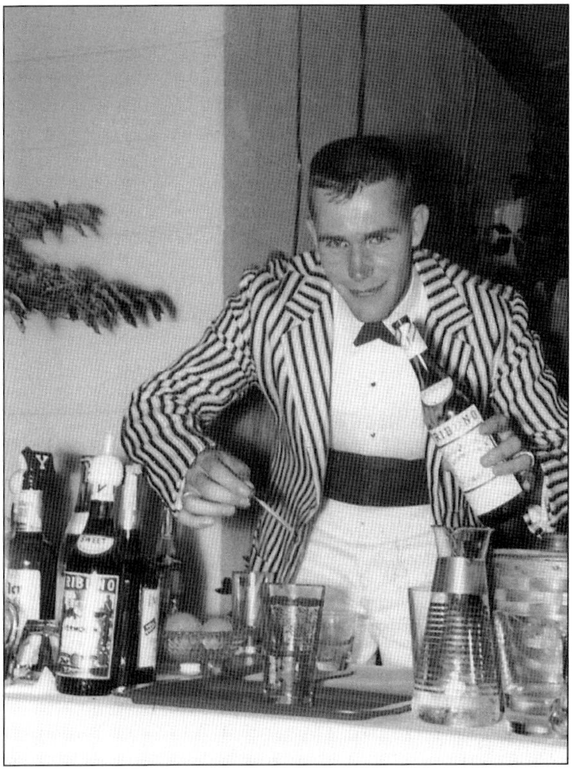

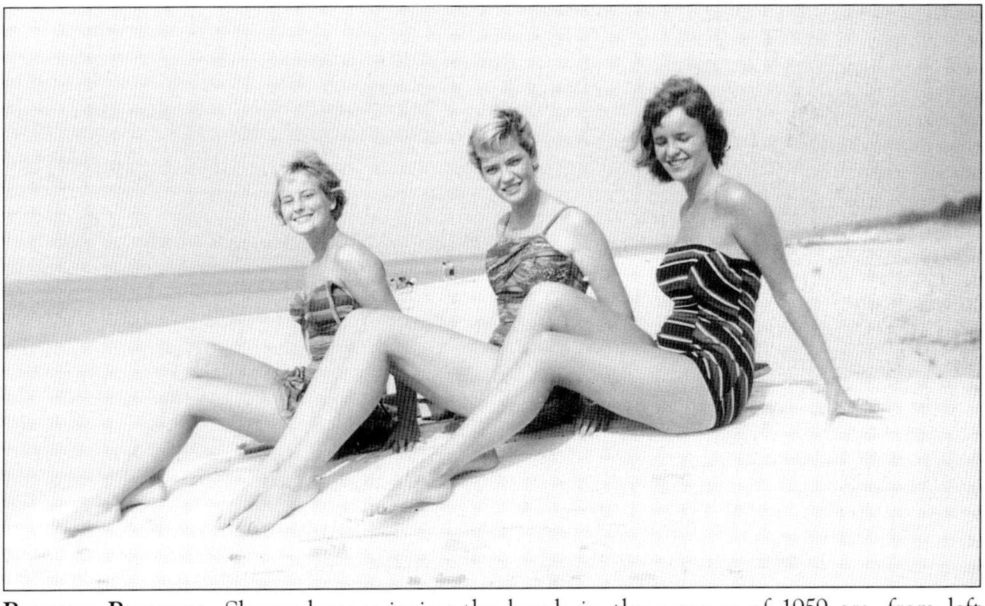

Bathing Beauties. Shown here enjoying the beach in the summer of 1959 are, from left to right, Libby Gray, an unidentified visiting friend, and Mary Lynn Burdick. The following September, Gray and Burdick were enrolled in college. Because of the middle-class character of the community, unlike in the larger society, almost all high school graduates went on to college. The *Sandpiper* listed 79 Ogden Dunes residents in college in September 1960. That same year, 87 students attended Portage High School. (Courtesy of George Svihla.)

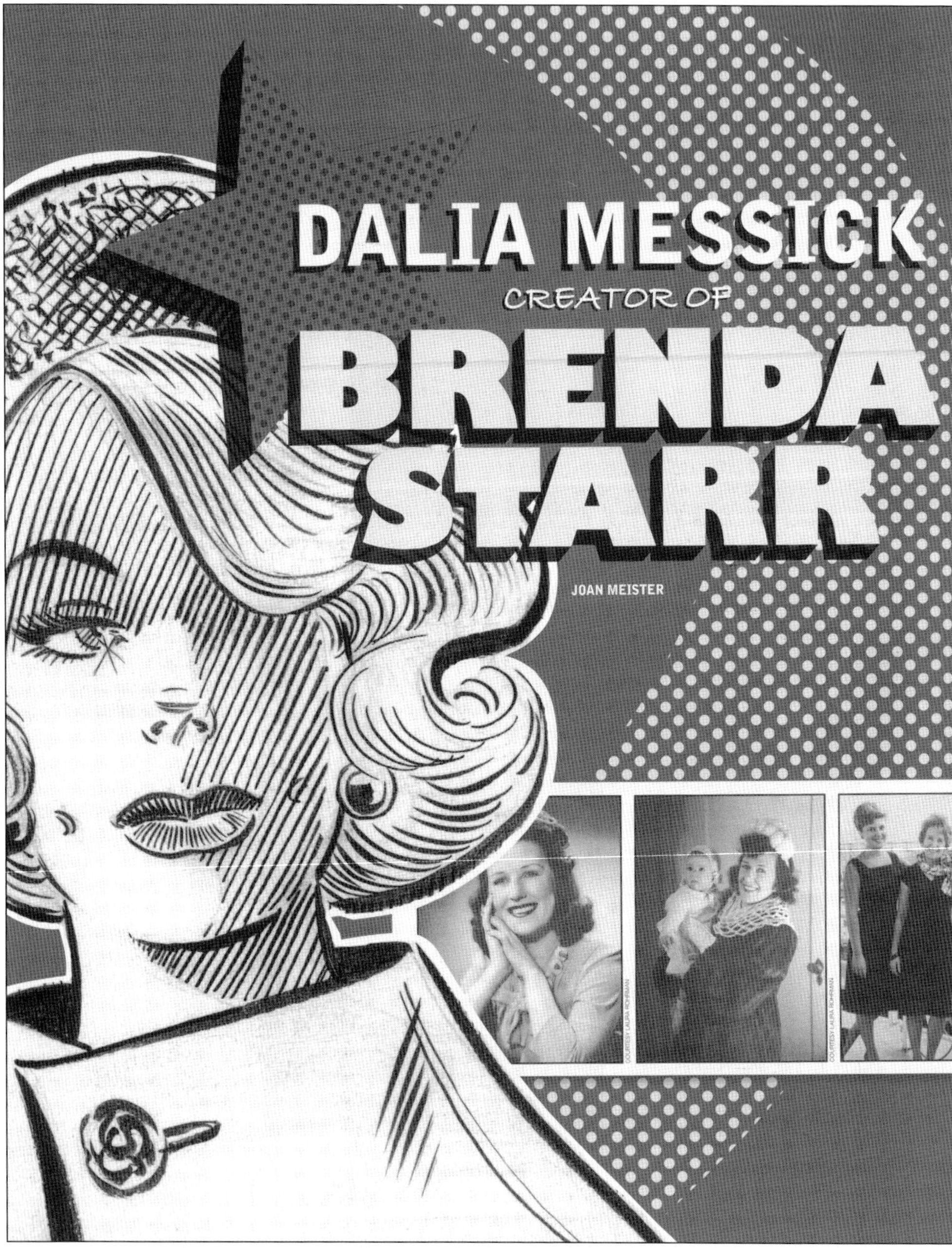

Dale Messick, Creator of Brenda Starr. Dalia Messick (1906–2005) was raised in Hobart, Indiana. After high school, she went to New York, changing her name to the masculine-sounding "Dale." In September 1940, *Brenda Starr: Girl Reporter* first appeared in the *New York Daily News*. For nearly 50 years, Messick led millions of readers through the adventures of Brenda Starr in more than 10,000 storyboards. Following the birth of her daughter, Starr, and later a divorce, Messick returned to Northwest Indiana in 1952, buying a home at 43 Shore Drive. That fall, her daughter entered fifth grade at Crisman (Portage) School. Dale and Starr remained part of the Ogden Dunes community until 1968. This image is from an article in *Traces: Indiana Magazine of Popular History*, written by Joan Meister. (Courtesy of the Indiana Historical Society.)

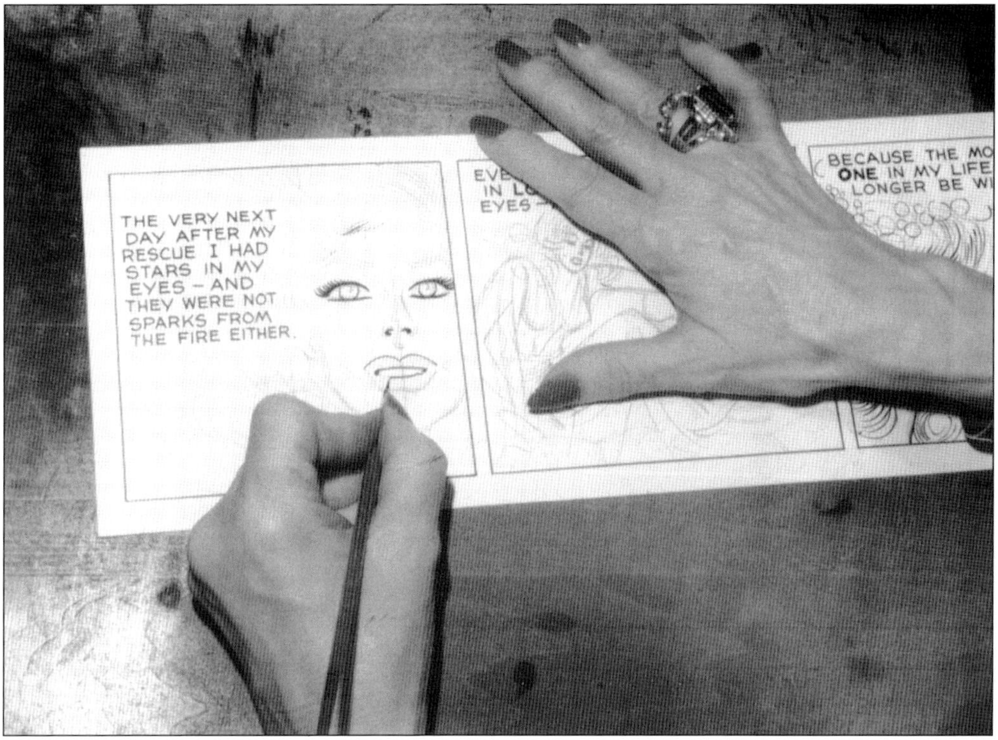

DALE MESSICK AT WORK. For more than 40 years, Dale Messick drew and wrote *Brenda Starr* at her home studio. This photograph shows her working on a storyboard. (Courtesy of Starr Rohrman.)

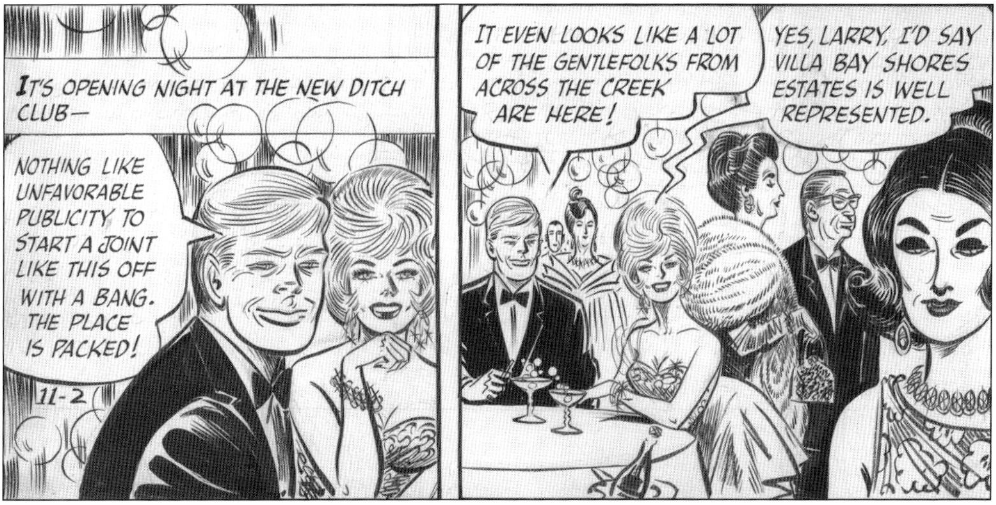

BATTLE FOR THE DUNES AND BRENDA STARR. In September 1961, Dale Messick began a story focusing on scantily dressed showgirls at a flashy nightclub, the Ditch Club. Brenda's nemesis is a gangster, Mr. Burns Ditch, who had opened the club across the creek from Villa Bay Shores Estates. This story continued for nearly three months. In response, an editorial in the Valparaiso *Vidette-Messenger* on September 23, 1961, attacked Messick. It saw the strip as part of the fight between, on one side, Save the Dunes Council and Ogden Dunes, and, on the other side, the steel mills and those advancing economic development. The strip's Villa Bay Shores Estate represented Ogden Dunes, and the nightclub stood in for Midwest Steel. (HSOD.)

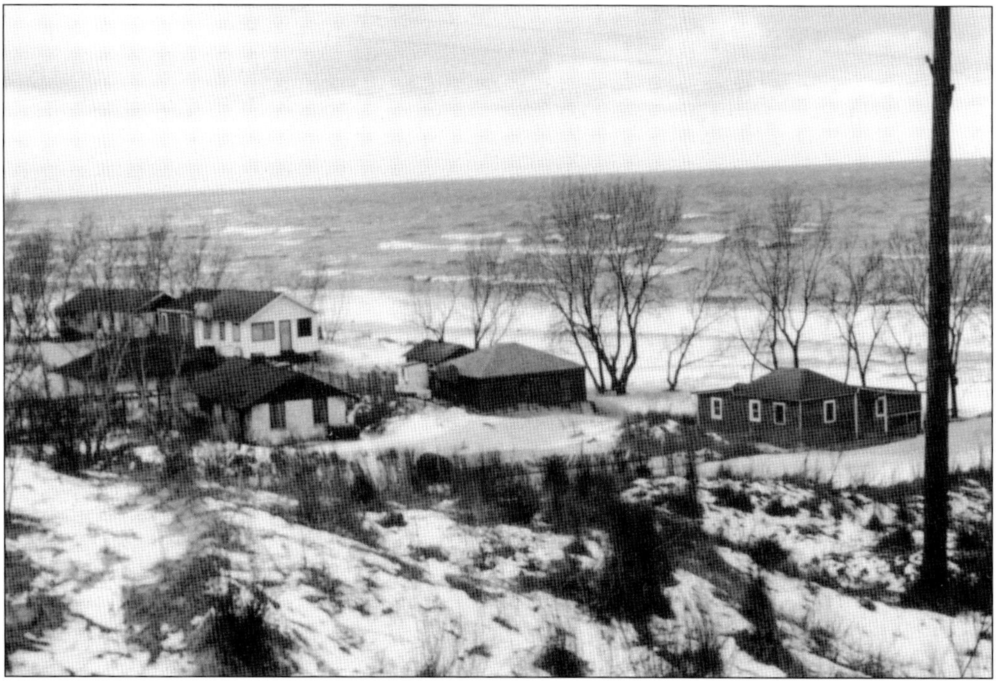

East End Cottages. The Ruppert family had a lease on Inland Steel property between Ogden Dunes and Burns Ditch. The land was directly west of the Gary Boat Club, established in 1936. Approximately 25 families had handshake agreements with the Rupperts to build small cottages. Many were members of the boat club. In 1959, the families were notified that they had 90 days to remove their belongings, as Midwest Steel was building a plant to the south. They received approximately $400 in compensation. The land, however, was never used for a steel mill. It became part of the Indiana Dunes National Lakeshore in 1966. (HSOD, Woodward.)

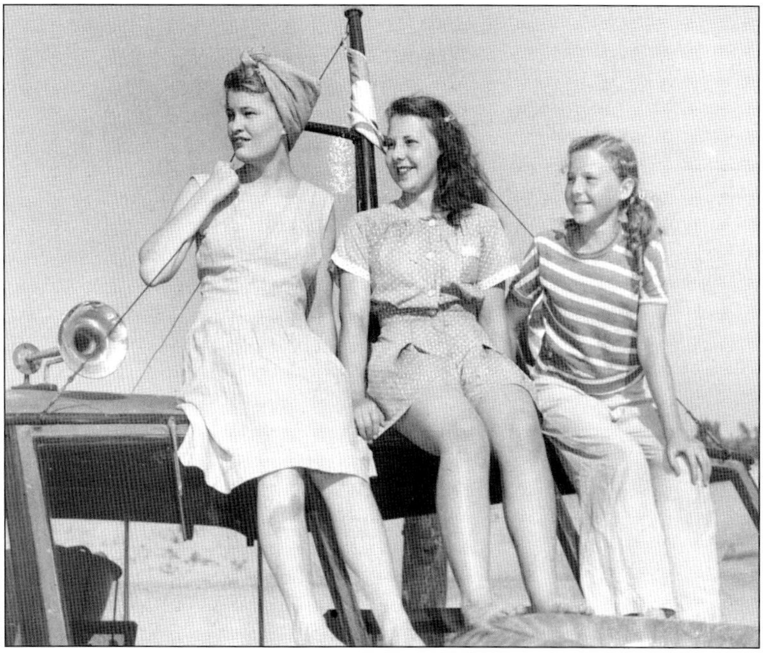

Sailing at the Boat Club. Shown here are, from left to right, Greta Landen, Annabelle Bucko, and Laura Bucko. They are on the Bucko family's boat, *Stardust*. In the 1970s, Laura Bucko, after her marriage, returned to the dunes and built a home in the Sixth Subdivision. (Courtesy of Laura Bucko Mallonee.)

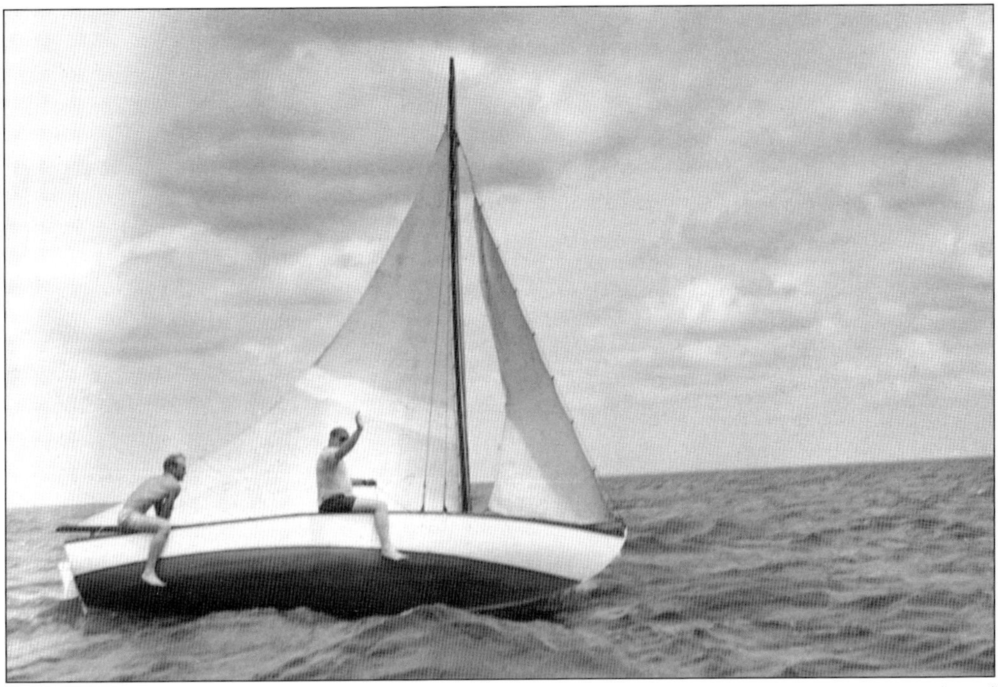

Enjoying Lake Michigan. In the Woodward family's Cape Cod knockabout, Tom Woodward (left) and Jack Orr sail off of Burns Ditch around 1950. Woodward's parents gave up their cottage on the East End and later bought a home in Ogden Dunes. (Courtesy of Tom Woodward.)

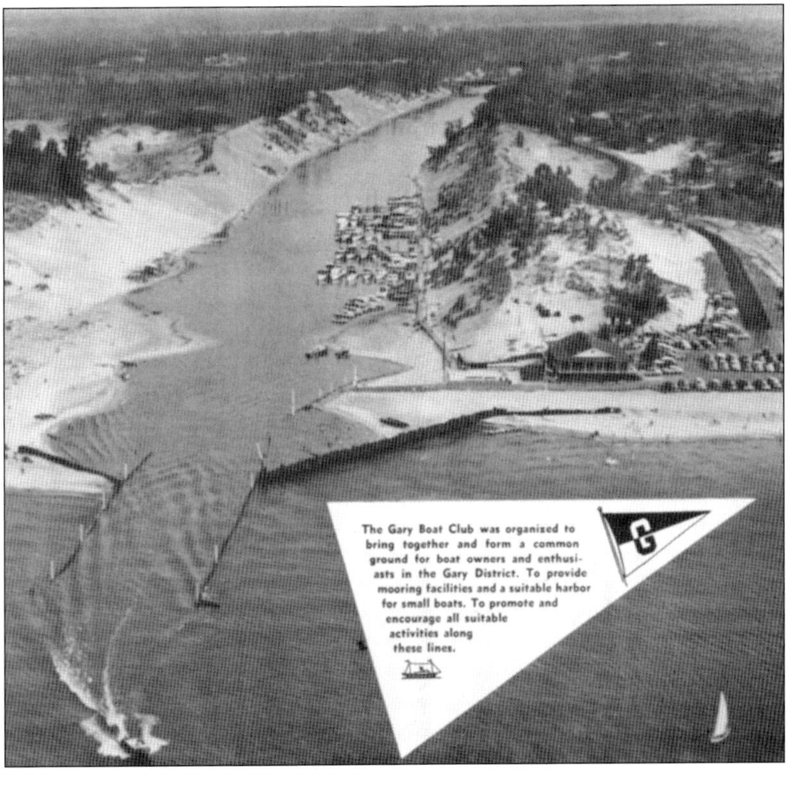

Gary Boat Club. This aerial photograph of the club shows its clubhouse and docks in the early 1950s. In the 15 years after World War II, the club expanded its membership and its facilities. Like the Ruppert cottages, the club in 1959 lost its lease and ultimately moved to New Buffalo. (HSOD, Tittle.)

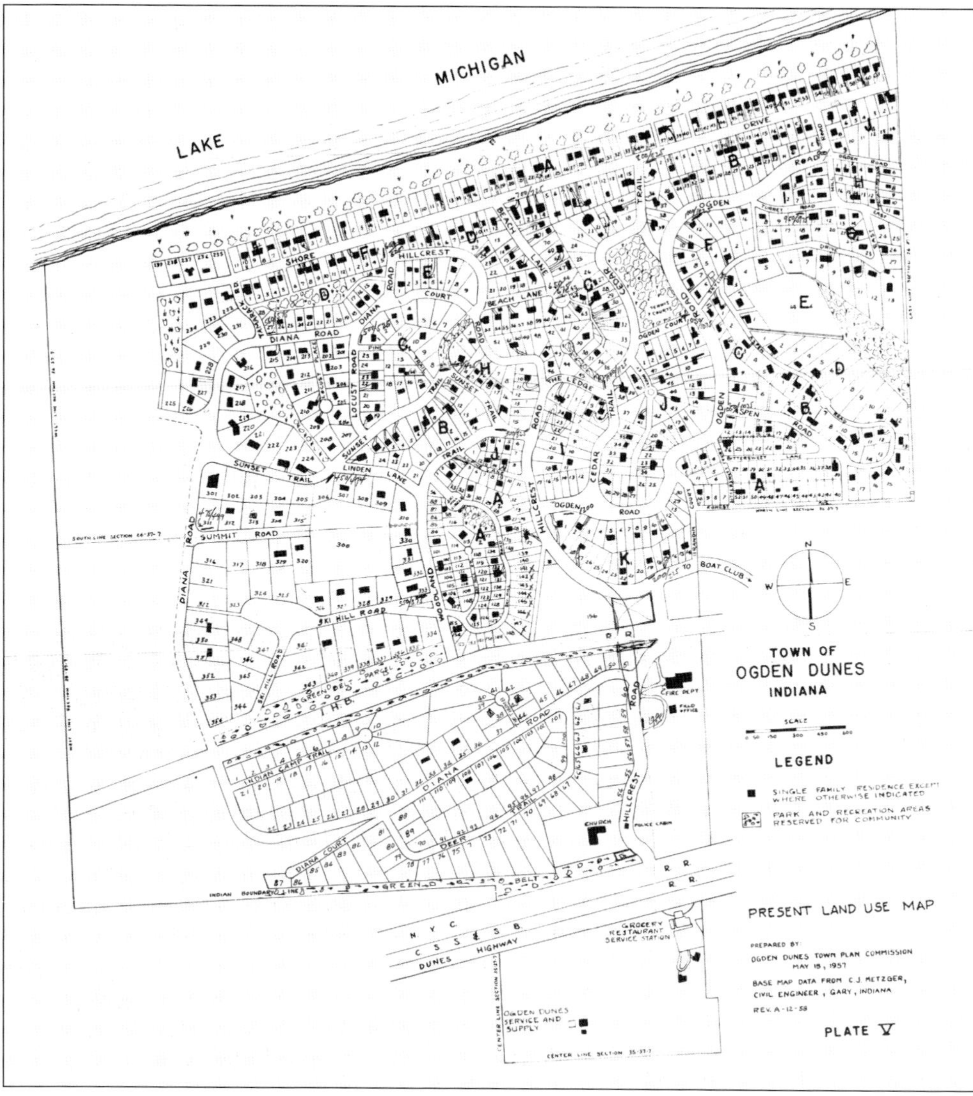

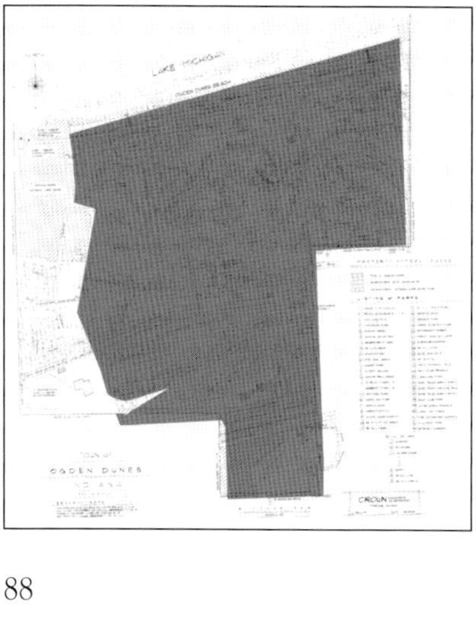

1959 Map. The map above shows nearly 400 homes and cottages. Growth occurred because of the addition of two new subdivisions, the Third and the Fifth. This extended the developed portion of the town to the west and the southwest. According to the 1960 census the population doubled, to 947 residents. The Portage Public schools enrolled 231 students in September 1960. Another 14 attended Catholic schools, and 79 students were in college, according to the *Ogden Dunes Sandpiper*. The 1959 map at left shows the town within the 1994 boundaries of Ogden Dunes, which remain the same today. (Both, HSOD.)

Seven

Turmoil and Resolution 1960s

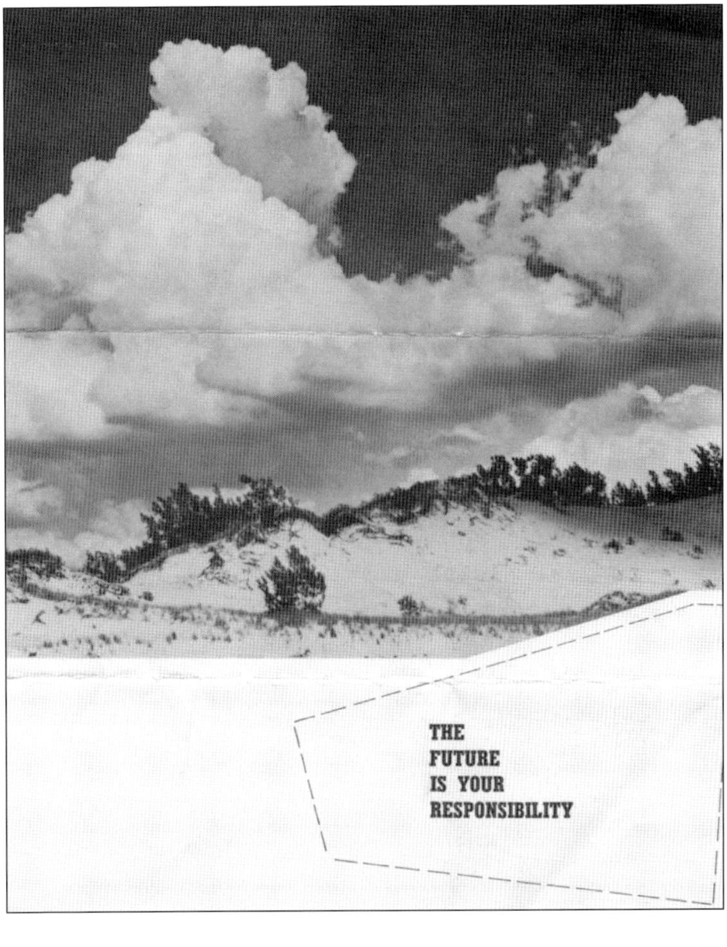

New Politics. During the latter part of the 1950s, the community became increasingly divided over the issue of industrial expansion. As a result, the consensus method of selecting the town board was replaced by a real election. The Republican Party slated six candidates, who ran on a platform of working with Midwest Steel and the new town of Portage to mitigate the changes ahead for Ogden Dunes. (HSOD.)

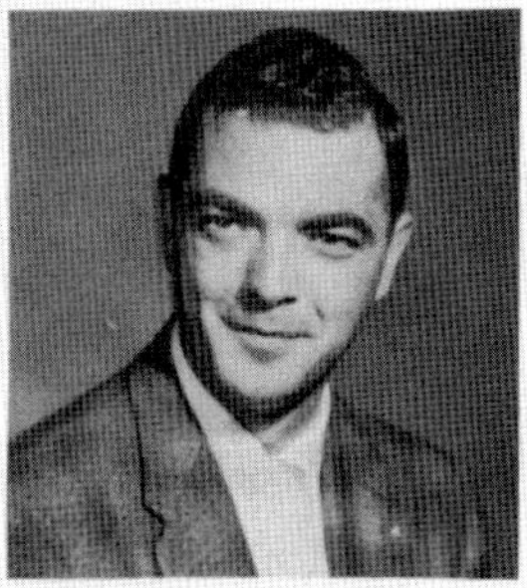

Jay Grantham, Jr., husband of Madronna, father of Jay, 6, Greg, 4 and Madronna, 2.
Republican candidate for Trustee, Ward 1, Town of Ogden Dunes.
Moved to Ogden Dunes 1954.
Member of Ogden Dunes Community Church (Presbyterian).
President Grantham Auto Corp., Vice President, Midwest Parts and Supply Co.
Member of Orak Shrine, South Bend Consistory, Gary Lodge No. 677 F. & A. M.
Past President, Gary Automotive Trade Association. Past Director, Automobile Dealer Association of Indiana. Director, Stewart Settlement House.
Hobbies: Guns, Hunting and Fishing.

Charles T. Graves; husband of Dody, father of Robert,16 and Marjorie, 14.
Republican candidate for Trustee, Ward 2, Town of Ogden Dunes incumbent Town Board President.
Moved to Ogden Dunes in 1944.
Chief of Design and Development; Railway Car Engineering Dept., General American Transportation Corporation for 23 years.
Charter member of the Ogden Dunes Community Church (Presbyterian).
Member of the Ogden Dunes Volunteer Fire Department.
Member of the Ogden Dunes Plan Commission.
Hobbies: Color slide photography and scouting.

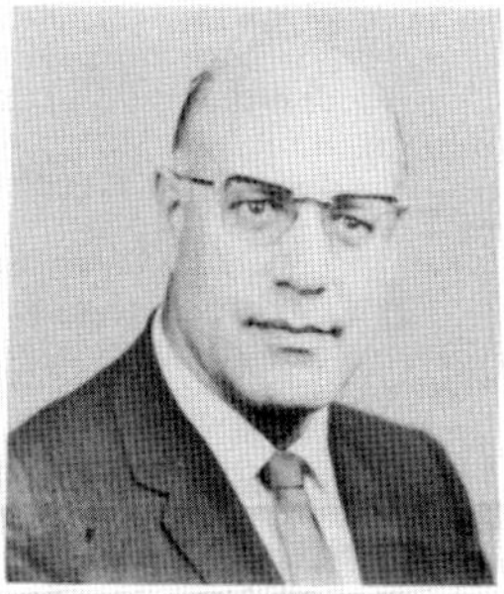

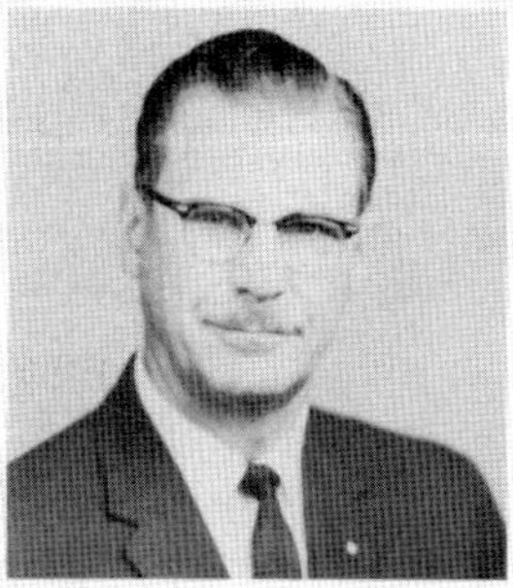

Julius M. Milach; husband of Dolly, father of Mark, 12 and Scott, 4.
Republican candidate for Trustee, Ward 3, Town of Ogden Dunes.
Moved to Ogden Dunes in 1953.
Salesman for Kahn Bros., Company, Chicago for past year. Salesman for Sears Roebuck and Company (Gary store) for 13 years.
Member of Marquette Methodist Church (Miller)
Member of the Ogden Dunes Volunteer Fire Department.
Member of the Ogden Dunes Lions Club.
Hobbies: Boating and wood-working.

Joseph J. Benson; husband of Mary, father of Joseph J. Jr., 10 and Mary Alice, 7.
Republican candidate for Trustee, Ward 4, Town of Ogden Dunes.
Moved to Ogden Dunes in 1956.
Member of St. Mary of the Lake Catholic Church (Miller).
Production Control Engineer for Taylor Forge.
Past Commander of Ogden Dunes American Legion Post No. 132.
Hobbies: "Do-it-yourself", bowling and golf.

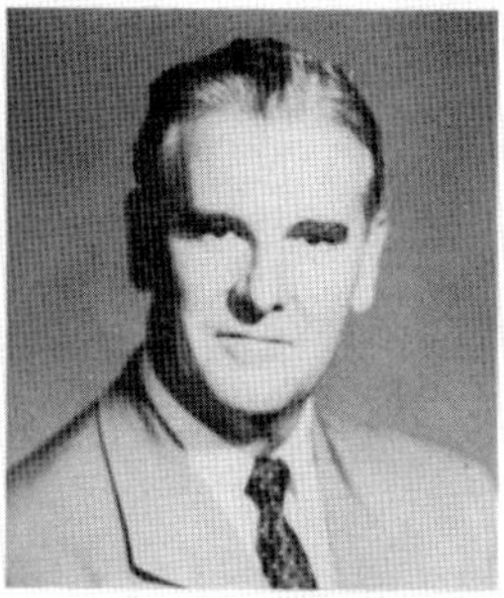

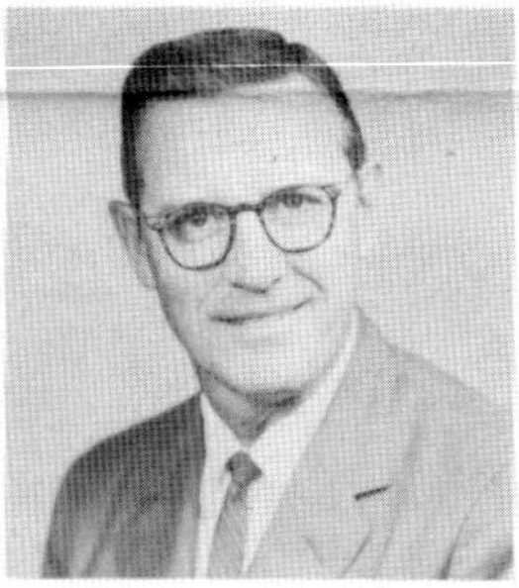

Sydney Young; husband of Jean, father of Gary, 13 and Wayne, 10.
Republican candidate for Trustee, Ward 5, Town of Ogden Dunes.
Moved to Ogden Dunes in 1956.
Roll Sales Engineer for the Blaw-knox Company, East Chicago.
Deacon of the Ogden Dunes Community Church (Presbyterian).
Member of the Adult Scout Advisory Committee in Ogden Dunes.
Hobbies: Boating and golf.

Lois M. Mueller; wife of Herbert P. Mueller, mother of Sharron White, 20 and Billy, 8.
Republican candidate for Town Clerk-Treasurer, Town of Ogden Dunes.
Moved to Ogden Dunes in 1950.
Owned and operated Ladies apparel shop and managed family business (retail grocery and meat market) for seven years.
Trained in retail accounting under A. H. Wahlen and Associates and E. E. Steinbrecker and Associates, Chicago.
Charter member of Ogden Dunes Community Church (Presbyterian).
Past president (3 terms) Portage High School P. T. A.
President, Ogden Dunes Volunteer Fire Department Auxiliary.
General chairman and business manager of O.D.V.F.D. "Fireman's Ball" (5 years).

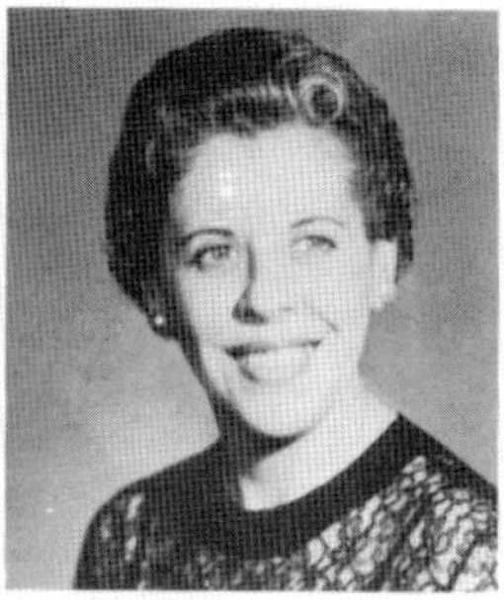

VOTE STRAIGHT REPUBLICAN NOVEMBER 3, 1959

TOWN BOARD ELECTION, 1959. The Republican slate advocated dropping the numerous lawsuits that opposed the new steel mill, the harbor, and the creation of the town of Portage. This was also the first election following the increasing of the size of the board from three to five members, plus the position of clerk-treasurer. (HSOD.)

MEL TRACHT, CANDIDATE. Mel Tracht ran on a slate that favored no compromise. The election was close in all the races, and the contest between Tracht and his opponent for the 1st Ward seat ended in a tie. The outgoing board had the authority to break the tie; it did, electing Tracht. Ralph Collins was elected clerk-treasurer. Tracht later described the election as a contest between the "resisters" and the "accommodators." (Courtesy of Mildred Tracht.)

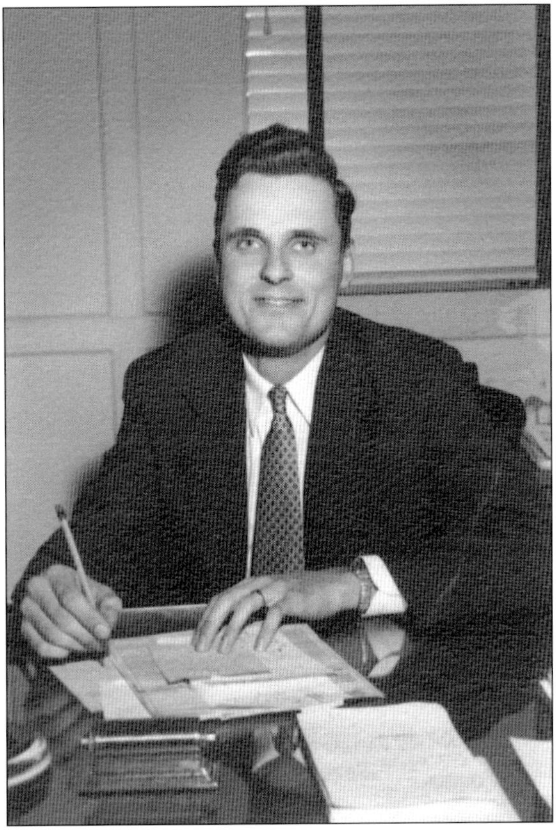

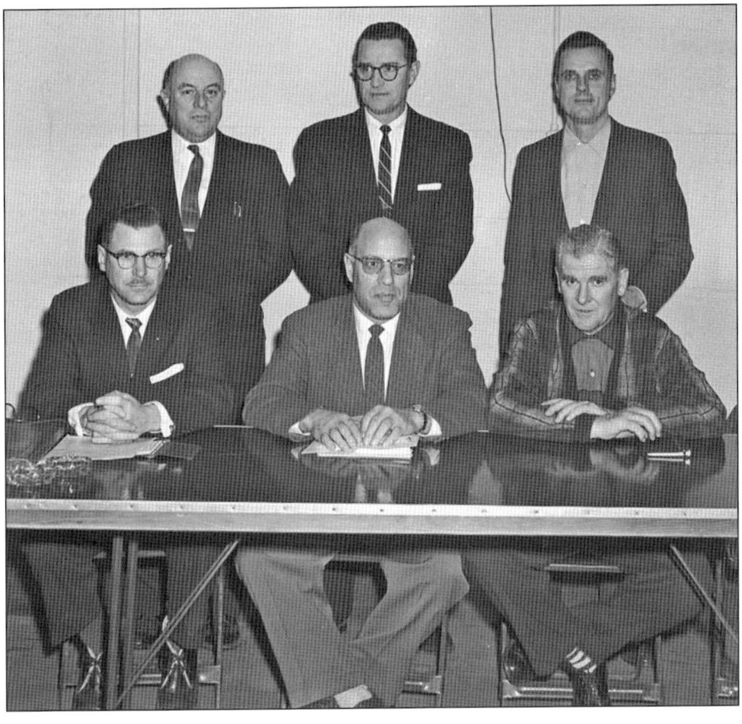

NEW TOWN BOARD, 1960. The new board elected Charles Graves as president, a position he held in the outgoing board. He oversaw the negotiations with Midwest Steel that resulted in successful efforts to mitigate air and noise pollution. Shown here are, from left to right, (seated) Julius Milach, Graves, and Joseph Benson; (standing) Ralph Collins, Syd Young, and Mel Tracht. (Courtesy of Steve Mark.)

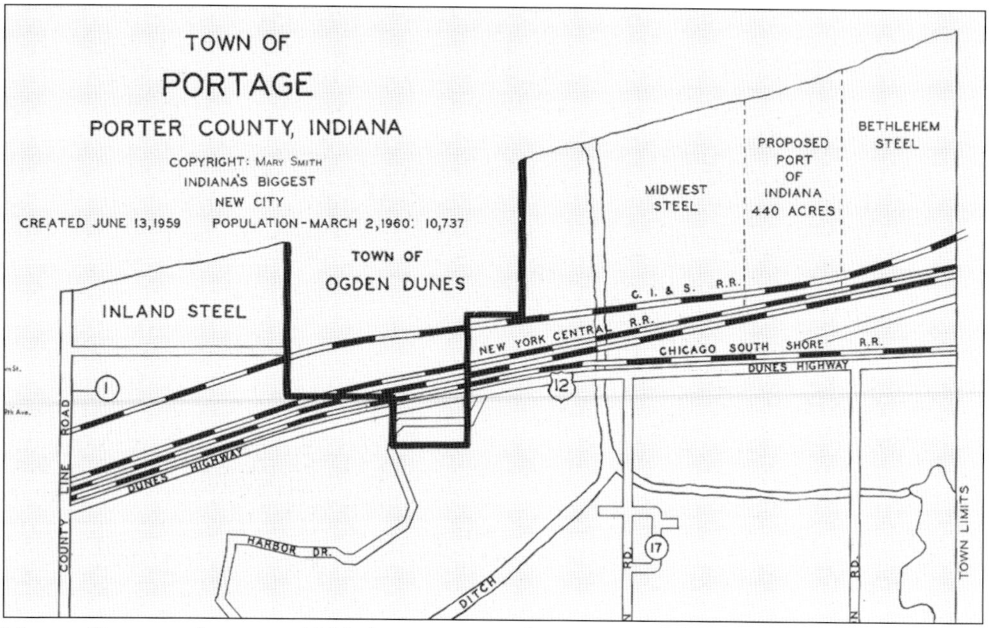

Map of Portage, Indiana, 1960. In reaction to the attempt of the Ogden Dunes Town Board to control land use within two miles of its boundaries, the Indiana state legislature repealed the 1947 law and expedited the incorporation of Portage in 1959. This map shows Ogden Dunes surrounded by the newly created town of 10,737 people. The Town of Portage was very supportive of new industry and a port. (HSOD.)

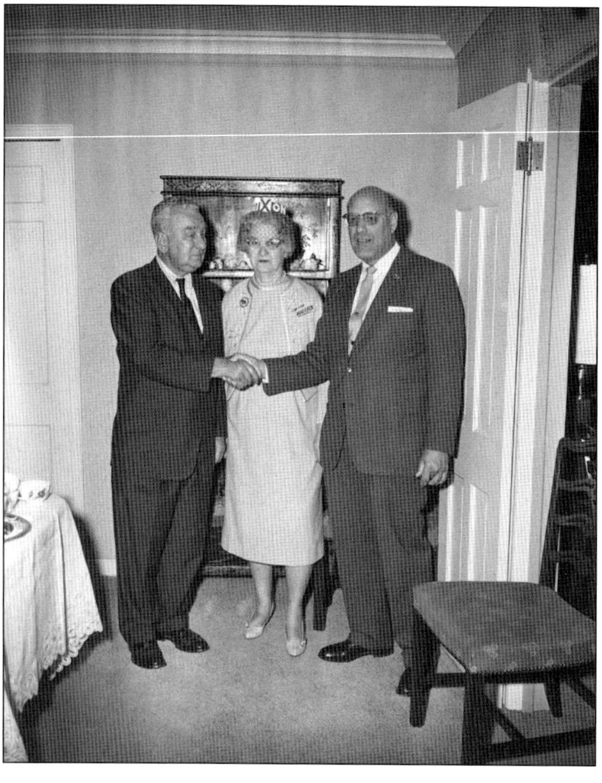

Accepting the Inevitable. Charles Graves, as president of the town board, worked to reduce the conflict with the neighbors. He is shown here at right with Rep. Charles Halleck and Mrs. John Vohr of Cedar Trail in 1959. Halleck led the fight on the federal level for a deepwater port. (Courtesy of Steve Mark.)

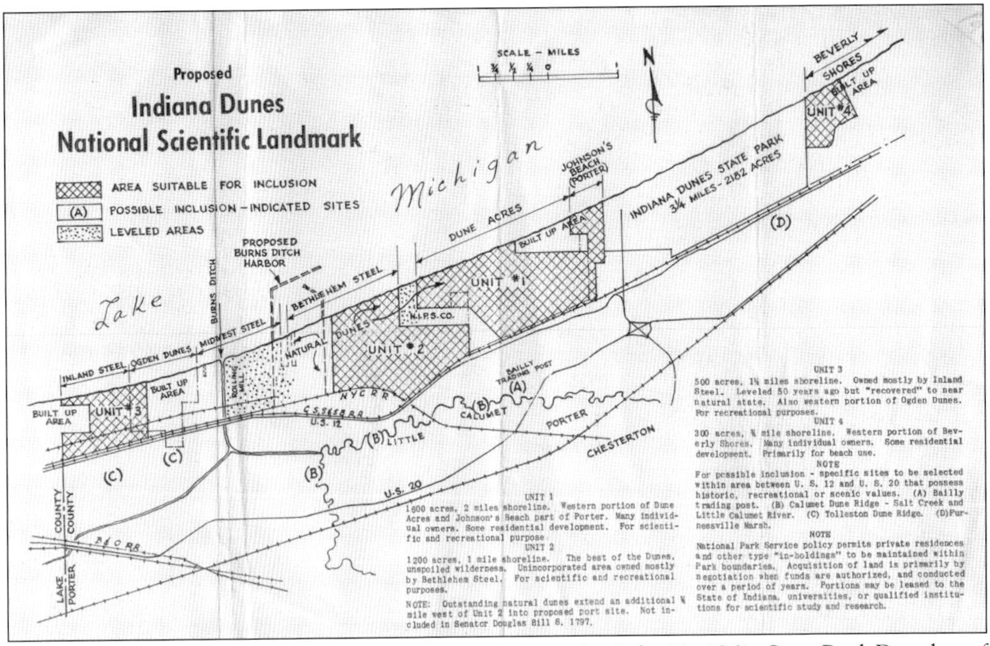

PROPOSED DUNES NATIONAL SCIENTIFIC LANDMARK. On July 23, 1961, Sen. Paul Douglas of Illinois introduced a proposal to create a national landmark. It recommended for inclusion almost all of the Central Dunes, except for land owned by National Steel (Midwest Steel) and Northern Indiana Public Service Company and land around the proposed port. The proposed park also included the west side of Ogden Dunes and the land west to Gary. (HSOD.)

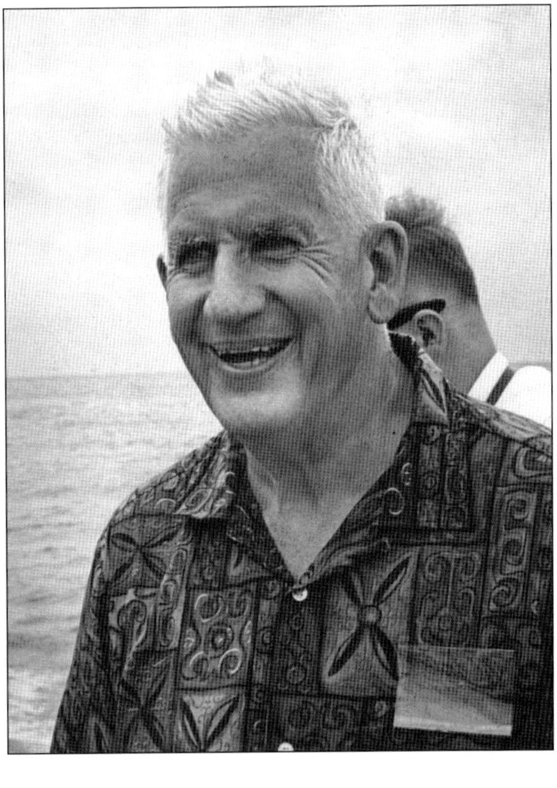

SEN. PAUL DOUGLAS. Paul Douglas, formerly a University of Chicago professor, was elected to the US Senate in 1948. At one time, he had a cottage in Dune Acres. Through mutual friends, Dorothy Buell enlisted Senator Douglas's support in 1959 for the Save the Dunes Council. From that time on, Senator Douglas led the fight in Congress to create a national park and to protect the Indiana sand dunes. (CRAIUN.)

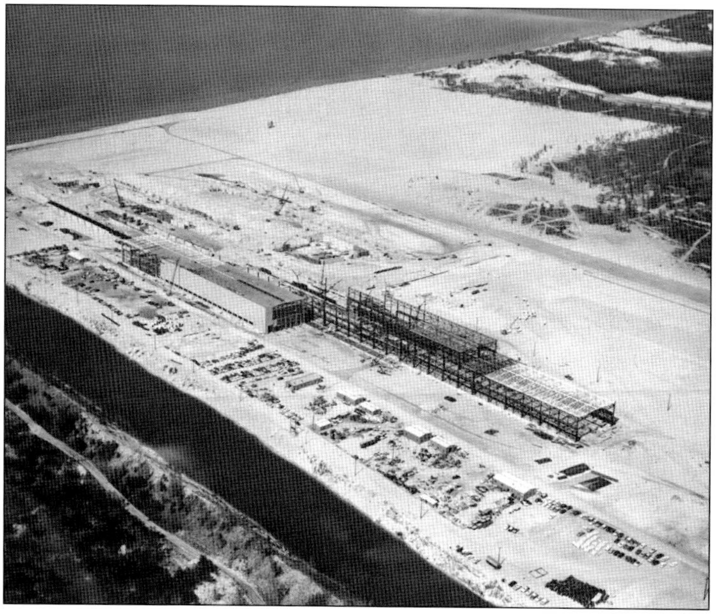

Midwest Steel under Construction. This aerial photograph, taken in the early 1960s, shows the construction of the mill east of Burns Ditch. The dunes were completely leveled, with the steel mill built right next to Burns Ditch. (WTHM.)

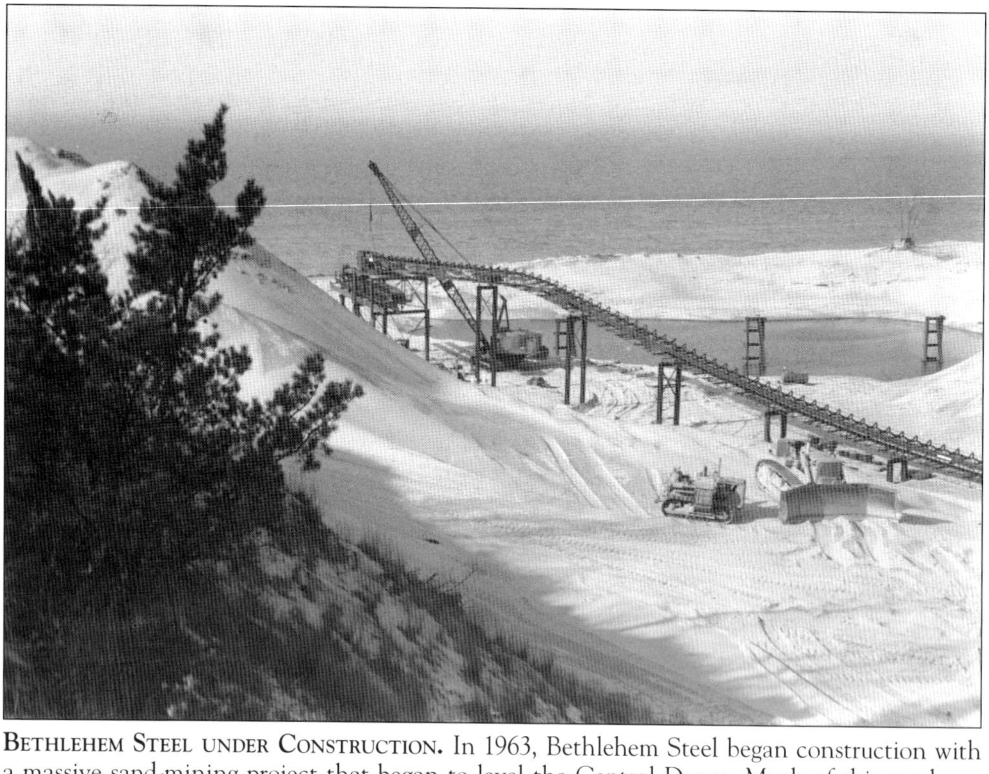

Bethlehem Steel under Construction. In 1963, Bethlehem Steel began construction with a massive sand-mining project that began to level the Central Dunes. Much of this sand was shipped by barge to Evanston for the purpose of expanding the Northwestern University campus at the expense of Lake Michigan. (CRAIUN.)

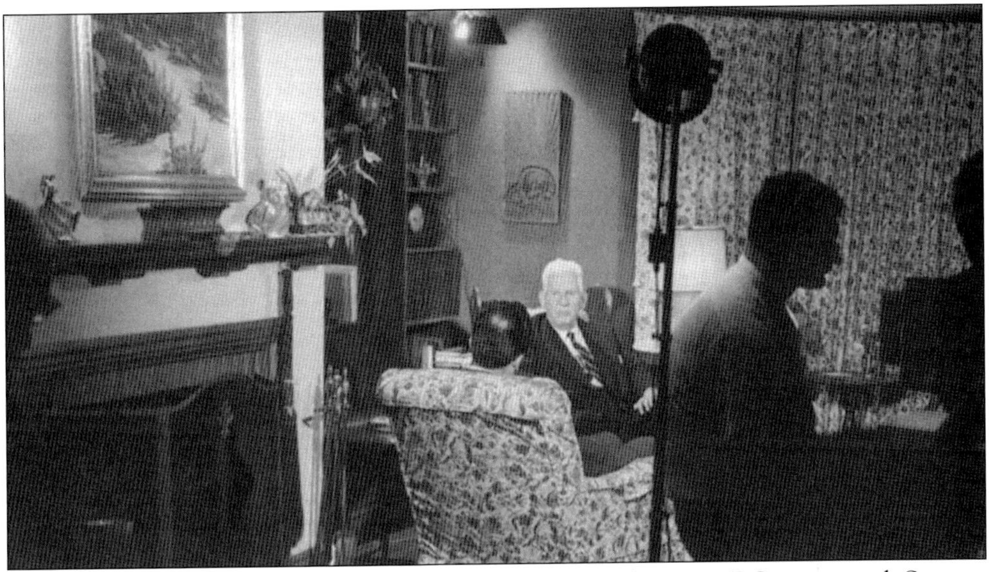

Press Conference at Buell Home. As the battle in Washington, DC, continued, Senator Douglas visited Ogden Dunes, holding a press conference in 1963 in Dorothy Buell's home on Cedar Court. A major issue at this time was the building of a public harbor east of Ogden Dunes. (WTHM.)

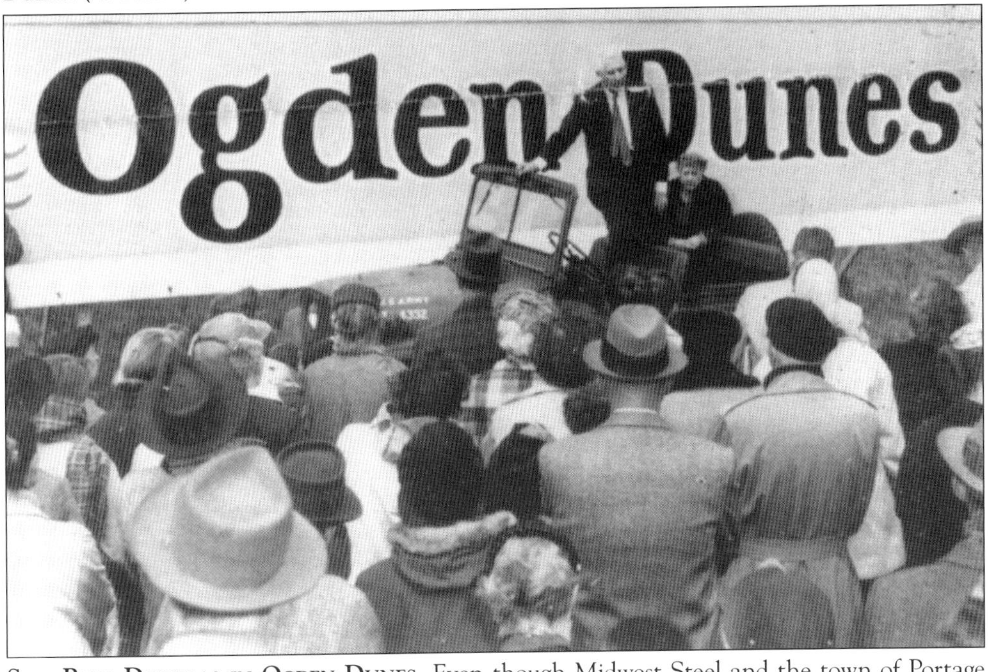

Sen. Paul Douglas in Ogden Dunes. Even though Midwest Steel and the town of Portage were realities, many residents continued the fight to save the dunes. Here, Senator Douglas speaks to supporters in Ogden Dunes while standing in a Jeep. Dorothy Buell is seen sitting in the Jeep. In 1966, Congress passed, and Pres. Lyndon Johnson signed into law, the "Great Compromise," which authorized the creation of the Indiana Dunes National Lakeshore as well as a deepwater harbor. Bethlehem Steel was allowed to continue to level the Central Dunes for a four-mile-long integrated steel mill. (HSOD.)

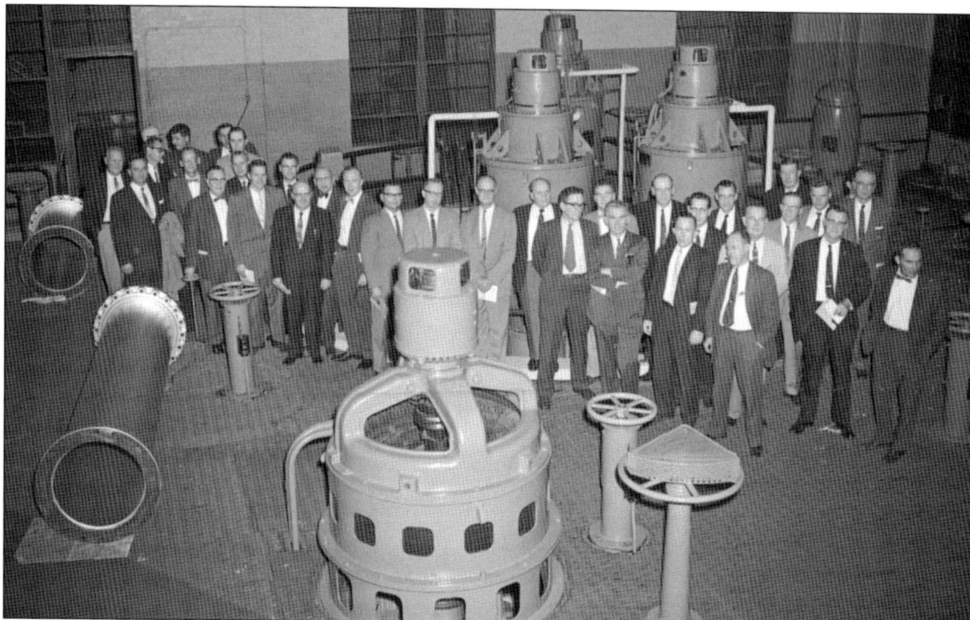

Ogden Dunes Waterworks. The building of Midwest Steel had the indirect effect of bringing to Ogden Dunes two public utilities. A natural-gas pipeline was extended to Midwest Steel, allowing Ogden Dunes to tap into this. This also led to the construction of a water-pumping station and filtration plant in 1960. In this photograph, residents of Ogden Dunes visit the Gary-Hobart Waterworks. (Courtesy of Steve Mark.)

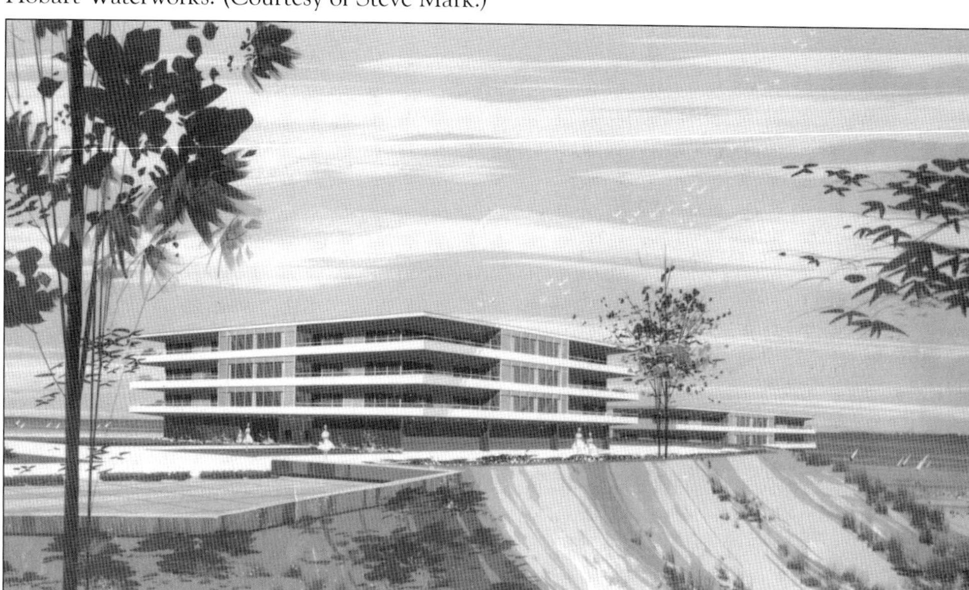

Western Horizon Development. The development of the Third Subdivision in the 1950s did not include the great dune known as Mount Everest. In the early 1960s, Ogden Dunes Realty developed two proposals, one calling for an 11-story high-rise on top of Mount Everest, and the other, the building of a condominium complex with four buildings and sixty units. This divided the community. The town board rejected both proposals. Soon after this, the Fifth Subdivision was platted. Mount Everest was leveled, and large lots were laid out along Summit Road. (HSOD.)

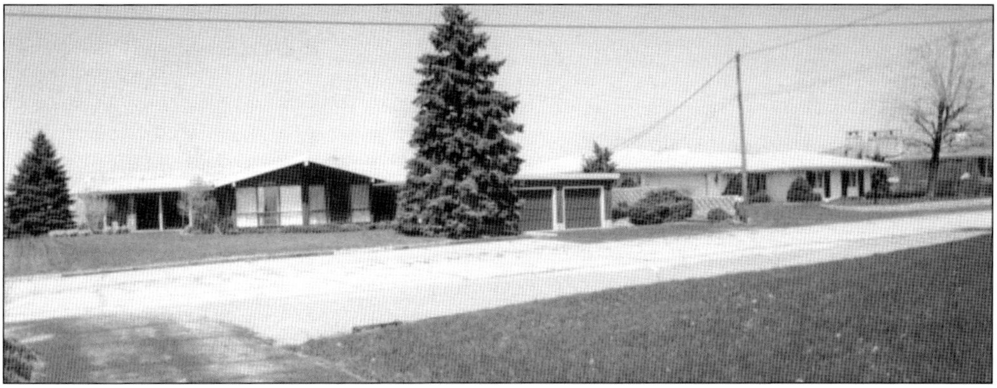

Fred Collins Home, 152 Shore Drive. In the late 1950s, Shore Drive was extended 500 feet to the west, just north of Polliwog Pond. Fred Collins (1915–2004), who had married Kathryn Monahan (1921–1999), was a very successful Gary architect. Beginning in 1946, he designed the first of the more than 30 homes that were built or remodeled in Ogden Dunes. These included a number of homes on or near Shore Drive, including his own. (HSOD.)

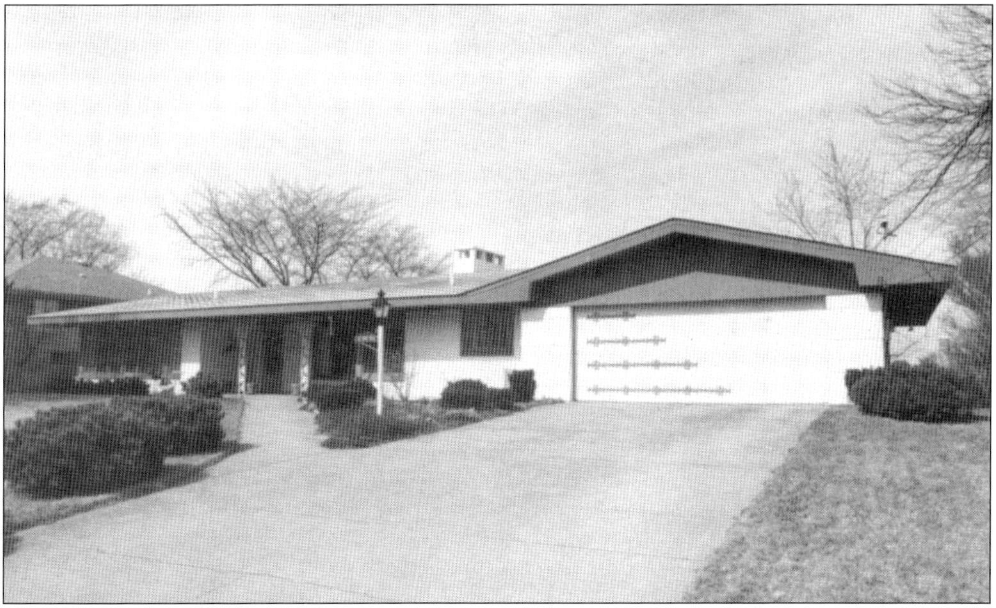

Sykes Home, 128 Shore Drive. Ralph and Alice Sykes, who built the home at 114 Shore Drive in 1940, sold it to their son William in 1957. They then built the home shown here. Ralph's sister, Edith Sykes Dorman, a widow since the late 1920s, built a home at 132 Shore Drive with her daughter and son-in-law, Sarah and Robert Bailey. Almost all the members of the extended Dorman/Sykes families were involved in the family businesses, Fifth Avenue Motors and Monarch Oil. (HSOD.)

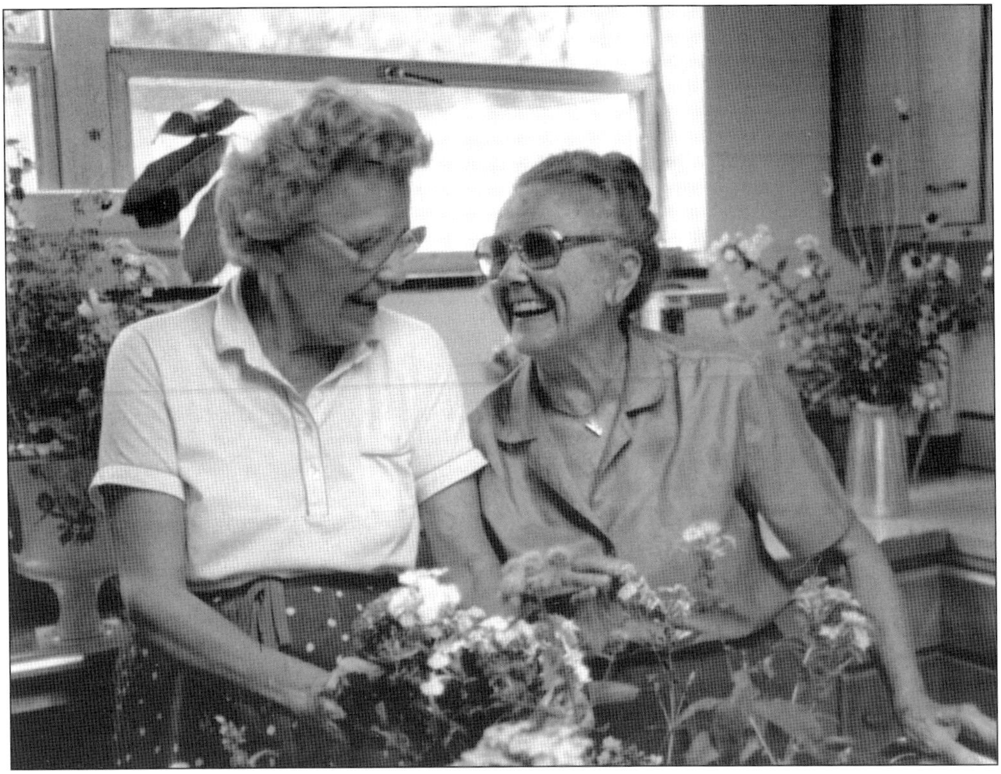

Margaret Benninger and Betty Mullin. Benninger (left) and Mullin were among the most active women in the community after World War II. They are shown here at an Ogden Dunes Community Church gathering. Margaret and her husband, Kester, purchased the home of Marion Sykes Stinson, at 113 Shore Drive, in 1957. Within a year of moving into the community, Benninger was an officer in the Book Club and the Woman's Club. Mullin, a music teacher in the Portage schools, served as the organist and choral director at the church for many years. (HSOD.)

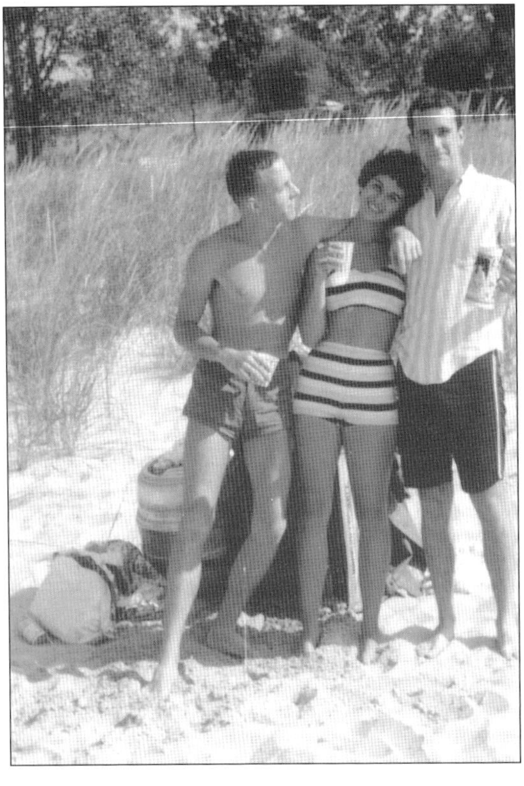

The Beach. Enjoying life on the beach are, from left to right, Hugh Moore, Jennifer Willis, and Bob Mullin. The Moore family moved into the community in 1948; his father, the historian Powell Moore, wrote *The Calumet Region*. The Willis family moved to Hillcrest in 1947, and the Mullin family came to Sunset Trail in 1943. (Courtesy of George Svihla.)

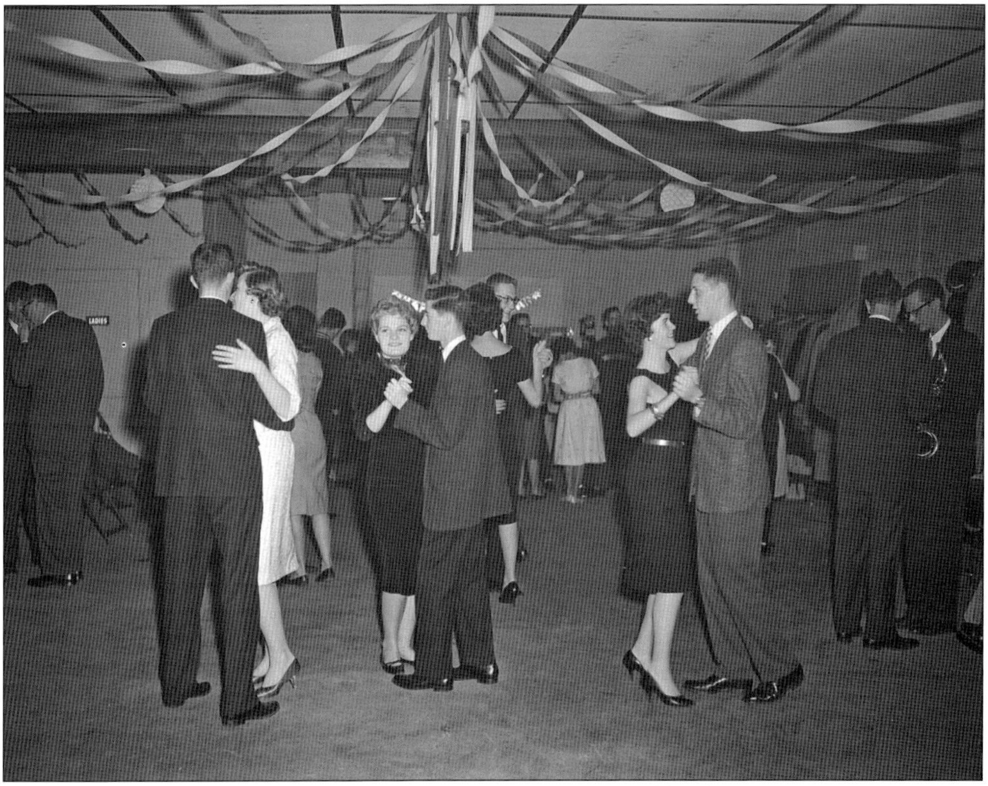

American Legion Dance. Among the various events sponsored by the active American Legion post in Ogden Dunes were dances at the fire hall. This dance was held in 1960. (Courtesy of Steve Mark.)

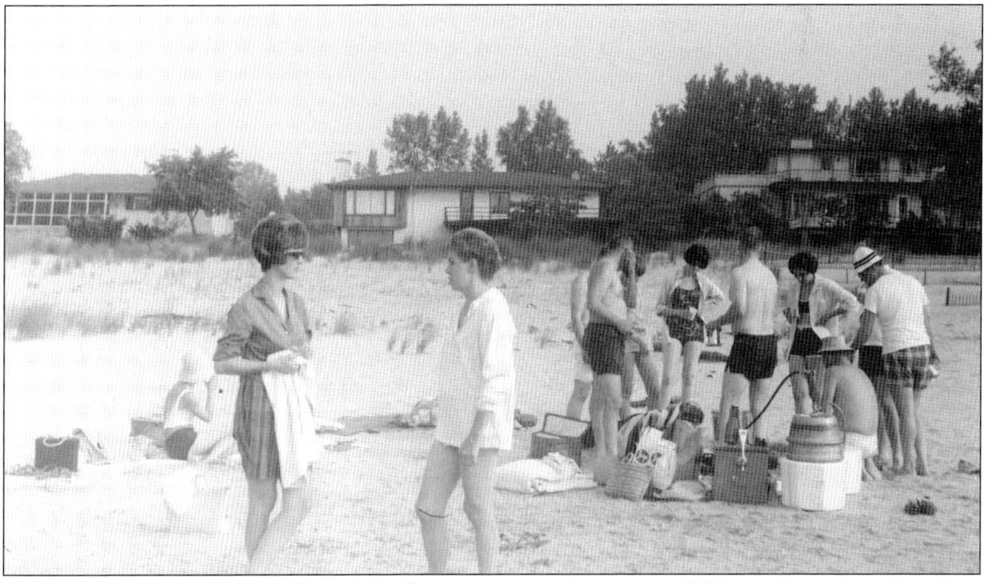

Community Beach Party. One of the last summer gatherings in 1968 was documented by Don Kurtz, as he did with scores of other events over a 40-year period. Don and Dorothy Kurtz moved to the community in 1964. (Courtesy of the Kurtz family.)

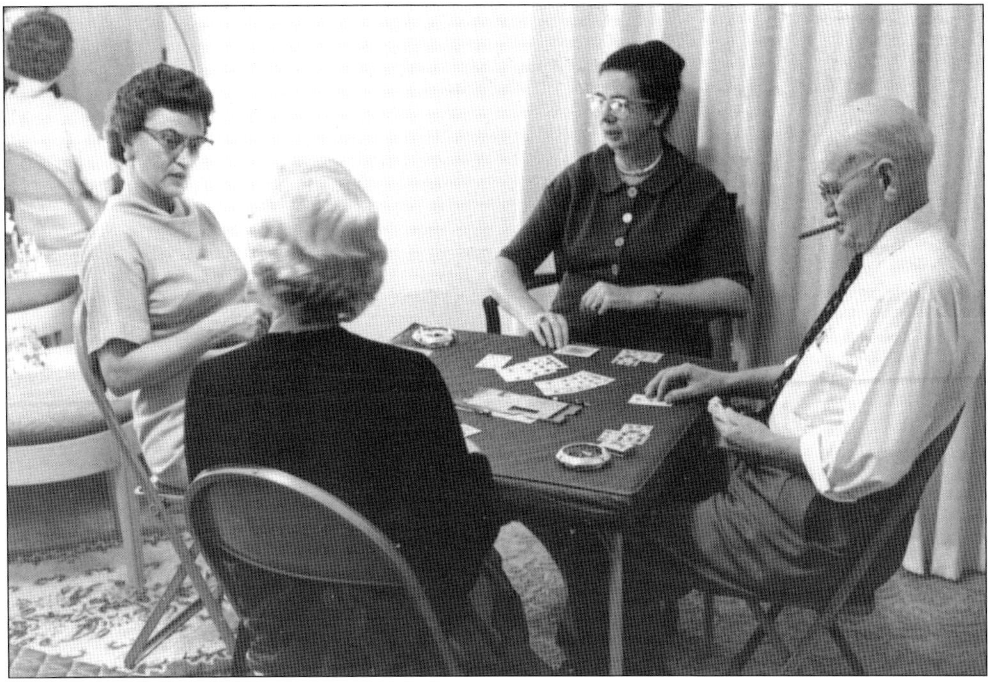

Bridge: A Winter Activity. In this photograph are, clockwise from lower right, A.L. Cash (with his famous cigar), Mary Fran Dittrich, June Bratton, and Dottie Foldessy. Cash built scores of homes in Ogden Dunes from 1930 to the 1960s. Ray and June Bratton bought a home on Beach Lane in 1946; he was a dentist, and she was a teacher in Portage and an artist. The Dittrichs and Foldessys moved to the community in 1957. (HSOD.)

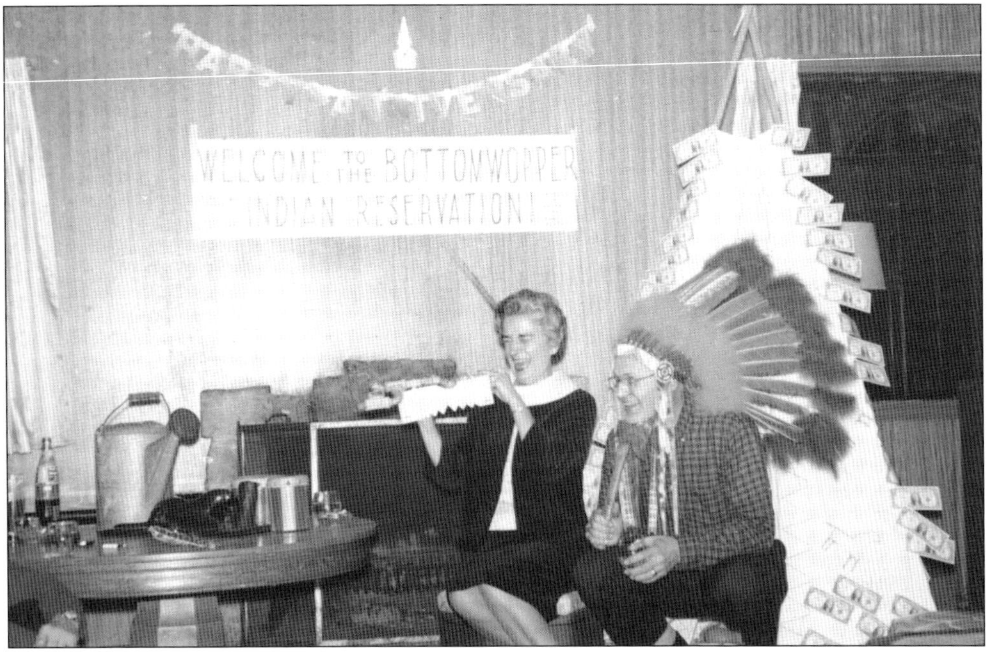

Willis Anniversary Party, 1964. The theme for this party was a common one for the time, but would not be popular today. (HSOD, Funkey.)

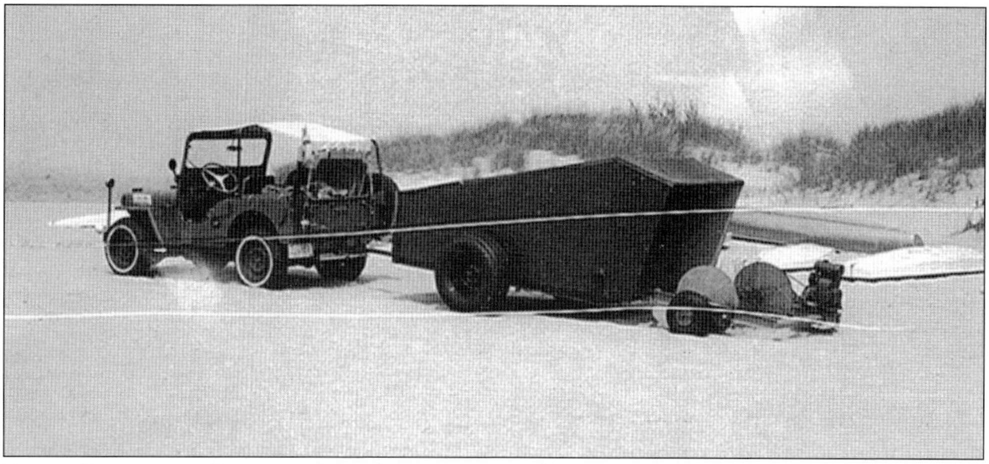

Beach Pollution. Because of the disappearance of predators, namely lake trout, the alewives nearly took over the Great Lakes in the 1960s. The seasonal die-off of alewives polluted the beaches. Volunteers spent countless hours cleaning up the beach in Ogden Dunes. To more efficiently keep the beaches clean, Ed Kratz invented a rotary rake to pick up the dead fish and other debris. In August 1968, he applied for a patent on his invention. (HSOD.)

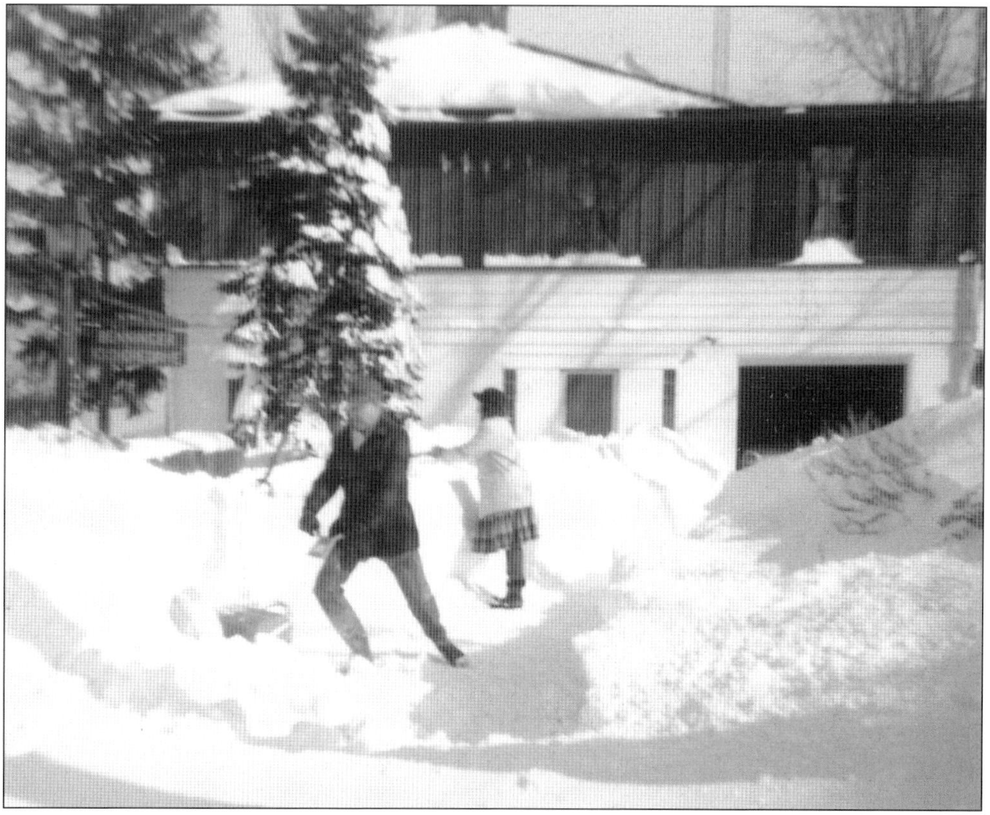

Snowstorm of 1967. On January 26 and 27, a massive snowstorm shut down the Chicagoland area for nearly a week. Almost two feet of snow fell in Ogden Dunes, with the wind creating eight-foot snowdrifts. Neighbors supported neighbors, as most contact with the outside world came to a halt. The Benninger home at 113 Shore Drive is shown here. (HSOD, Tittle.)

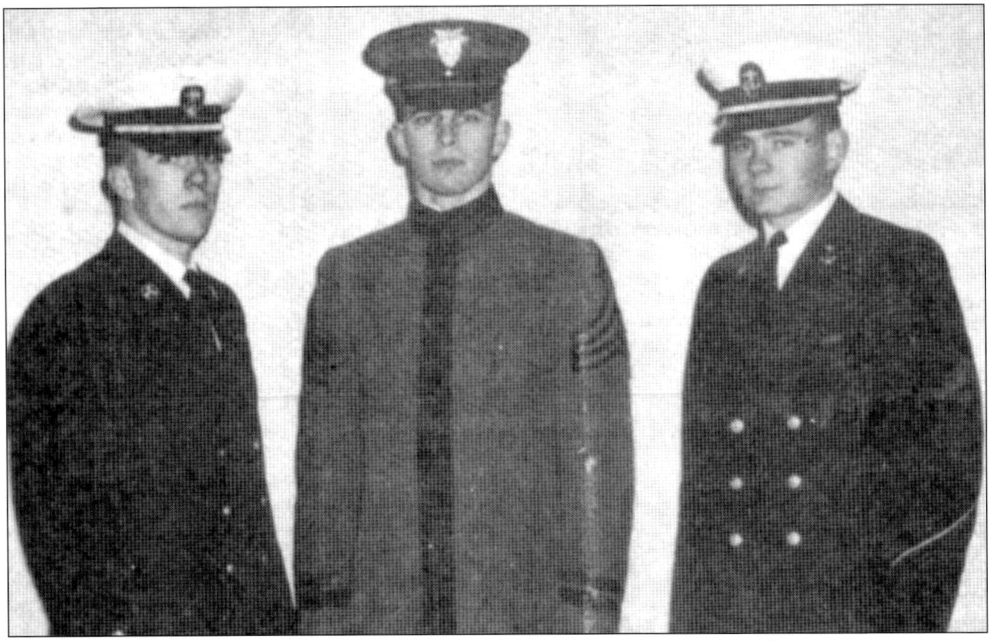

COLD WAR. In November 1960, the charismatic John F. Kennedy was elected president. American patriotism and optimism was at its peak. Ogden Dunes, a community of 974, reflected this patriotism, as four of its young men had appointments to the military academies. The three who spent the 1960 Christmas holidays with their families are shown in this photograph. They are, from left to right, Richard Amos, first year, Merchant Marine; Michael Brady, fourth year, West Point; and George Vermef, second year, Annapolis. The fourth local academy appointee was Frank Midnight, who spent Christmas with his parents at the Air Force Academy. (Courtesy of Steve Mark.)

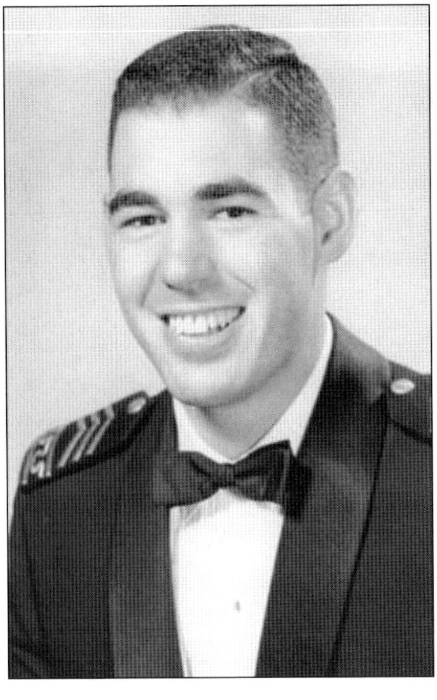

FRANK MIDNIGHT. On August 23, 1967, Captain Midnight's plane was shot down over North Vietnam. His body has never been recovered. During the war, two other young men from Ogden Dunes also died. Paul Strange, who enlisted in the Army, died on September 13, 1967, in a firefight in Dihn Tuong, South Vietnam. James Giegel joined the Marines in 1967 in New Jersey, where his family had moved in 1965. On May 26, 1970, he died in Quang Nam, South Vietnam. (HSOD.)

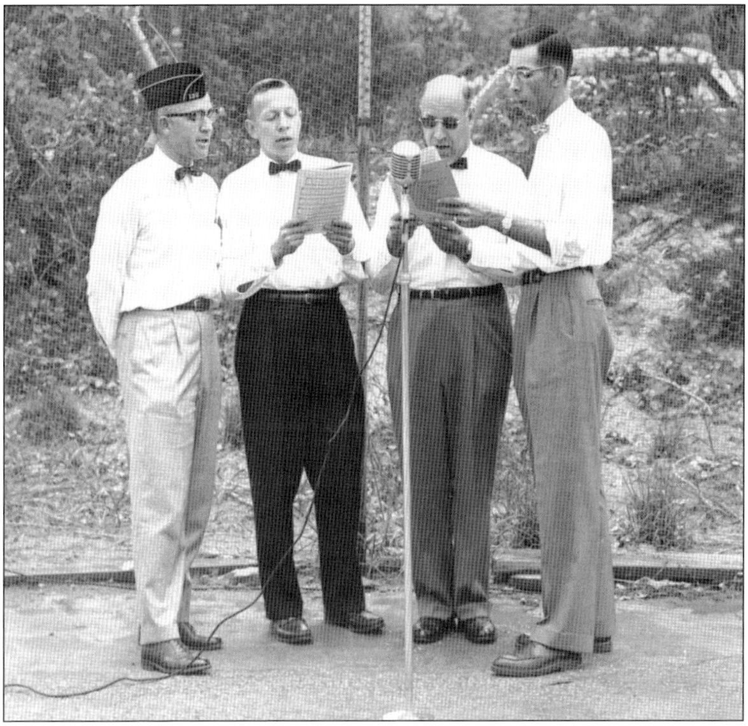

Memorial Day, 1960. The annual Memorial Day parade, ceremony, and picnic became increasingly special during the 1960s. Each ceremony was opened with the singing of the national anthem. Shown here are, from left to right, Paul Van Leuven, Bob Gasser, Charlie Graves, and Lee Ross. (HSOD.)

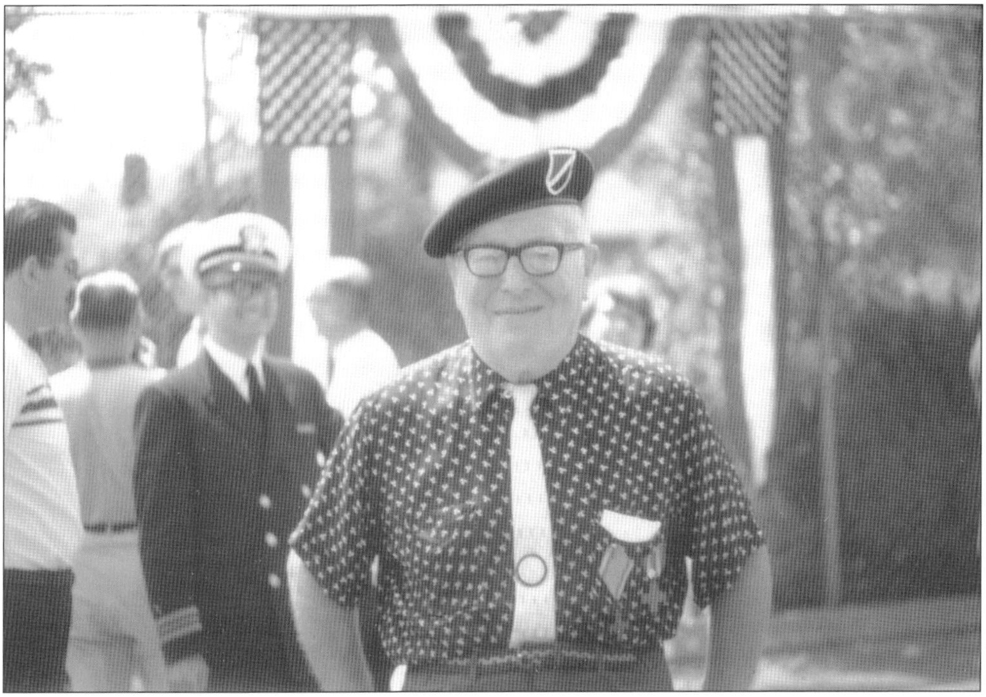

Memorial Day, 1969. For 25 years, beginning in 1947, World War I veteran George Washington Kowalski (1894–1971) read "In Flanders Fields" at each Memorial Day ceremony. The ceremonies during most of these years were held at the tennis courts in Juniper Park, now Nelson Reck Park. Kowalski died in a fire at his home on Ogden Road in 1971. (HSOD.)

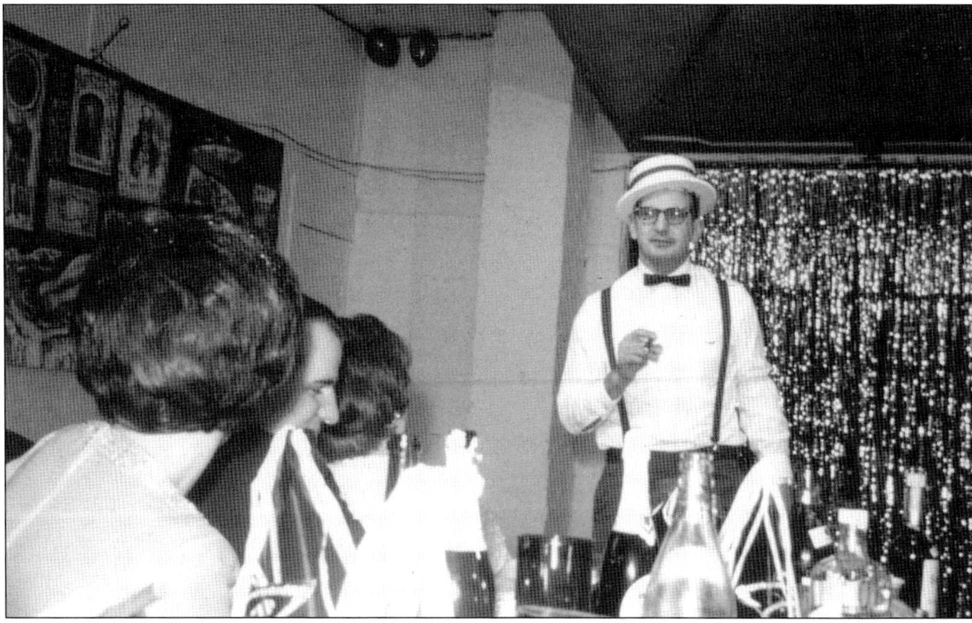

New Year's Eve Follies. Beginning in 1967, a group of creative women added a musical revue to the annual Woman's Club party. They scripted the program, built scenery, and spent hours at rehearsal. Each party had a theme. In 1968, Lynne Schroeder was the writer, director, and referee of "Come to the Cabaret." Pictured here is Joe Costanza, a young attorney who moved to Ogden Road in 1964. He was the emcee and "barker" for the production. (Courtesy of the Kurtz family.)

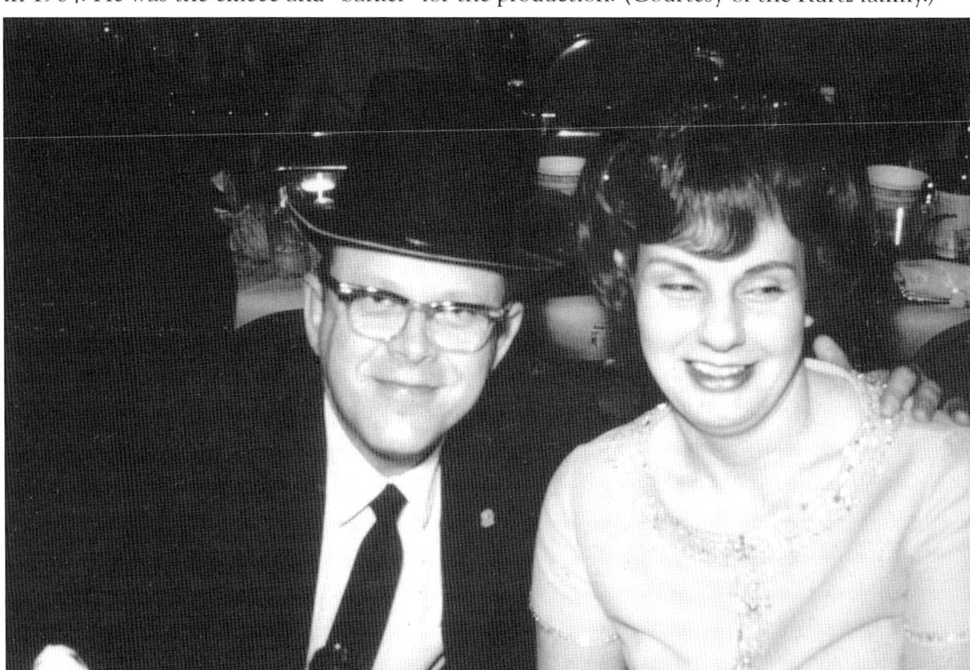

Rapt Audience. The annual party, held at the fire hall, drew large audiences. Pictured here in 1968 are Jim and Barb Homme. They, like many of the other attendees and performers, had moved to the community in the 1960s. (Courtesy of the Kurtz family.)

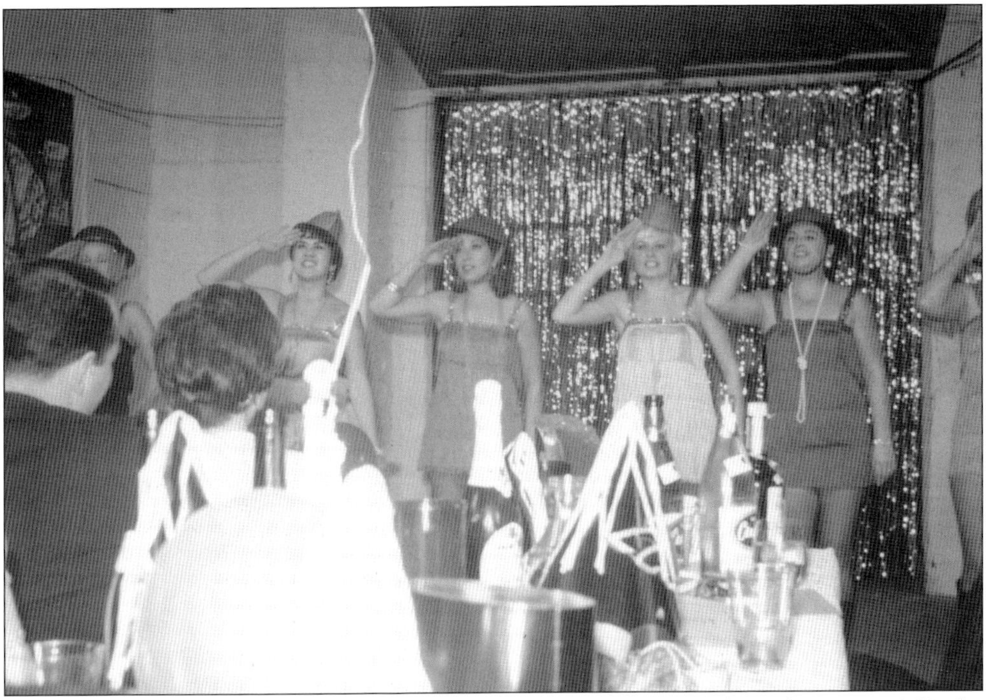

Chorus Line. Each musical revue had its chorus line. In "Come to the Cabaret" in 1968, the chorus line included, from left to right, Barbara Ahrens, Barbara Beiser, Jeanne Gaydos, Kathleen Given, Marleen Kopp, and Marilyn Senour. Themes of the following years were "A Night in Old Baghdad (or, oh! what a bag dad had)" in 1969, "Those Were The Days, My Friends" in 1970, and "This Was Burlesque" in 1971. (Courtesy of the Kurtz family.)

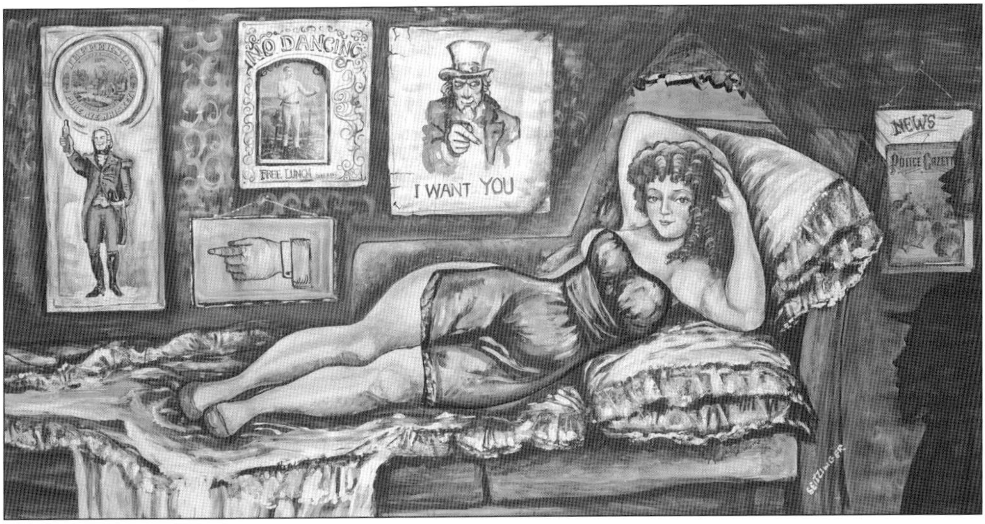

Goya's Nude: Different Context. Arlene Seitzinger, a noted Ogden Dunes sculptor and painter, moved into a new home with her husband, Melvin Miller, at 116 Diana Road in 1960. He, like her, was artistic, working as art director for a Chicago advertising firm. Arlene developed sets for the "Follies," one of which was a takeoff on Francisco Goya's *The Nude Maja* and *The Clothed Maja*, both painted in Spain around 1800. Arlene combined the paintings. It became *Ogden Dunes Slightly Dressed Nude*. (Photograph by Emilie Cardoso-Seerup; HSOD.)

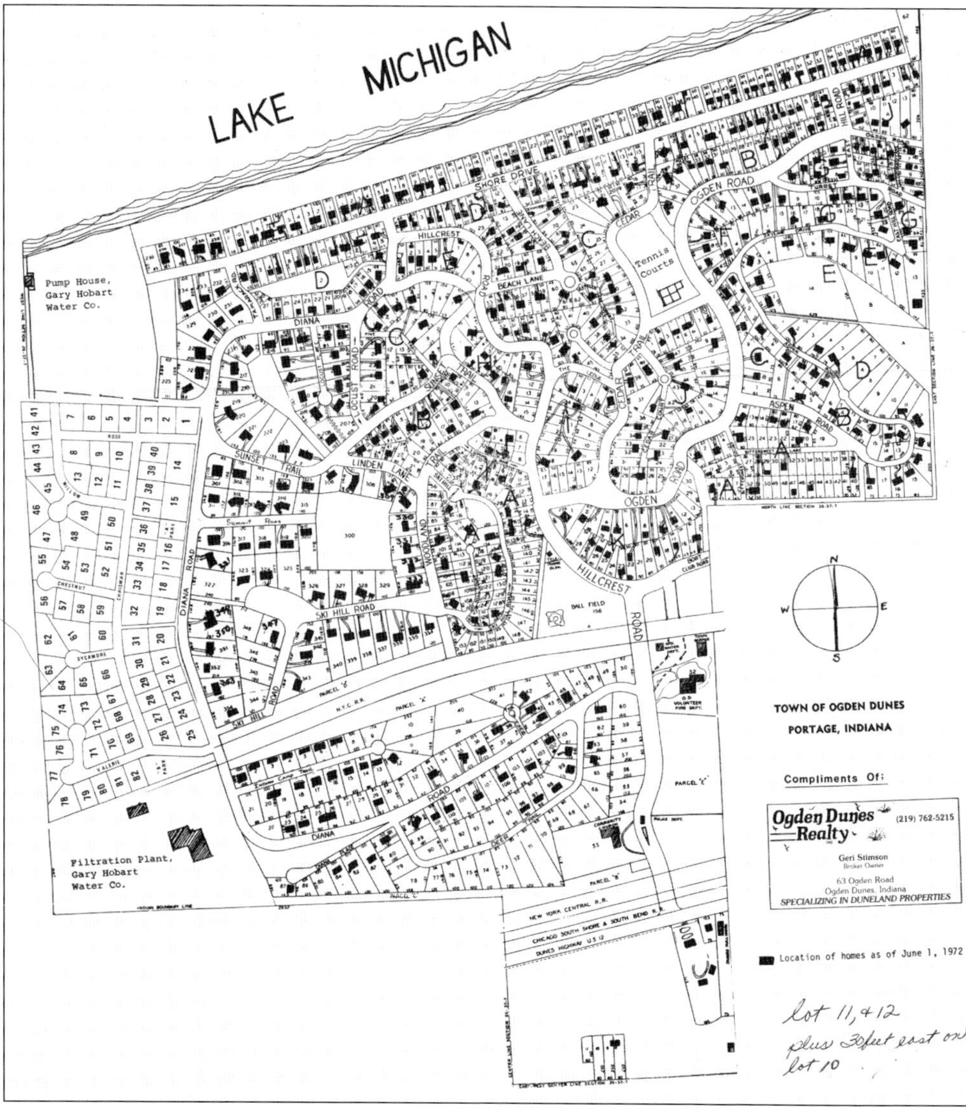

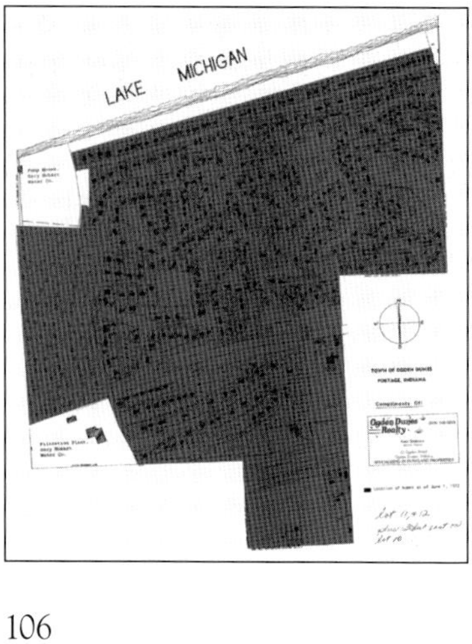

1972 Map. The map above includes the proposed Sixth Subdivision on the West Side of town and shows about 600 homes and cottages. According to the 1970 census, 1,361 people were full-time residents of Ogden Dunes. In September 1970, 345 students were enrolled in the Portage schools, including 23 in kindergarten, according to the last issue of the *Ogden Dunes Sandpiper* (Spring and Summer 1970). It also lists 35 children in private schools and 86 students in college. The 1972 map at left shows the town within the 1994 boundaries of Ogden Dunes, which remain the same today. (Both, HSOD.)

Eight

ADJUSTING TO NEIGHBORS
1970s AND AFTER

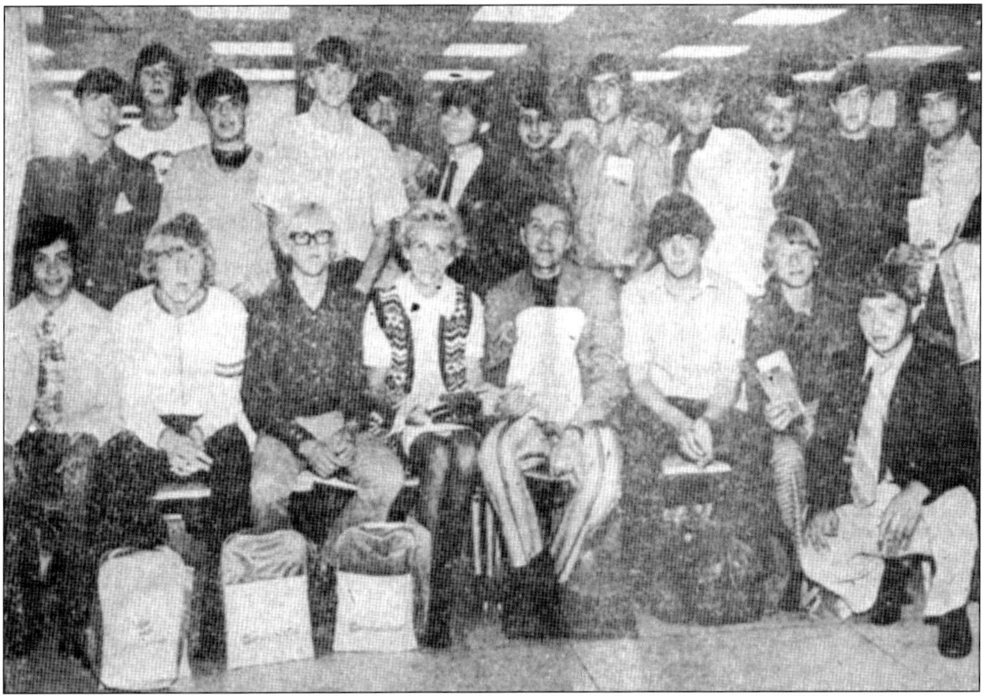

OPENING THE IRON CURTAIN. In August 1971, in the midst of the Cold War, a group of young men from Northwestern Indiana and their sponsors flew from Chicago to Russia to play soccer, as a sign of friendship through sports. The primary organizers of this trip were Connie Daley, who headed the $20,000 fundraising campaign, and Nick Matavuli, who coached the team. Both were from Ogden Dunes, as were many of the young players. (HSOD.)

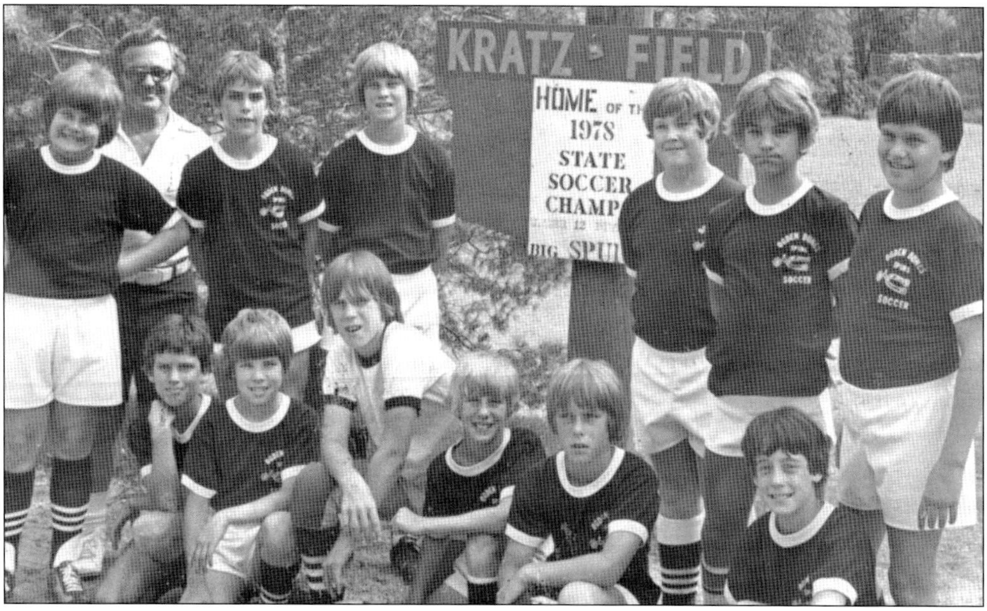

Boys' Soccer, 1978. Soccer developed as a major pastime in Ogden Dunes during the late 1960s. Games were played on Kratz Field, which had been the end of the ski jump, and later a Victory Garden. Shown here is coach John Petrou with his team. Petrou and his wife, Sharon, moved to Ogden Dunes in 1962. He taught at Gary Emerson and coached freshman football. In the 1970s and 1980s, both he and his wife coached youth soccer. (HSOD.)

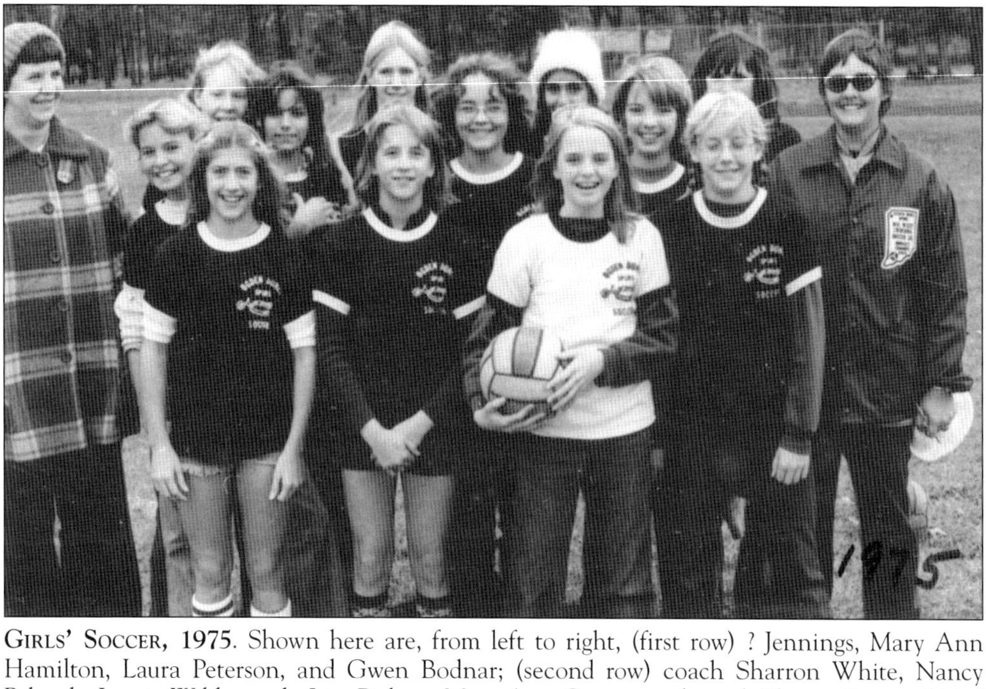

Girls' Soccer, 1975. Shown here are, from left to right, (first row) ? Jennings, Mary Ann Hamilton, Laura Peterson, and Gwen Bodnar; (second row) coach Sharron White, Nancy Ribordy, Laurie Wildermuth, Lisa Pickart, Mary Ann Groves, and coach Sharon Petrou; (third row) Missy Stimson, Barb Homme, Carol Homme, and an unidentified girl. (HSOD.)

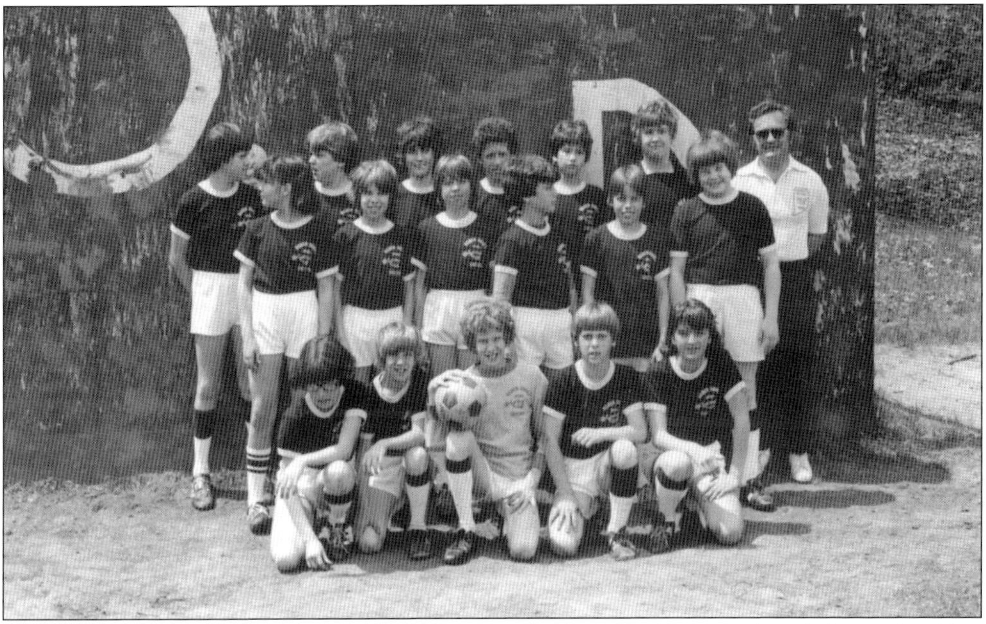

Co-ed Soccer. Some beginning-level teams were co-ed. Posing here are, from left to right, (first row) Bobby Walls, Mike Pocza, Duncan Hines, John Mario, and Mia Costanza; (second row) Lisa Compton, Bo Marriott, Ken Kopp, Jaime Butcher, Dan Ialeggio, and John Plunkett; (third row) Billy White, Tim Sampson, David Torrence, Tim Schuler, Brian Dudenski, Andy Petrou, and coach John Petrou. (HSOD.)

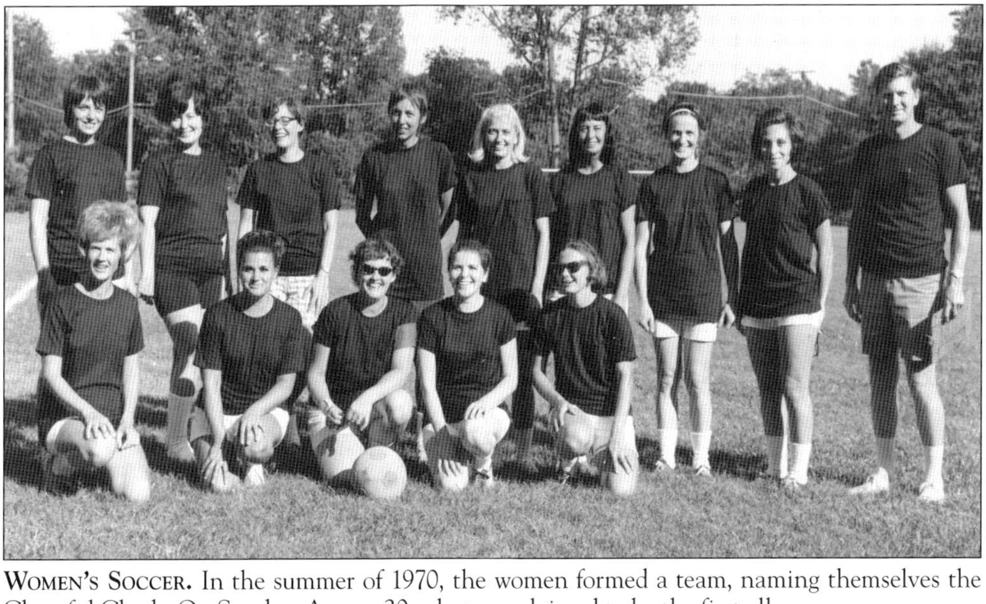

Women's Soccer. In the summer of 1970, the women formed a team, naming themselves the Cheerful Chads. On Sunday, August 20, what was claimed to be the first all-women soccer game in the United States was held in Ogden Dunes before over 400 fans. Dale Messick returned to Ogden Dunes to kick the first ball. The Chads won 2-1. Shown here are, from left to right, (first row) Jennie Gravis, Maycel Mirr, Sharon Petrou, Eunice Chadwick, and Dorothy Kurtz; (second row) Helen Phillips, Ruth Rondinelli, Linda Kelly, Mary Bush, Marleen Kopp, Carolyn McGirr, Joan Froman, Marge Tittle, and coach Norm Chadwick. (HSOD.)

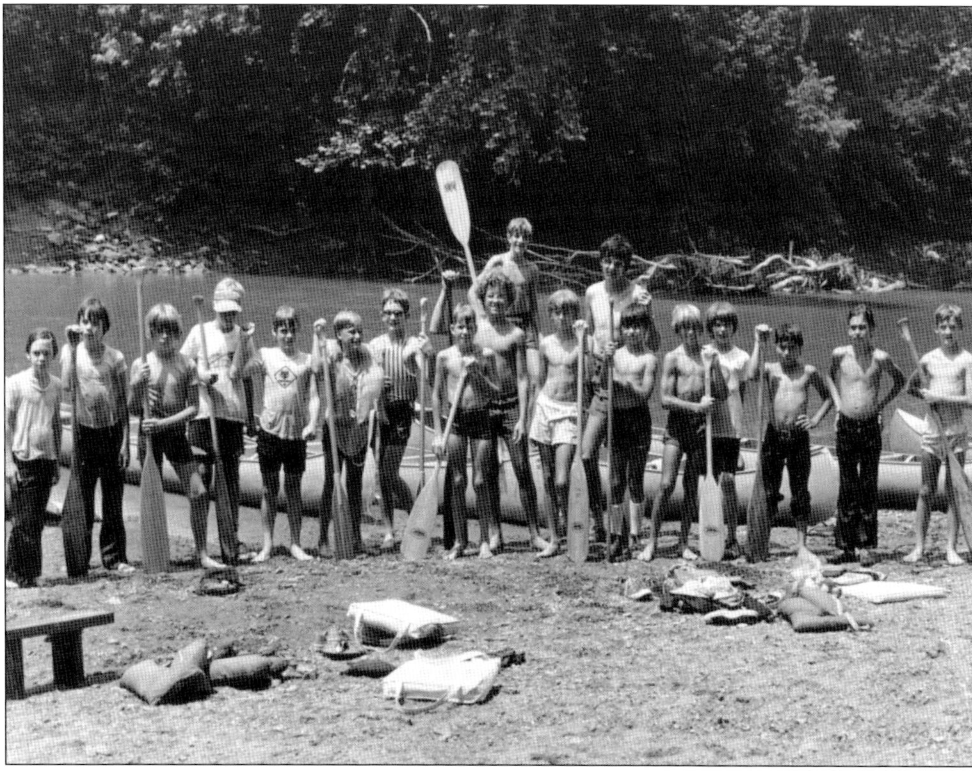

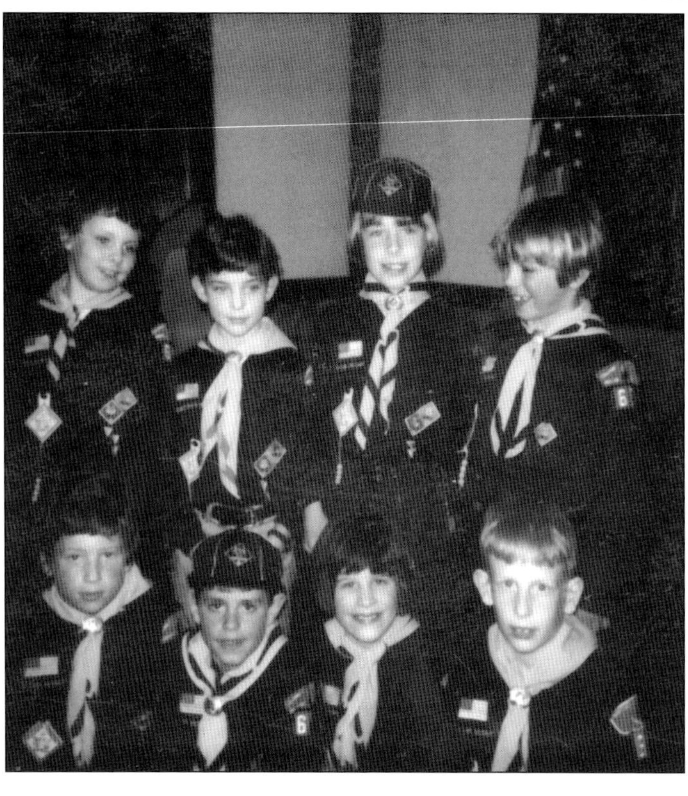

TAKING ON NATURE. Troop 68, under the leadership of scoutmaster Don Kurtz, supported by Duane Hibbs and Dick Hallman, completed a 28-mile canoe trip on Sugar Creek in Parke County, Indiana. Scouting, like soccer, involved many of the families in the community during the 1970s. (Courtesy of the Kurtz family.)

CUB SCOUTS. To prepare future Boy Scouts for excursions into the wilderness, moms were responsible as den mothers for the younger boys, the Cub Scouts. (HSOD.)

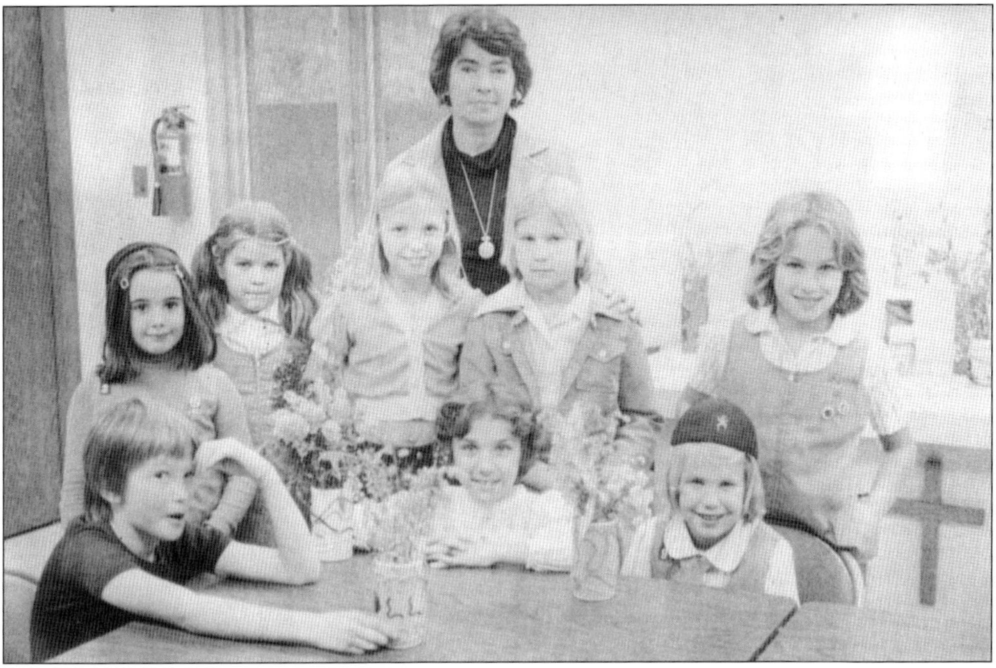

Brownies and Girl Scouts. This photograph, taken on October 27, 1977, includes Scout leader Pat Kleim. The girls are, from left to right, (seated) ? Smith, Jennifer Patellis, and Krissy Jensen; (standing) Heidi Grenchik, Kelly Olson, Chrissy Waite (Girl Scout), Beth Jensen (Girl Scout), and Lori Kleim. (HSOD.)

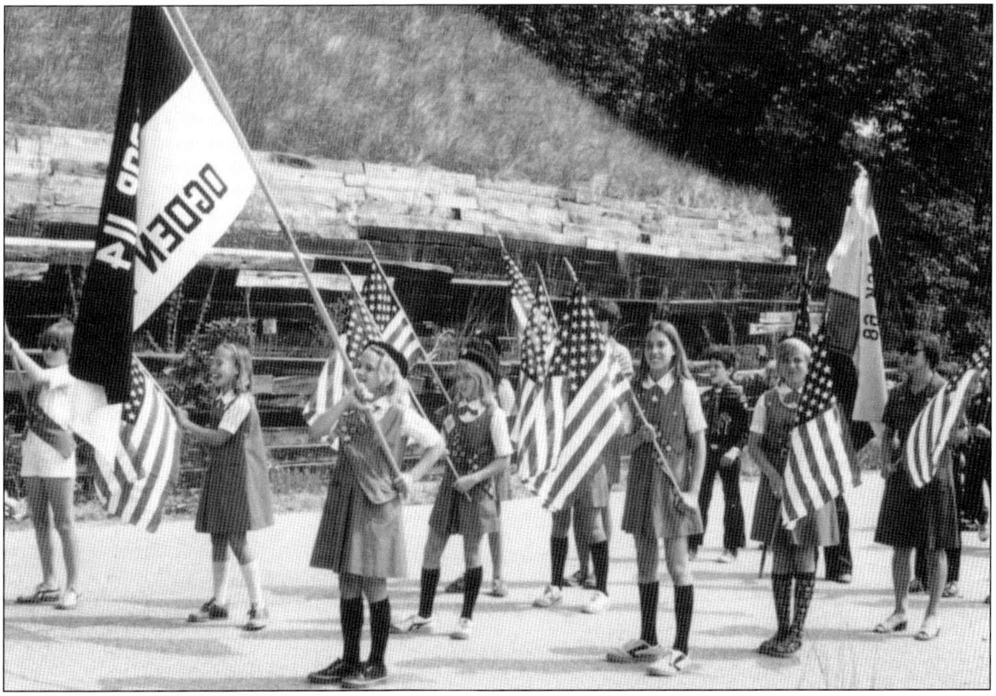

Girl Scouts on Parade. On Memorial Day and other holidays, the Town of Ogden Dunes held parades, with the Scouts participating. (Courtesy of the Kurtz family.)

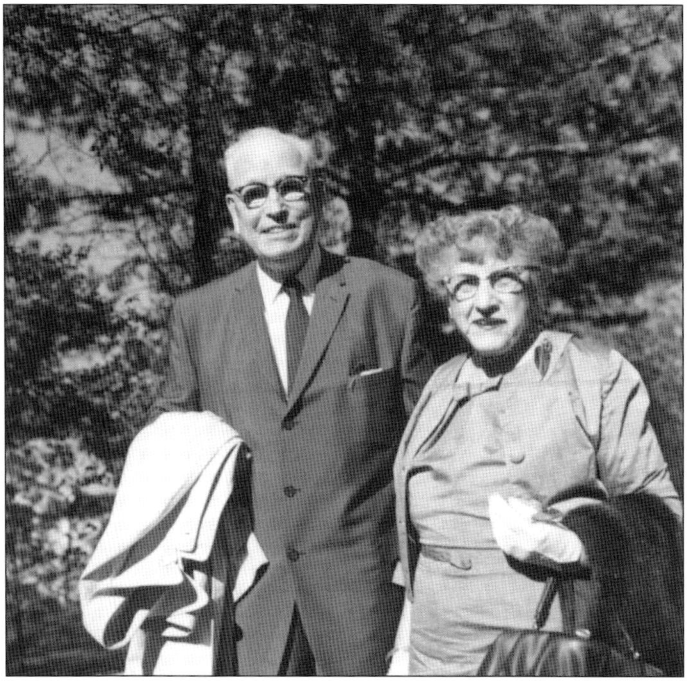

JAMES HAL AND DOROTHY BUELL. James Hal Buell (1881–1970), better known as Dorothy's husband, had a distinguished career as an engineer. After living in many areas of the country, the Buells in 1941 built a home in Ogden Dunes. After the creation of the National Lake Shore in 1966, they retired to California. (CRAIUN.)

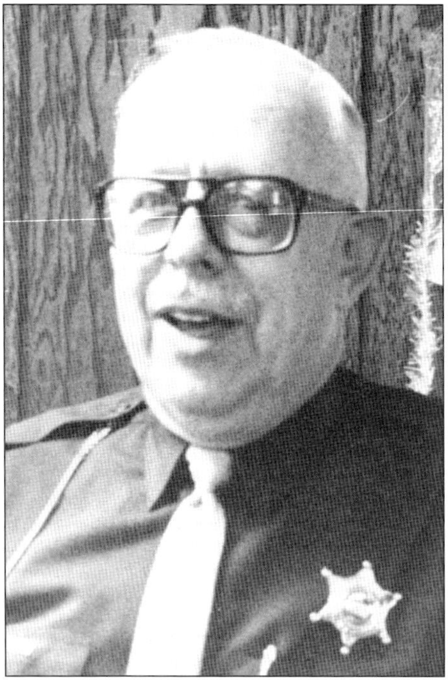

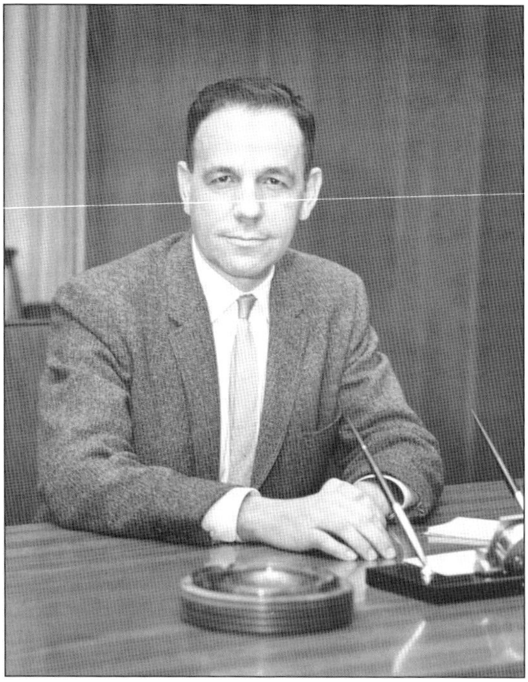

PUBLIC SERVANTS. Beginning in 1957, Ed Moore (1915–1999) worked for the town as deputy marshal, water superintendent, street commissioner, daytime fire chief, and marshal. After 17 years as marshal, Moore, shown in the left photograph, retired on December 31, 1980. Steve L. Collins and his wife, Anne, moved to 128 Diana Road in 1963. Steve (right) was safety director of Midwest Steel. He served as president of the town board in 1971 and then as state representative from 1972 to 1982, the first person from Ogden Dunes to hold a statewide position. (Both, HSOD.)

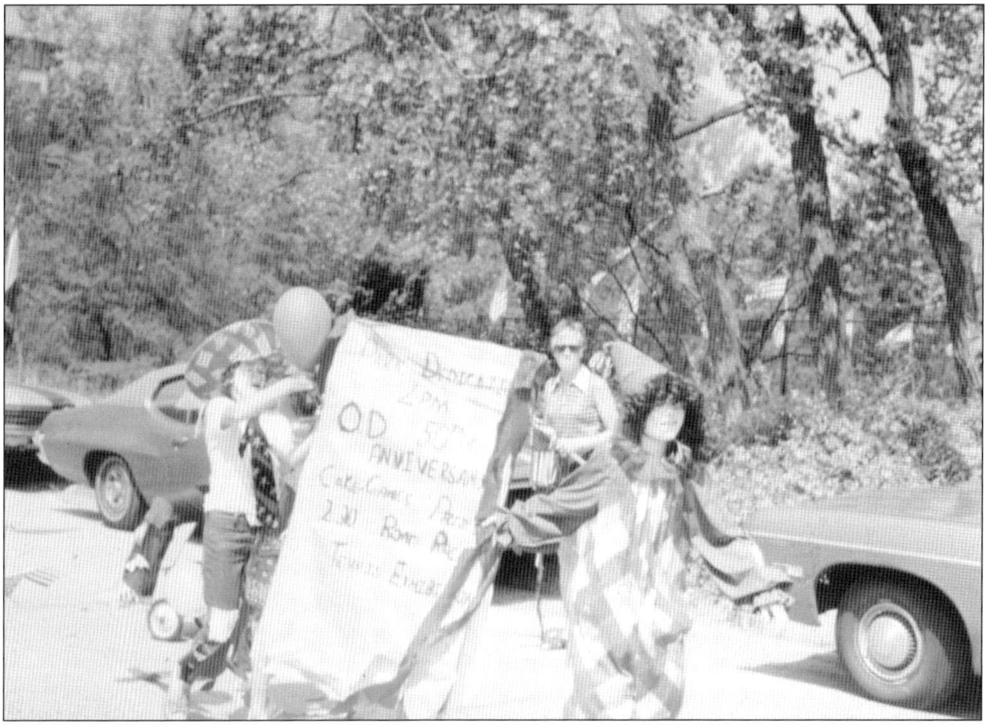

OGDEN DUNES' 50TH ANNIVERSARY. In the mid-1970s, the town had much to celebrate. In 1975, the town turned 50 and held a major community party, including this parade. To commemorate its birthday, Joe Thomas, a journalist with the *Gary Post-Tribune*, edited the first *History of Ogden Dunes.* (Courtesy of the Kurtz family.)

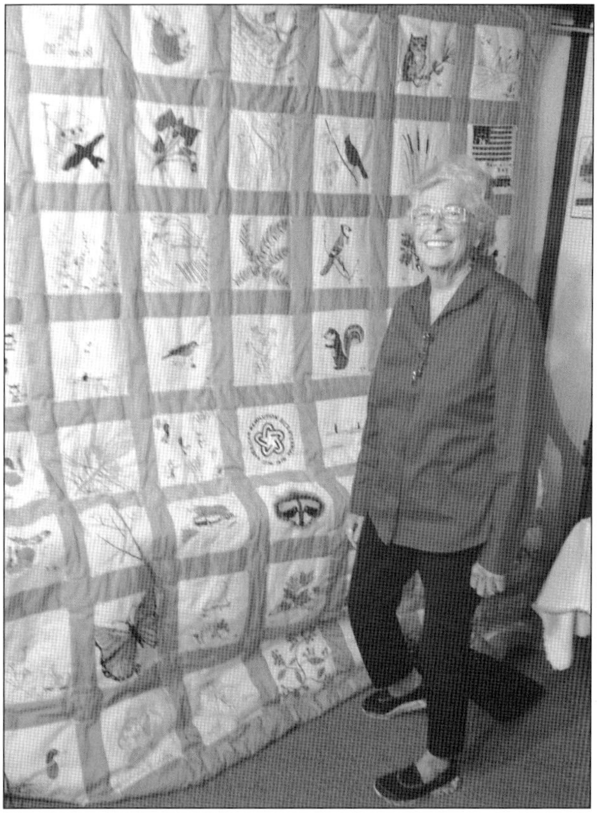

BICENTENNIAL QUILT. The celebration of the bicentennial of the United States in 1976 ended with a massive Fall Festival on Kratz Field. Nearly 50 families contributed to making this quilt, which is composed of 56 squares, depicting life in Ogden Dunes. Carolyn Ribordy, shown here, coordinated the completion of the quilt. The Bjorklund family won it at the raffle and later donated it to the historical society. (HSOD.)

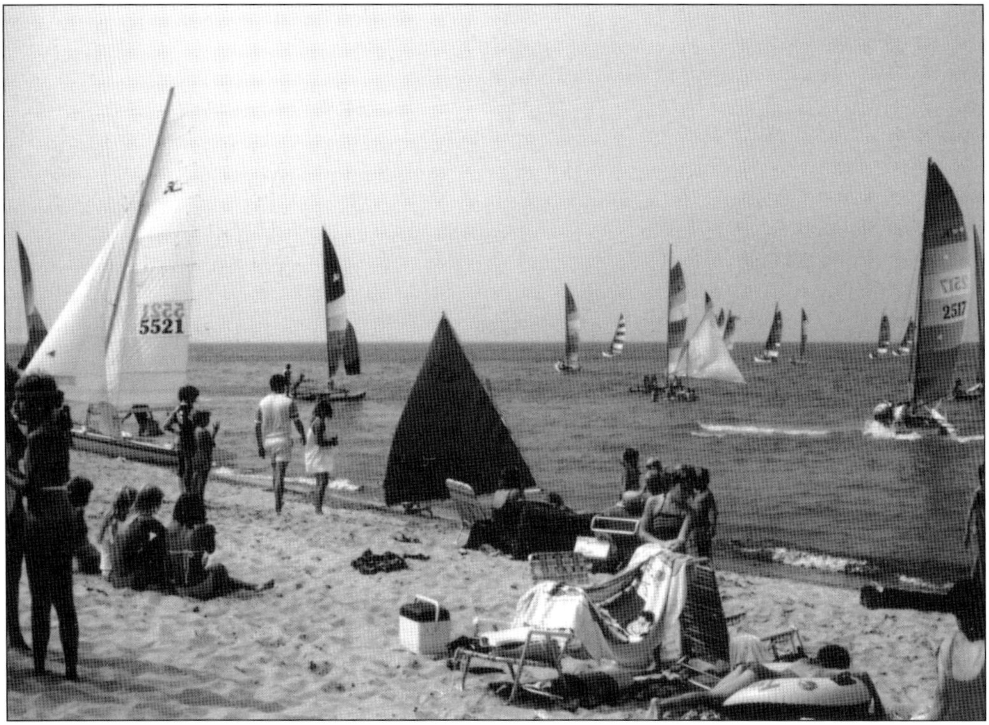

Sailing Races and Windsurfing. In the 1980s, the children of the families who moved into the community in the 1960s became young adults. The beach was no longer a place just to play in the sand. Instead, it became a site to challenge nature. Sailing, especially organized races, was a favorite pastime (above). Hank Kazmier, a college science teacher, his wife, Manda, and their family moved to 141 Shore Drive in 1970. In the early 1980s, he organized the sailing competitions. In 1983, he became the first commander of Hobie Fleet 505, with over 30 charter members. Another area of competition in the 1980s was windsurfing (below). (Both, HSOD, Kazmier.)

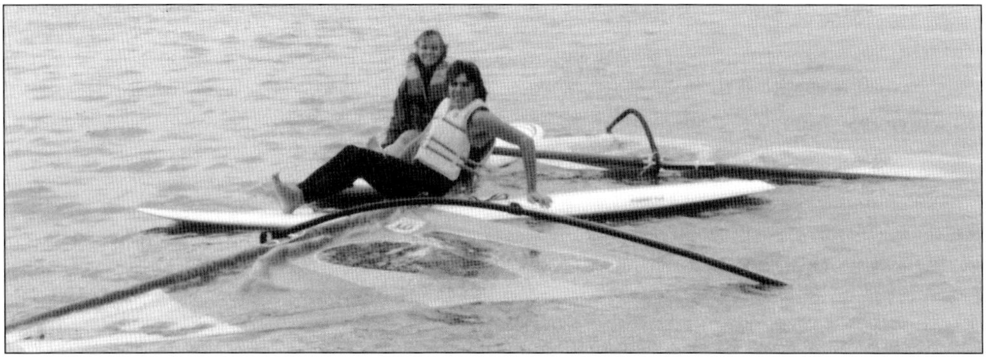

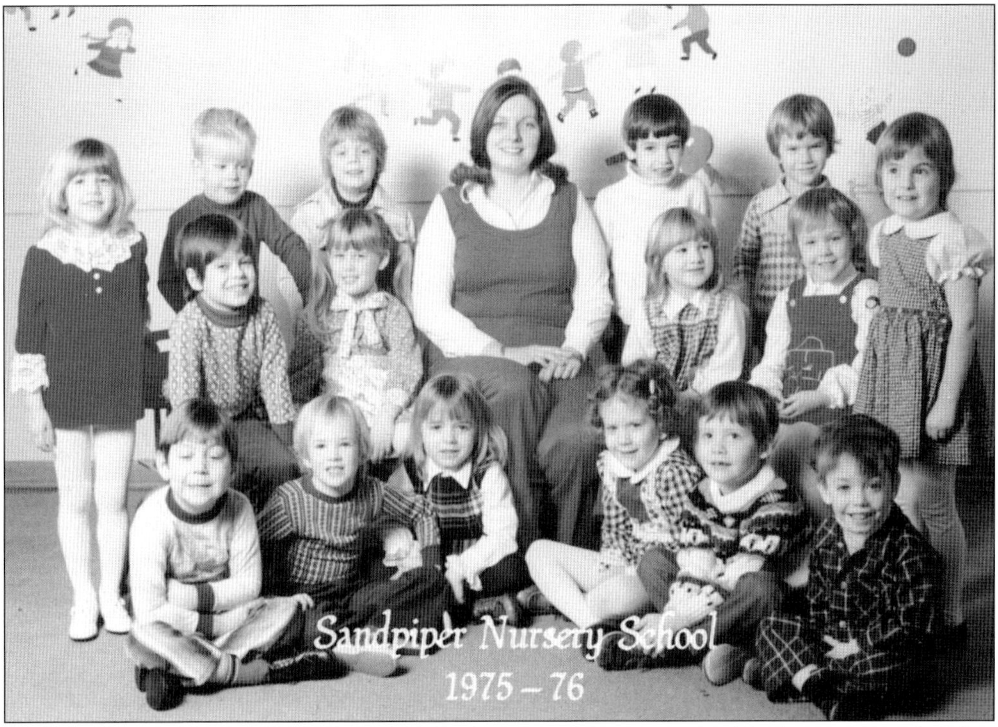

Sandpiper Co-op Nursery. In 1973, the Ogden Dunes Community Church recommended that the congregation support the establishment of a nondenominational co-op nursery school. That year, the church provided the facilities and two teachers, Lee Hibbs and Joan Froman. Lee and Duane Hibbs moved to 79 Ski Hill Road in 1964, and Joan and Charles Froman moved to Ski Hill Road in 1969. Lee is pictured here with her students in 1975. (Courtesy of Lee Hibbs.)

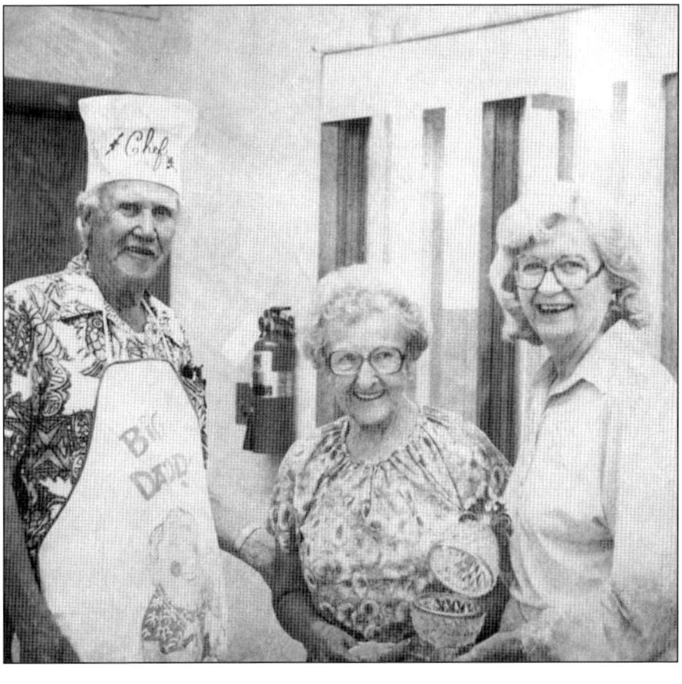

Prime Timers. A few years later, the Ogden Dunes Community Church established the Prime Timers program, which brought together the retirees of the community. Since 1979, the group has shared a luncheon and program almost every month at the Community Church. One of the programs in 1981 featured culinary skills. Here, Carl Lundquist poses with two unidentified friends. (HSOD.)

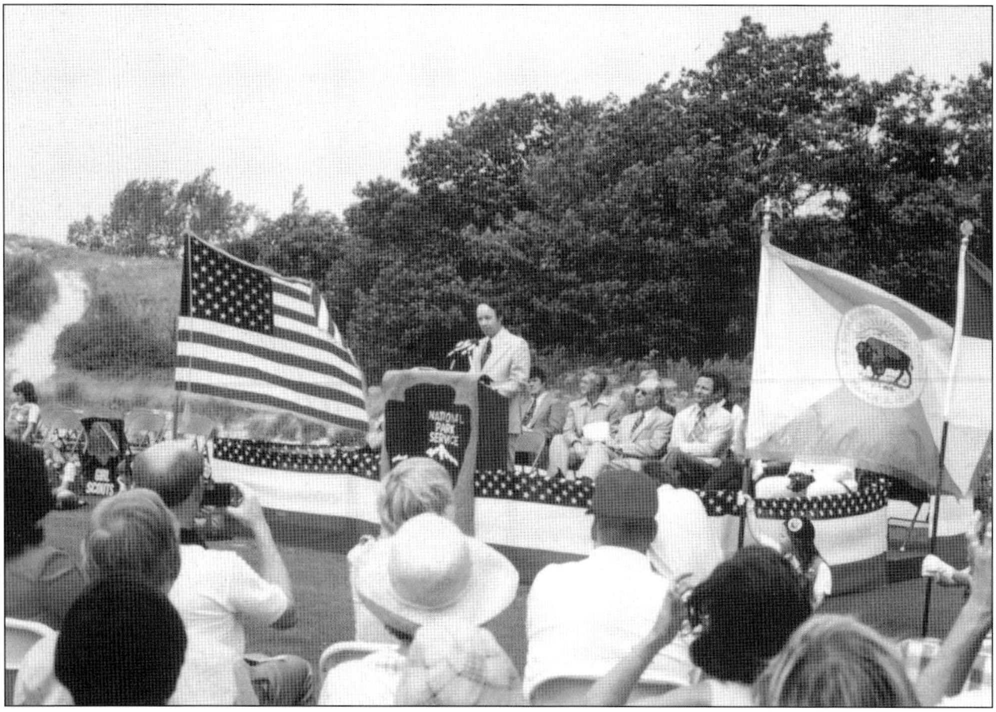

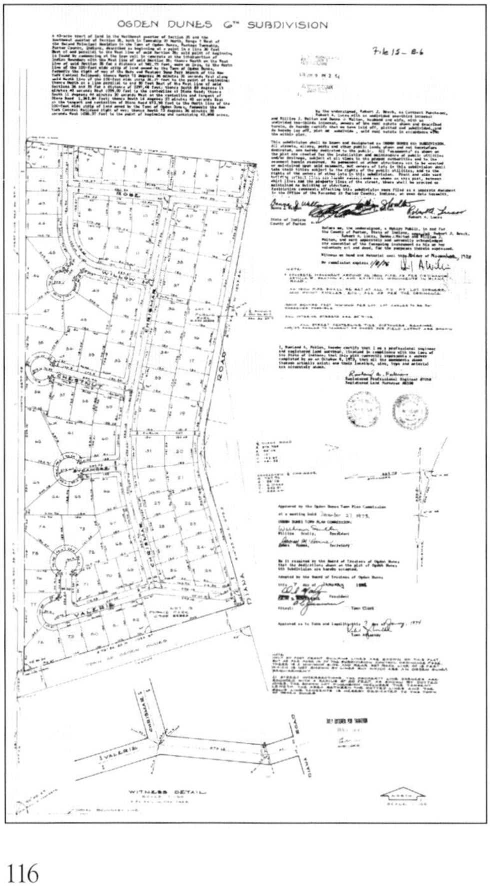

West Beach: A New Neighbor. On May 21, 1977, the West Beach of the Indiana Dunes National Lakeshore was formally opened, with Congressman Floyd Fithian giving the remarks. This area of the park was selected because it was closer to Chicago and had been leveled by sand mining earlier in the century. (Courtesy of the Kurtz family.)

The Sixth Subdivision. In 1967, Nelson and Helen Reck donated the 43 acres west of Diana Road to the University of Chicago. After nearly 50 years of being part of the community, the Recks retired to California in 1972. The university sold this land to developers in 1973, who divided it into 82 large lots. It is interesting to note that the president of the town board was Colin Mackenzie, whose father played a critical role in establishing Ogden Dunes in 1923–1924. (Courtesy of Alec Mackenzie.)

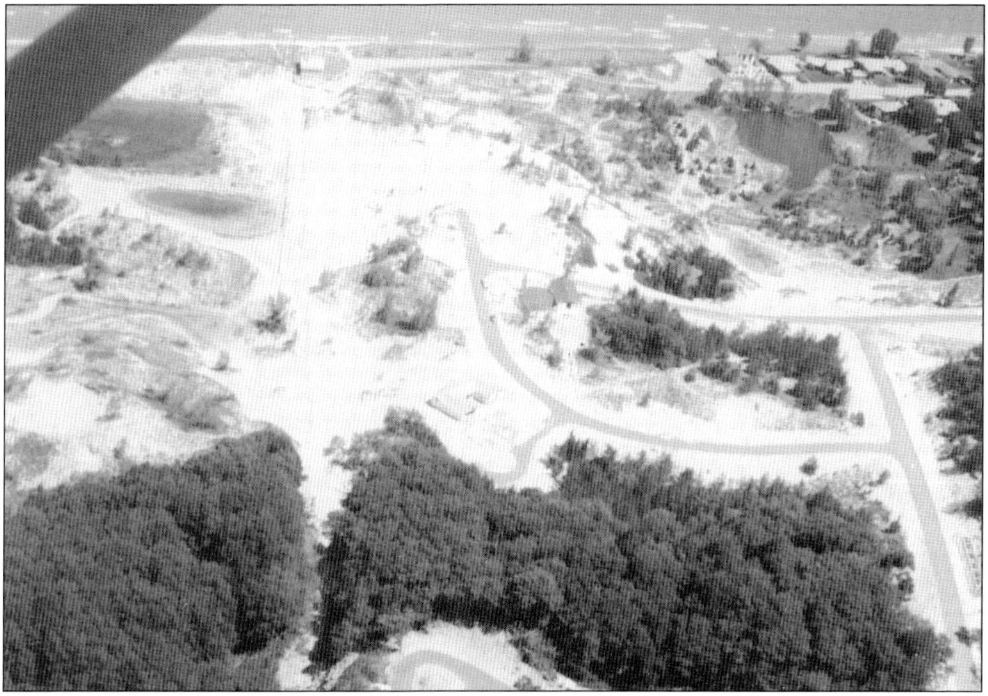

Northern Half of Sixth Subdivision. The pond on the left is in the National Lakeshore, and the pond on the right is Polliwog. In 1976, Congress appropriated funds to purchase this area for the Indiana Dunes National Lakeshore. Much to the dismay of Ogden Dunes and the seven homeowners who had recently moved into their homes, the park service used its power of eminent domain to purchase 34 lots and 7 homes in this section. (Courtesy of Dena Green.)

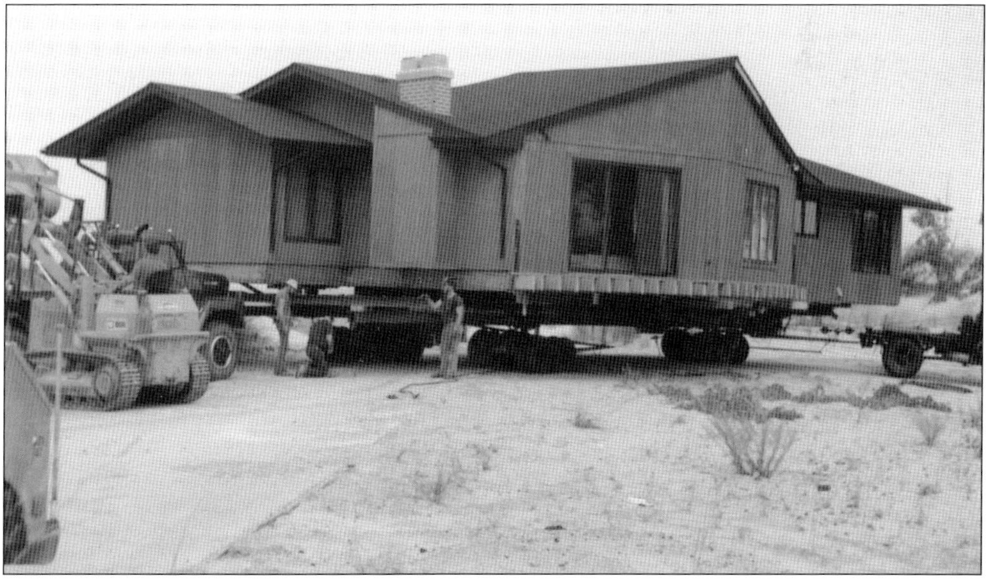

Relocating Homes. The seven homeowners had the opportunity to move their homes. Dena and Albert Green moved their house from Willow to a lot on Indian Camp Trail. The home shown here was moved to Summit Road, approximately a quarter-mile east. (Courtesy of Dena Green.)

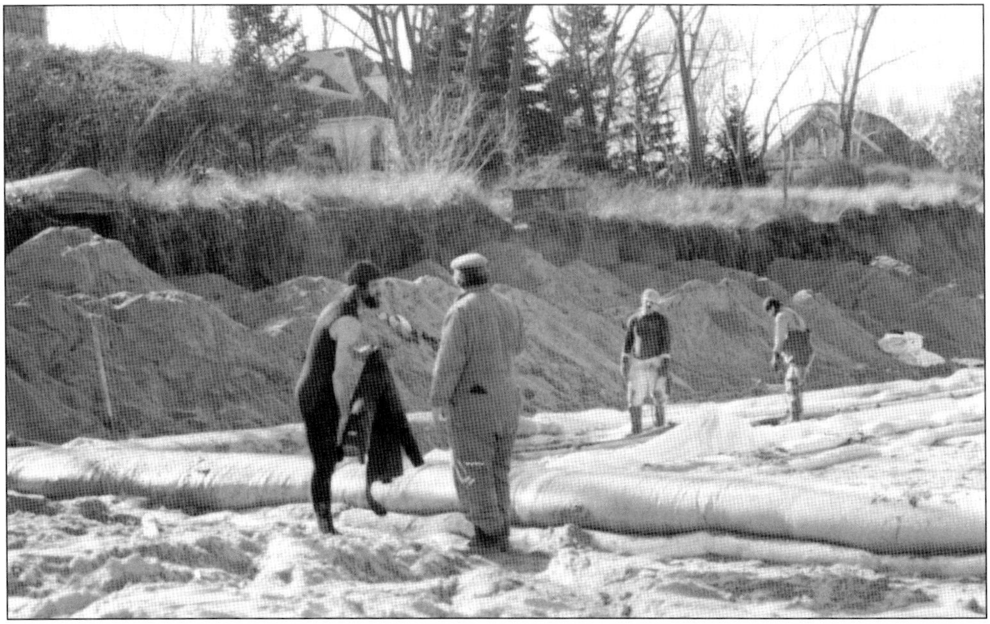

COST OF INDUSTRIALIZATION. With the completion of Midwest Steel, a long breakwater was installed on both sides of Burns Ditch in the 1960s. A few years later, an even longer breakwater was built to protect the international port that was constructed two miles to the east. These two artificial structures, approved by the Army Corps of Engineers, prevented the natural replenishment of sand along the southern shore of Lake Michigan. Thus, Ogden Dunes began to lose its beach. (HSOD.)

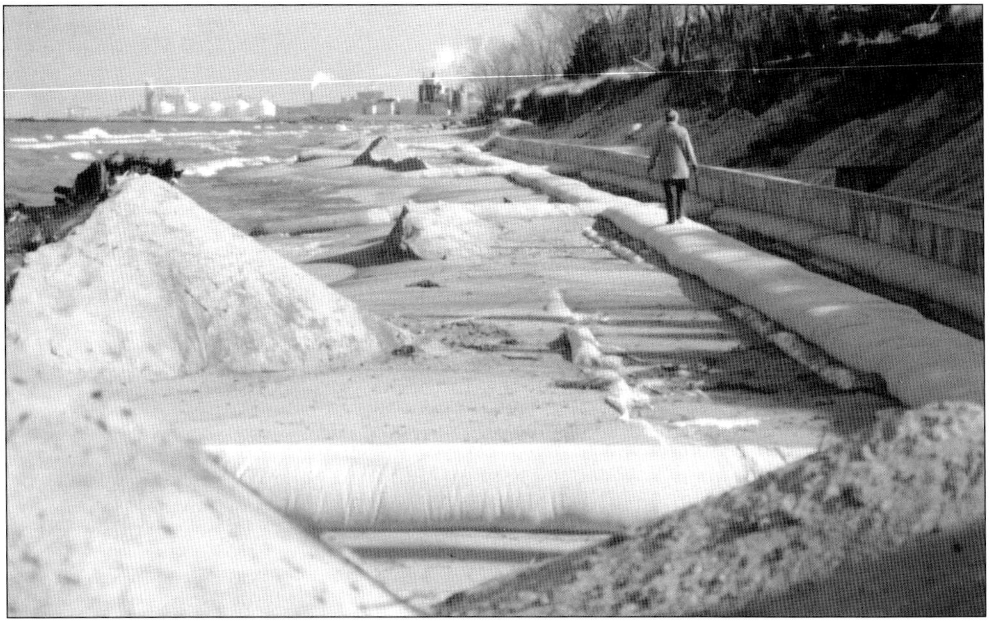

BEACH EROSION. The seriousness of the erosion became evident in the 1970s, but it was not until the mid-1980s that it became a crisis. The town sued the Army Corps of Engineers and began work on mitigating the erosion through a series of cement groins. This failed to halt the erosion. (HSOD.)

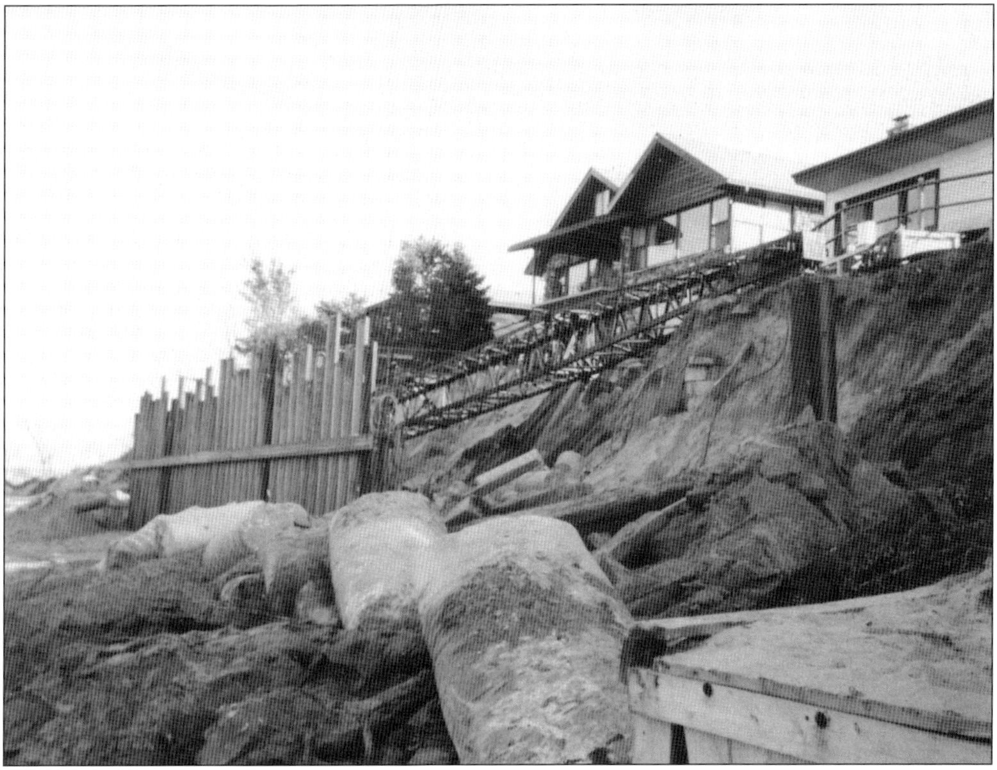

Return of Erosion. The storms of the mid-1990s removed not only the beach but also the first low-level dune that protected the homes on Shore Drive. Thus, as elsewhere along Lake Michigan, homes in Ogden Dunes were in danger of falling into the lake. This time, the answer was an expensive wall of steel pilings. (HSOD.)

Wall of Steel. The immediate danger to homes was lessened during the first part of the 21st century. This was achieved as a result of three actions: the addition of a second wall of steel pilings; the replenishment of the beach by dumping sand, conducted by the Army Corps of Engineers; and lowering lake levels due to mild winters. (HSOD.)

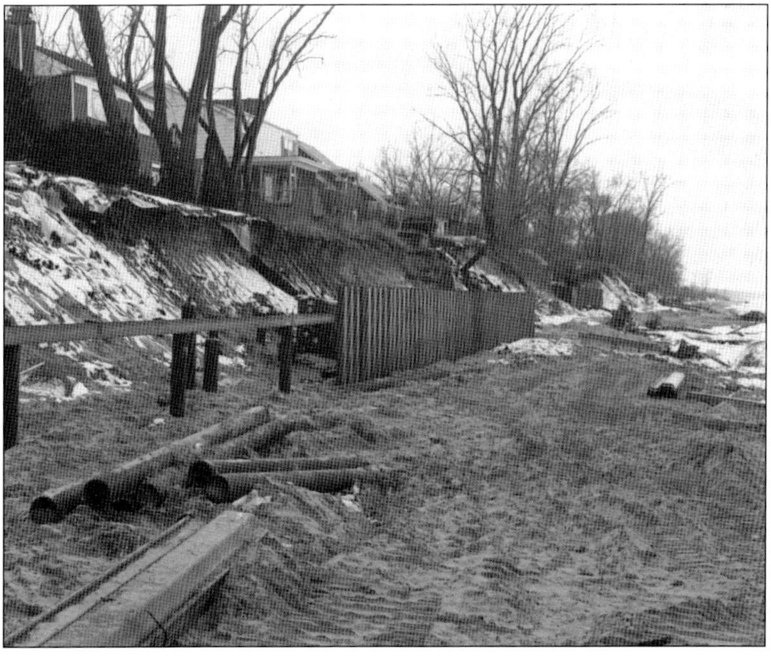

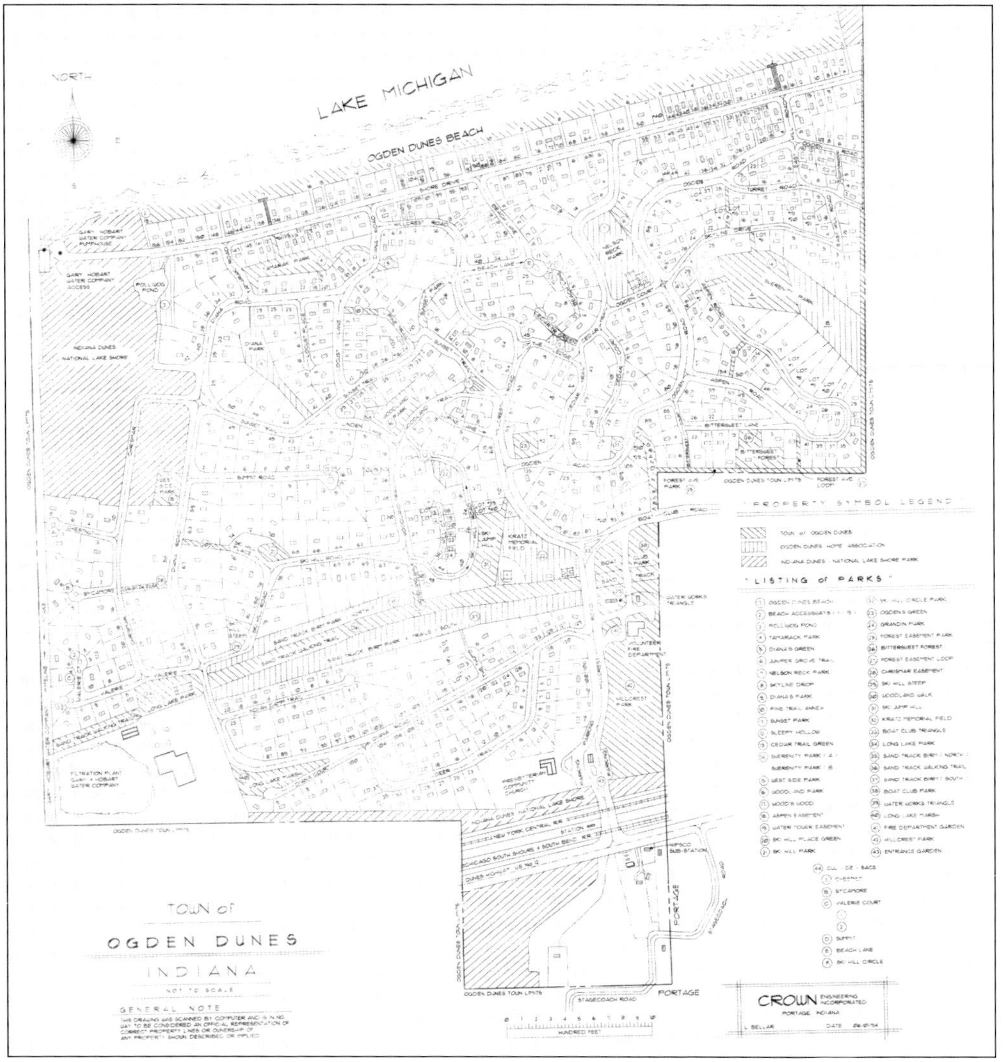

1994 Map. This map shows a reduction of the size of Ogden Dunes due to the acquisition by the National Park Service of approximately 20 acres, including 34 lots and 7 homes, plus other undeveloped sections of land in Ogden Dunes. The 1994 map shows about 700 homes and cottages. According to the 1990 census, 1,499 residents lived full-time in Ogden Dunes. The number decreased to 1,110 in 2010. Below, from left to right, these maps show the growth and decline of the developed areas of the town in the years 1924, 1939, 1959, and 1972 within the 1994 boundaries of Ogden Dunes. (Both, HSOD.)

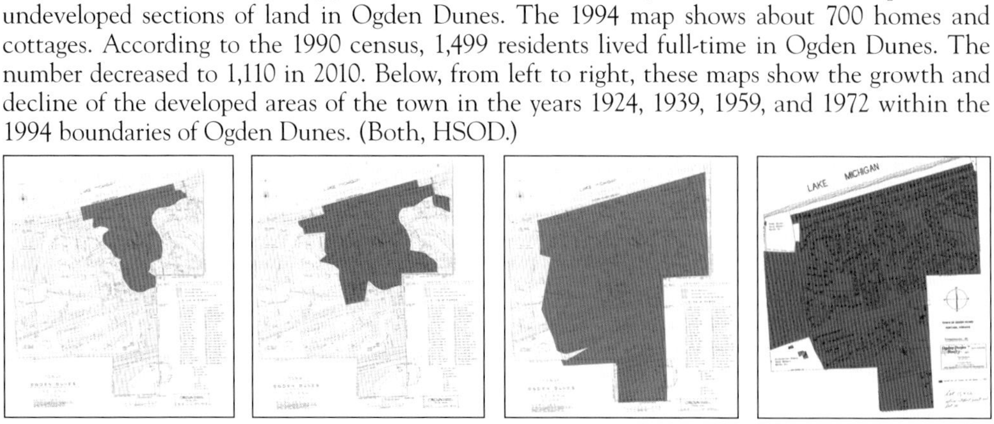

EPILOGUE

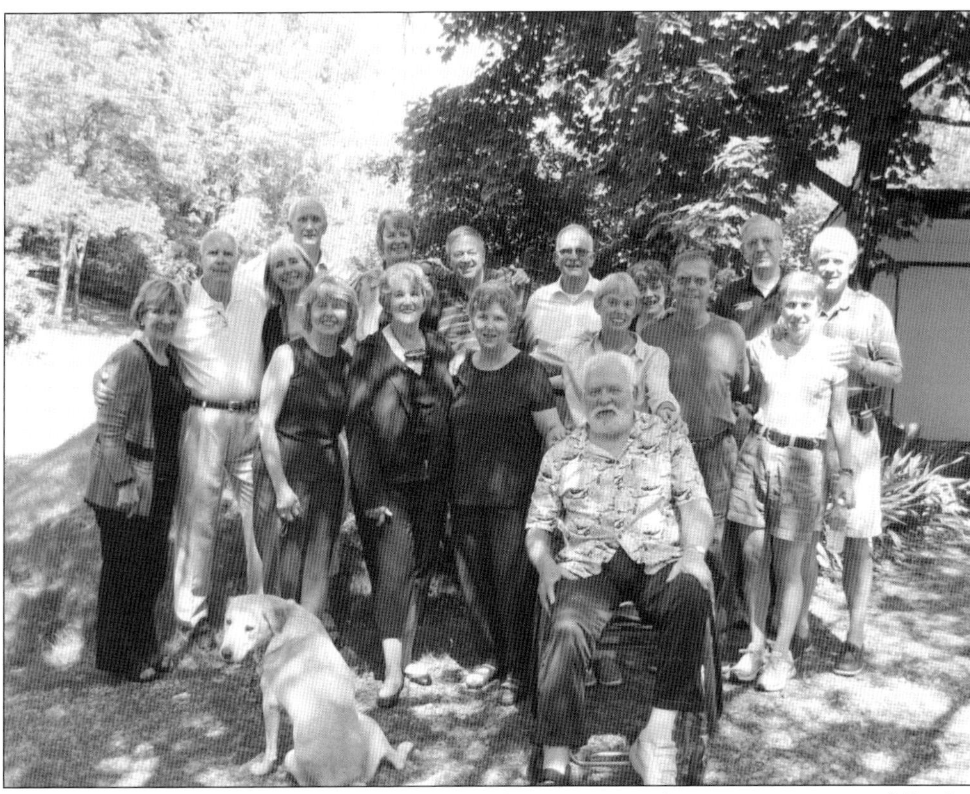

REUNION, 2007. In the latter part of the 20th century, Ogden Dunes was a middle-class community, white and primarily Republican. Almost all of the families sent their children to the Portage Schools, a school system that primarily served blue-collar families. A high percentage of Ogden Dunes graduates went on to attend college and to have successful careers. Most left the area. Yet, many kept their ties to the community, first returning to visit family and then to come together when the community celebrated Memorial Day. The group of friends seen here grew up in the late 1950s and made a commitment a number of years ago to return every two years. They have kept this pledge. (Courtesy of Richard Hallman.)

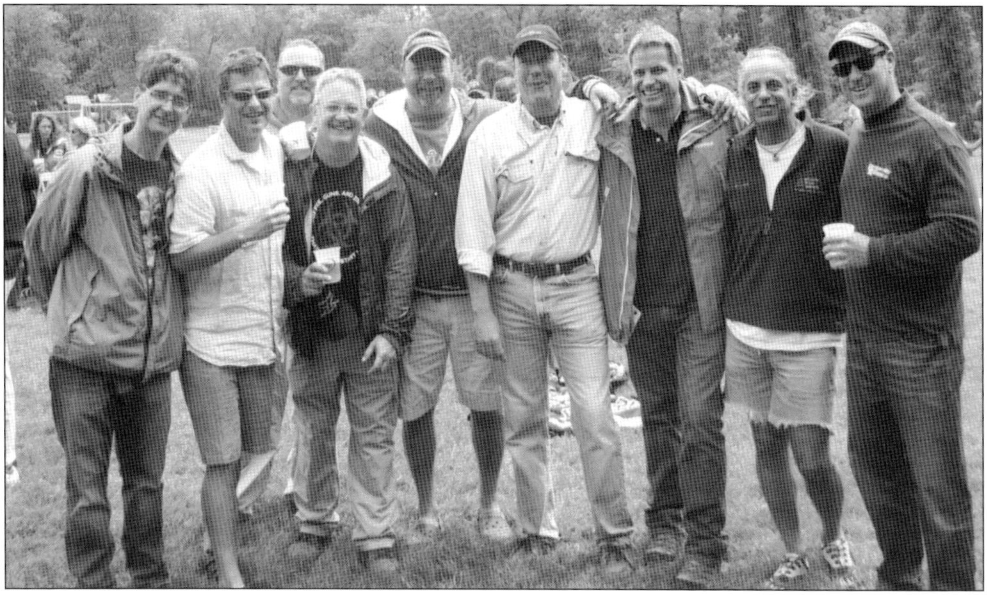

Memorial Day, 2013. Young men who grew up in the 1970s and 1980s came together in 2013. They are, from left to right, Chris Hoham, Steve Hallman, John Olsen, D.J. Petrou, Mark Ribordy, Brad Wood, Tom Froman, Jerry Savel, and Bill Pendleton. (Courtesy of Richard Hallman.)

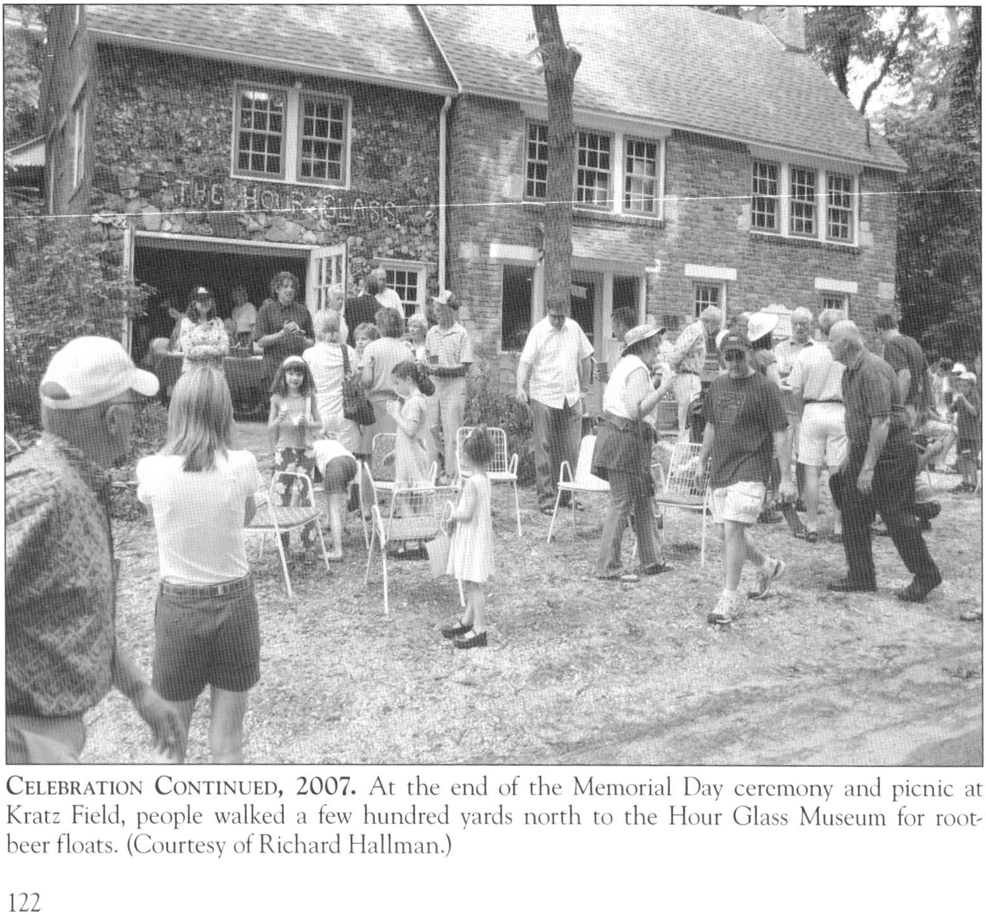

Celebration Continued, 2007. At the end of the Memorial Day ceremony and picnic at Kratz Field, people walked a few hundred yards north to the Hour Glass Museum for root-beer floats. (Courtesy of Richard Hallman.)

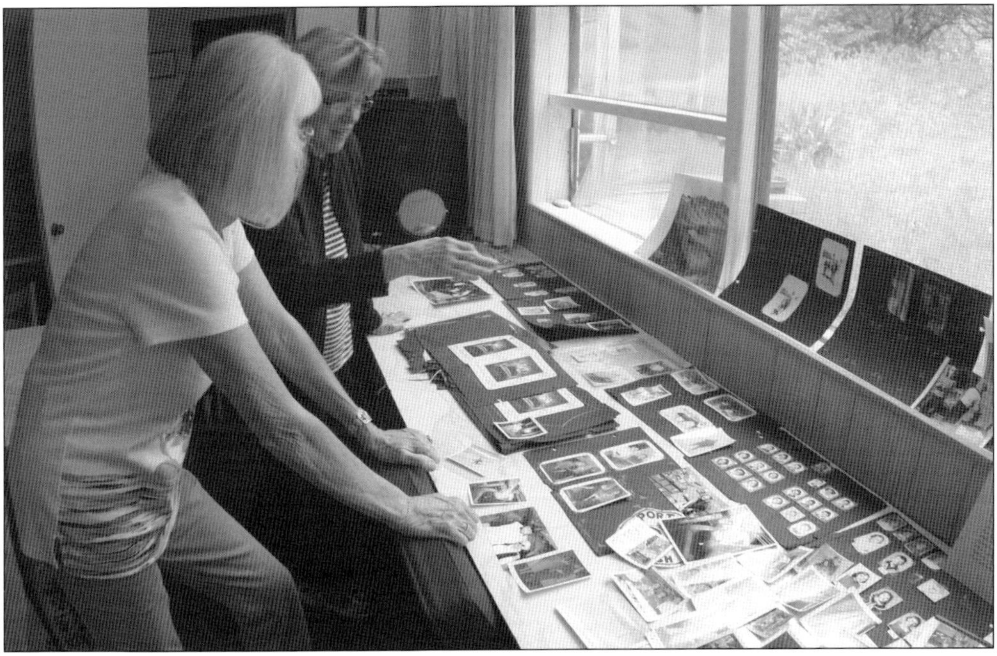

Remembering. Every two years, when the kids of the 1950s return, George Svihla Jr. returns from Austin, Texas, to open his parents' home to the reunion attendees. They spend the Memorial Day weekend in and out of the Svihla home on Ogden Road. Part of their ritual is to revisit the past through photographs. (Courtesy of Richard Hallman.)

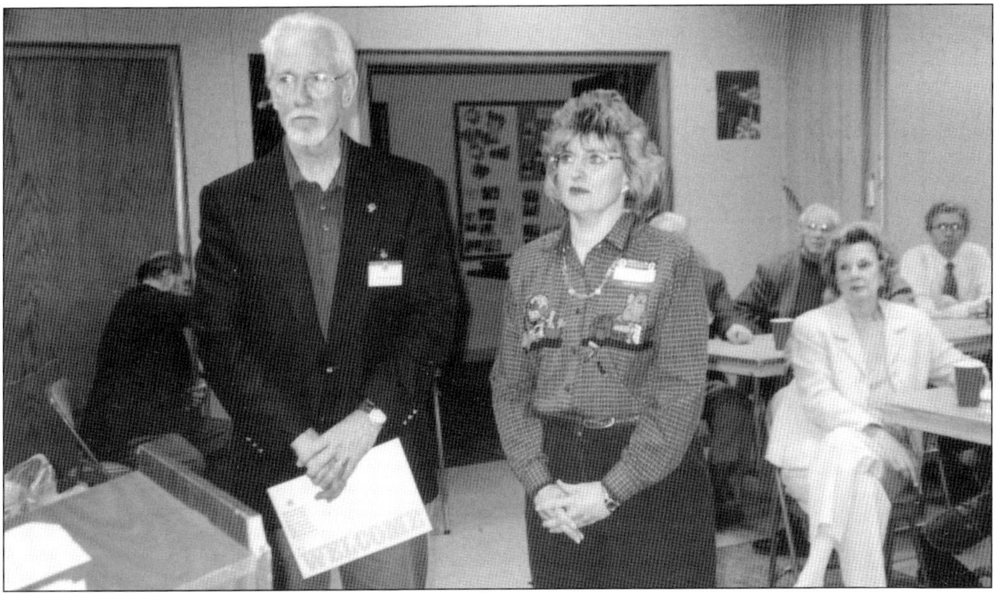

Lions Club. Since its founding in 1959, the Lions Club has provided support for many in need in Porter County, especially those who have sight disabilities. When the American Legion post disbanded, the Lions Club also became the sponsor of the Memorial Day parade, ceremony, and picnic. In this 2000 photograph, Mike Becker, president, inducts the first woman into the Ogden Dunes chapter. Debby Bailey is a third-generation member of the extended Dorman, Sykes, and Bailey families. (Courtesy of Tom Hendrix.)

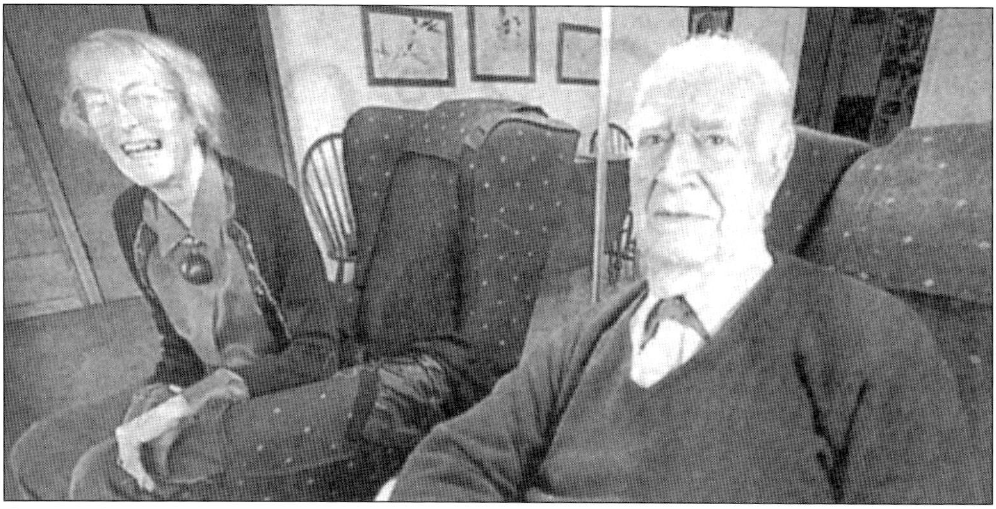

George Svihla and Naomi Svihla. Although many individuals have contributed to the establishment of the Historical Society of Ogden Dunes, the Svihlas deserve special mention. George (1915–2002), a retired scientist at Argonne Laboratories, took the lead in saving artifacts and collecting oral histories. In 1973, after his wife, Beth, died, he married Naomi Ireland (1917–2006). She had a long history as a community leader in the League of Women Voters, Save the Dunes Council, and the historical society. It should also be noted that the first president of the historical society was Margaret Benninger (1911–1999). Her photograph is on page 98. (HSOD.)

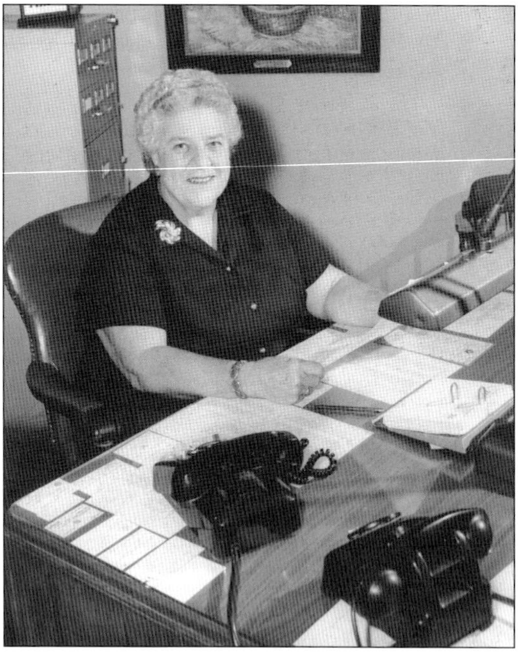

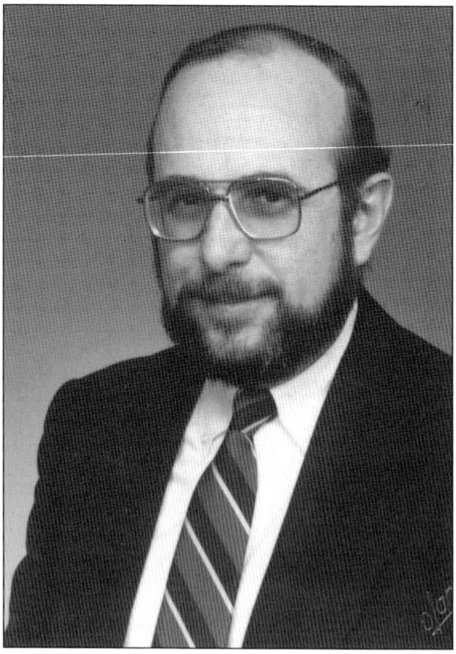

Sue Mechtersheimer (1905–1993). Sue, a teacher, principal, realtor, and benefactor, lived in Ogden Dunes for more than 60 years. In 1993, after she purchased The Hour Glass from the descendants of O.D. and Tillie Frank, Mechtersheimer (left) donated the building to the historical society. Don Kurtz (right), a founding member of the society, was the official photographer and the early curator of the photographs. (Left, HSOD; right, courtesy of the Kurtz family.)

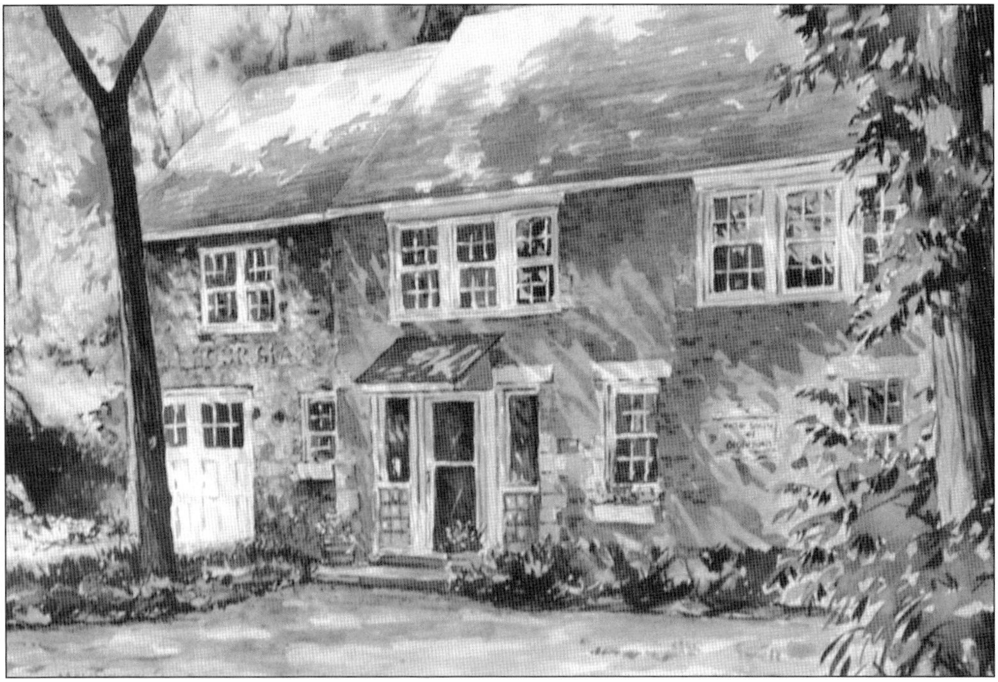

The Hour Glass. Jack Simmerling (1936–2013) painted this watercolor of The Hour Glass in 2008. A graduate of the University of Notre Dame, Simmerling dedicated his life to art and to salvaging the past. He and his family had a home and an art gallery in Chicago's Beverly neighborhood and a second home in the dunes. His many watercolors and prints of Ogden Dunes are his legacy to the community. (Photograph by Emilie Cardoso-Seerup; HSOD.)

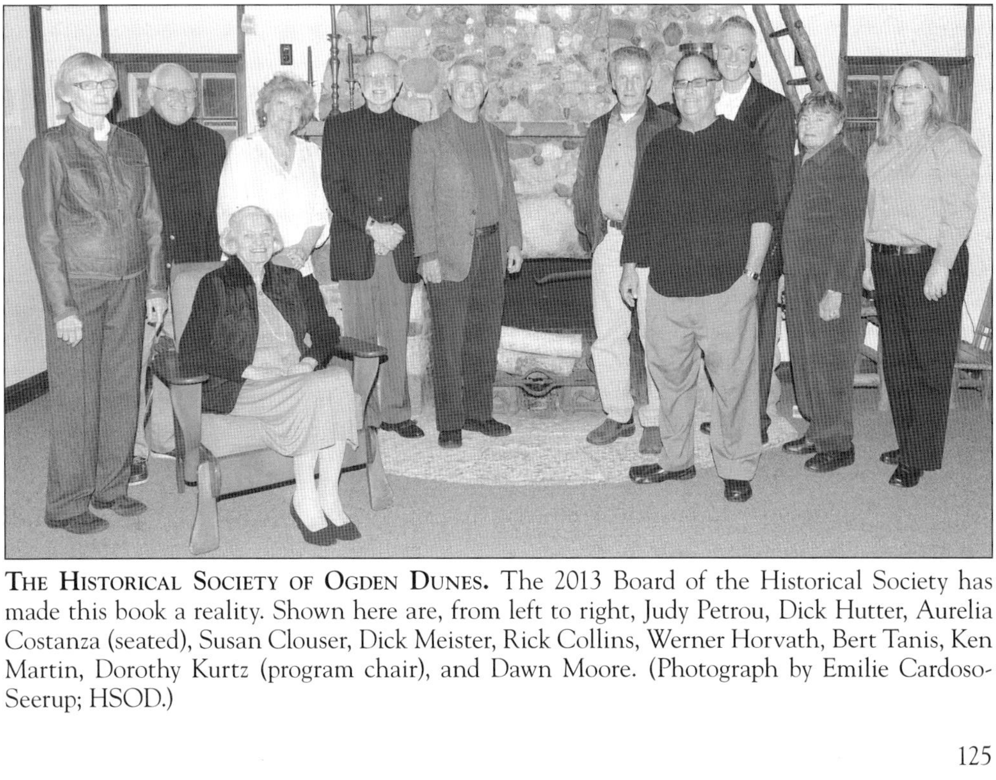

The Historical Society of Ogden Dunes. The 2013 Board of the Historical Society has made this book a reality. Shown here are, from left to right, Judy Petrou, Dick Hutter, Aurelia Costanza (seated), Susan Clouser, Dick Meister, Rick Collins, Werner Horvath, Bert Tanis, Ken Martin, Dorothy Kurtz (program chair), and Dawn Moore. (Photograph by Emilie Cardoso-Seerup; HSOD.)

Bibliography

Cohen, Ronald D. and McShane, Stephen G., eds. *Moonlight in Duneland: The Illustrated Story of the Chicago, South Shore and South Bend Railroad*. Bloomington, IN: Indiana University Press, 1998.

Edwards, Janet Zenke. *Diana of the Dunes: The True Story of Alice Gray*. New Castle, PA: Hermes Press, 2010.

Engel, J. Ronald. *Sacred Sands: A Struggle for Community in the Indiana Dunes*. Middletown, CT: Wesleyan University Press, 1983.

Franklin, Kay and Norma Schaeffer. *Duel for the Dunes*. Urbana, IL: University of Illinois, 1983.

Lane, James B., ed. *Tales of Lake Michigan and the Northwest Indiana Dunelands*. Gary, IN: Indiana University Northwest, 1998.

Messick, Dale. *Brenda Starr, Reporter: The Collected Dailies and Sundays: 1940–1946*. New Castle, PA: Hermes Press, 2012.

Moore, Powell A. *The Calumet Region: Indiana's Last Frontier*. Indianapolis, IN: Indiana Historical Bureau, 1959.

Schoon, Kenneth J. *Calumet Beginnings*. Bloomington, IN: Indiana University Press, 2003.

———. *Dreams of Duneland: A Pictorial History of the Indiana Dunes Region*. Bloomington, IN: Indiana University Press, 2013.

Simon, Linda and Jane Ammeson. *Miller Beach*. Charleston, SC: Arcadia Publishing, 2012.

Svihla, George, compiler. *The Ogden Dunes Sandpiper 1938–1970*. Ogden Dunes: Ogden Dunes Historical Society.

Thomas, Joseph, ed. *A History of Ogden Dunes*. Gary, IN: Ad-Craft, 1976.

Index